THE U.S.-SOVIET TRADE SOURCEBOOK

William S. Loiry
Editor

St J
St James Press

Chicago and London

ISBN 1-55862-142-3

Printed in the United States of America

1   2   3   4   5   6   7   8   9   0

TABLE OF CONTENTS

To Mikhail S. Gorbachev

Who Beat Swords Into Trade Shares

ACKNOWLEDGMENTS

Many thanks to all those who were generous with information, including the American Translators Association; APCO Associates; Baker & McKenzie; BLOC Magazine, the Center for Foreign Policy Development at Brown University; the International Section of the American Bar Association; and the Institute for Soviet-American Relations.

This edition benefited greatly from the expert editorial skills of Laura Goldenberg and Lynn A. Wildman and from the extraordinary word processing efforts of Cynthia Wallace.

A heartfelt thanks to my associates who supported this project: David Cutler of David Cutler & Associates; Peter C. Linzmeyer of Foley & Lardner; and Terence W. Dittrich, President of Global Trading Associates, Inc.

A warm thanks to Reverend Helice C. Green, for special guidance, and to Diane Light and Gayle Darden for increased capacity.

And special thanks for the personal support from my wonderful family: Dr. and Mrs. David A. Loiry, Jan Bearty, and her adorable children Andrea, Brett, and Michelle.

INTRODUCTION

Imagine you are in a business looking for new global markets and living in a country with a staggering trade deficit. And imagine a new market opening with almost 300 million potential consumers, who want and need everything from syringes to computers and who have oil, natural gas, gold, high technology, and hundreds of other products and services to trade with.

Imagine the Soviet Union.

Never again in our lifetimes will there be such a market with so many opportunities. And yet, in my travels throughout the Soviet Union, I consistently get asked, "Where are the Americans?" The Soviets would rather deal with American business than with the Germans or Japanese, but American business has hardly make a scratch in the Soviet marketplace.

The 1991 U.S.-Soviet Trade Directory is designed to provide you with the information you need to profitably enter the Soviet marketplace. The myriad of consultants, attorneys, government agencies, financing sources, and other resources listed here will help you plot a course for trading victory.

It goes without saying that to achieve that victory, you will have to ignore those cold and timid souls who incorrectly state that the Soviets have nothing to trade and who moan that even if they did, there is no way we can conduct profitable trade because the ruble is inconvertible. America did not create the largest consumer market in the world, invent the automobile and the airplane, or land a man on the moon by being meek. We have the capacity to create the world's greatest trade arena - the Soviet/American marketplace - a marketplace that will provide the people of both nations not only prosperity but also peace. Let's do it!

William S. Loiry
Washington
September, 1990

11

*We offer the whole world, including the world of capitalist states,
a broad, long-term and comprehensive program of
mutually beneficial cooperation,
a program incorporating new opportunities which are being
opened before mankind by the age of scientific
and technical revolution.*

Mikhail S. Gorbachev

THE
U.S.-SOVIET
TRADE
SOURCEBOOK

SECTION 1

CONSULTANTS AND TRADING COMPANIES

This section contains a wide range of consultants who specialize in areas ranging from legal expertise and structuring joint ventures and contracts to market research and industry analysis. To find a firm whose capabilities and experience match your company's requirements, it is suggested that you ascertain the following information about any consulting group you are considering for assistance.

• What is the range of the firm's services (i.e., consulting, travel assistance, legal counsel, translation, interpretation, research, etc.)
• What is the background of the firm's principals in the field (academic, government, consulting, business, trade, language)?
• Does the staff include Russian speakers?
• How many years has it been in operation?
• Does it have a presence in Moscow (office and/or representatives)?
• Have they successfully concluded agreements with Soviet counterparts?
• Can they provide references?
• On what basis do the consulting companies work (success fee, commission, consulting fees, retainer)?
• Does the firm operate in countries aside from the USSR, Eastern Europe?

CONSULTANTS

Accord Consulting Group
444 Castro Street
Suite 400
Mountain View, CA 94041
Phone: (415) 940-1896
FAX: (415) 969-8660
Contact: Keith Rosten
Services: ACG provides practical advice to U.S. companies on Soviet trade and law. ACG evaluates prospective partners, negotiates business and trade agreements, evaluates proposals for cooperation agreements and joint ventures, structures joint ventures, and provides implementation support.

American-Ukrainian Trade Corporation, Inc.
2509 Rio DeJaneiro Avenue
Port Charlotte, FL 33983
Phone: (813) 627-5800
FAX: (813) 624-4023
Contact: Misha Nywelt

Amtrade Associates International
420 Lexington Avenue, Suites 1624-27
New York, NY 10170
Phone: (212) 697-2467
FAX: (212) 599-0839
Telex: 6503764897
Contact: Stephen B. Van Campen, President
Services: The firm identifies new business opportunities; conducts feasibility studies and trade and joint-venture proposals; provides liaison and administrative support; and arranges key introductions to Soviet contacts.

APCO Associates
The Arnold and Porter Consulting Group
1155 21st Street, NW
Suite 1000
Washington, DC 20036
Phone: (202) 778-1015
FAX: (202) 331-9832
Telex: 248303 ARPO UR
Contact: Randy Bregman, Director, Soviet and Eastern European Services
Services: APCO offers its clients the skills of experienced specialists in Soviet and East European trade and commerce, culture, language, and international joint venture formation. APCO can assess the potential for joint ventures or other strategic alliances; identify and provide introductions to potential partners; assist with the development of letters of protocol; help with the structuring and negotiation of joint ventures or other strategic alliances; help prepare feasibility studies; facilitate the registration of a venture under the laws of the host country; and provide logistical and other on-location support.

Aranda Corporation
18 East Canal Avenue
Paoli, PA 19301
Phone: (215) 296-0111
FAX: (215) 640-0619
Contact: Michael S. Tomczyk, President
Services: Aranda provides trade development services including strategic planning, identification of opportunities, trade negotiations, market research, marketing, and distribution. The company also publishes a quarterly business report on East Europe and the Soviet Union.

ASET Consultants, Inc.
American-Soviet Exchange and Trade
in Washington:
8350 Greensboro Drive
Suite 805
McLean, VA 22102
Phone: (703) 790-1922
FAX: (703) 883-1305
Telex: TWX 510-660-8023
Contact: Erika D. Nobel, President
in Moscow:
Ul. Vernadskogo, 33/153
117331 Moscow

Phone: 201-50-21, 138-05-04
FAX: 201-72-47
Telex: 412230 MPSM SU
Contact: Holly Smith, Director, Moscow Operations
Services: Drawing from its databases and U.S.-and U.S.S.R.-based research teams, ASET provides a wide range of information and business services to companies exploring sales, joint venture, and other trade opportunities in the Soviet Union, as well as to law firms and other trade consulting firms that represent clients in the U.S.S.R.. ASET's staff is experienced in tracking down information on Soviet industry, individual organizations and enterprises, regulations, legal charters, industrial standards and other topics. The scope of the research services range from preparing comprehensive industry or market analyses to obtaining the telephone number of a plant in Irkutsk. ASET can quickly provide the information crucial for sound business planning and development. Other professional services include: business contact development and planning, negotiation support, seminars and personnel training, translation and interpretation.

Aviation Consulting Inc.
90 Moonachie Avenue
Teterboro, NJ 07608
Phone: (201) 288-1235
FAX: (201) 288-8400

Telex: 134408
Contact: John Dugan, Executive Vice President
Services: ACI provides economic, management, and technical consulting services for the aviation industry.

Baltic Ventures, Inc.
1075 Washington Street
West Newton, MA 02165
Phone: (617) 527-2550
FAX: (617) 527-2823
Telex: 49605791 BALTIC
Contact: Paul D. Kalnins, President
Services: Baltic Ventures Inc. is a consulting firm assisting business organizations and research institutions in the Baltic republics to market their products in North America, as well as aiding Western companies to establish business operations in the Baltic republics. Baltic Ventures Inc., featuring a multilingual staff, offers a variety of services including: project analysis, market research, locating Baltic business partners, development of market entry strategies and translation.

Bethesda Institute for Soviet Studies (BISS)
4400 East-West Hwy.
Suite 806
Bethesda, MD 20814
Phone: (301) 652-2722
FAX: (301) 951-6435
Contact: Isaac Tarasulo

Services: The organization offers consulting on joint venture agreements, seminars on Soviet industrial ethics and business culture, telephone, fax, and computer communications between the U.S. and U.S.S.R., translations, and language training.

Cambridge East-West Consulting Group, Inc.
University Place
124 Mt. Auburn Street
Harvard Square
Cambridge, MA 02138
Phone: (617) 576-5724
FAX: (617) 547-1431
Contact: David J. Kramer
Services: The firm provides research, information, and other services to companies and financial institutions interested in doing business in the Soviet Union and Eastern Europe. CEWCG offers customized reports and presentations as well as valuable contacts with officials, businesses, and organizations in the region.

CAWT
245 Park Avenue
New York, NY 10167
Phone: (212) 856-1228
FAX: (212) 856-1694
Contact: Donald Asadorian, Senior Manager
Services: CAWT provides Soviet joint venture consulting and market research, as well as the structuring of hybrid transactions combining trade finance and countertrade.

C & M International LTD
1001 Pennsylvania Avenue, NW
Washington, DC 20004-2505
Phone: (202) 624-2895
FAX: (202) 628-5116
Contact: Doral S. Cooper
Services: C & M offers consulting services to companies doing business with the Soviet Union. Affiliated with the law firm Crowell and Moring.

Consulting Commodities Marketing International, Ltd.
1880 Commonwealth Avenue, Suite 6
Brighton, MA 02135
Phone: (617) 731-3433
FAX: (617) 731-3433
Telex: 940103 WU PUBTLX BSN
Contact: Amrit Russ
Services: The firm offers marketing and feasibility studies for Western companies seeking to enter Soviet market. The firm also aids in negotiating and establishing joint ventures with and in the Soviet Union.

Delphic Associates, Inc.
7700 Leesburg Pike
Suite 250
Falls Church, VA 22043
Phone: (703) 556-0278

20

FAX: (703) 556-0494
Contact: Gerold Guensberg, Director
Services: Delphic Associates has published over 120 studies on Soviet science and technology which are based primarily on the eyewitness accounts of Soviet emigres. Delphic also publishes a bi-weekly newsletter on Soviet science, technology, and trade.

Design Dynamics
5525 Twin Knolls Road
Suite 323
Columbia, MD 21045
Phone: (301) 995-3022
FAX: (301) 995-0805
Contact: Alex Koorbanoff
Services: The firm provides full-service support to businesses entering the Soviet/Eastern European markets. Services include consulting and negotiating for American/Soviet transactions; language services - interpreting, translating, and abstracting; market research; training of key personnel; full-service Russian and East European language graphics; business planning; and development and identification of potential business partners.

Dhalfelt International
in the U.S.:
120 Potter Road
Scarsdale, NY 10583
Phone: (914) 472-2084

Contact: Ulf Nofelt, President
in Moscow:
ICA-Soviet-American Foundation
Moscow, 170778, B-87
Phone: 245-02-03
Contact: Alexander Churkin, Associate
Services: The firm offers consulting services in joint ventures, strategic planning, marketing, representation, cost analysis, import/export advice, industry research, feasibility studies, business contacts, and guide and translation services.

Diomedes, Inc.
3105 Washington Street
San Francisco, CA 94115
Phone: (415) 563-4731
FAX: (415) 931-0915
Telex: 4931349 ESAL UI
Contact: Jim Garrison, CEO
Services: Diomedes, Inc., is a California Corporation established to assist American and Soviet entrepreneurs in formulating, establishing, and managing profitable relationships in the Soviet Union and Eastern Europe. Jim Garrison started the firm after working in Soviet-American relations professionally for ten years, during which time he cultivated contacts at high levels in the Soviet government.

Dr. Dvorkovitz & Associates
P.O. Box 1748
Ormond Beach, FL 32175-1748

.

Phone: (904) 677-7033
FAX: (904) 677-7113
Telex: 4940321
Contact: Anne Klenner
Services: The firm is a technical search organization with representatives located throughout the world, as well as a service organization prepared to provide additional data, prototypes, samples, and assistance in arranging meetings, and if requested, help in negotiations. The firm has established technology transfer centers in the U.S.S.R., C.S.S.R., Europe, and Asia.

East-West Concepts, Inc.
196 Tamarack Circle
Skillman, NJ 08558
Phone: (609) 924-6789
FAX: (609) 466-0864
Telex: 408568 EWC/HVS
Contact: Janos Samu
Services: The company's services include joint ventures, representation, credit references, background checks, on-site inspections, translation, interpretation, legal assistance, research, consultation, special assignments.

East-West Initiatives, Inc.
30 South 17th Street
Philadelphia, PA 19103
Phone: (215) 636-4961
FAX: (215) 636-4990
Contact: Julie Swift, President
Services: East-West Initiatives, Inc., a member of the U.S.-U.S.S.R. Trade and Economic Council since 1986, focuses on establishing and developing commercial relations between American and Soviet businesses. East-West Initiatives, Inc. is affiliated with the law firm of Ballard, Spahr, Andrews & Ingersoll with broad expertise in energy, life sciences, and all areas of corporate and public finance.

East-West Trade Development, Ltd.
2025 I Street, NW
Suite 606
Washington, DC 20006
Phone: (202) 296-3598
FAX: (202) 296-3599
Contact: William Barlow, President
Services: The company is involved in the construction industry (technology, devices, tools), petroleum industry, (technology of oil extraction EOR) consumer goods industries (reconstruction and retooling of production facilities), general consulting (market surveys, sales planning, step-by-step marketing). Willing to represent companies in the timber and building materials industry.

Ernst & Young
East European Division
787 7th Avenue
New York, NY 10019
Phone: (212) 830-6000

FAX: (212) 977-9359, 977-9159
Telex: 7607796
Contact: James E. Searing, National Director of International Business Services
Services: The firm's East European Division helps Western companies assess business opportunities and assists in implementing business strategies in Eastern Europe and the U.S.S.R.. The firm also provides services to Soviet organizations such as the Academy for Foreign Trade in Moscow. They advise on all issues related to joint ventures, and also on turnkey projects, compensation arrangements, and countertrade.

Expertech
in the U.S.
c/o Wavetech International
1600 Broadway
Suite 550
Denver, Colorado 80202
Phone: (303) 839-9488
FAX: (303) 839-9497
Contact: Edward Gendelman
in Moscow:
Ul. Krasikogo, 32
117418 Moscow
Phone: 095-129-16-33
FAX: 129-26-27
Contact: Dr. Igor N. Shokin, Director General
Services: Expertech, a business development firm, assists Western companies in analyzing investment possibilities in the Soviet market, carries out detailed analyses of

proposals for joint projects, and provides a full range of consulting, communications, and agent services. Its current projects are in forestry, oil and gas exploration, chemical manufacturing, publishing, real estate, and commercial fishing. Expertech is JV #1086.

Export Network Inc.
7315 Wisconsin Avenue, Suite 300W
Bethesda, MD 20814
Phone: (301) 961-8770
FAX: (301) 961-8775
Contact: Linda Price
Services: The firm is an on-line desk-top management system providing exporters with a single-screen solution to the worldwide intelligence needs of any sized company.

Feshbach, Murray
232 Poulton Hall
Georgetown University
37th & P Street, NW
Washington, DC 20057
Phone: (202) 687-6811
Contact: Murray Feshbach
Services: Feshbach is a consultant active in the fields of medical equipment and pharmaceuticals.

Field, Mark G.
Harvard Russian Research Center
Harvard University
1737 Cambridge Street
Cambridge, MA 02138

Phone: (617) 495-1719, (617) 495-4037,
(617) 862-8322, (603) 284-6437
FAX: (617) 495-8319
Telex: 4948261
Contact: Mark G. Field
Services: Field is an authority on the Soviet health care system and has served as a consultant in the areas of Soviet medicine and pharmaceuticals. Field's experience with Soviet health care includes testimony presented in the U.S. Congress concerning the Soviet drug industry. Field is a Fellow in the Russian Research Center and an Adjunct Professor at the School of Public Health at Harvard University. Field's consulting activities are not connected with the Harvard Russian Research Center.

FYI Information Resources
735 8th Street, SE
Washington, DC 20003
Phone: (202) 544-2394
FAX: (202) 543-9385
Contact: Jonathan Halperin
Services: The firm provides a range of services, including consulting services, proprietary research and marketing reports, travel briefings, Sovscan- a syndicated research and reporting service, and a telephone reference service which provides answers to questions on cultural, political, and economic topics.

Georgian-American Medical & Economic Development Corporation
3419 Barger Drive
Falls Church, VA 22044
Phone: (703) 941-5264
FAX: (703) 658-2807
Contact: Alexander M. Van Doren-Shulkin
Services: Advises a number of Soviet ministries and state enterprises on the subjects of trade and investments. Operates a business clearinghouse in the U.S.S.R. Provides business facilitating and other consulting services to Western firms involved in trade with entities in the U.S.S.R.

Geotech International
714 S. Dearborn
Suite 3
Chicago, IL 60605
Phone: (312) 939-7162
FAX: (312) 427-4504
Telex: 271 001 GEOTECH UR
Contact: Dr. Marshall Silver, President
Services: Geotech International coordinates feasibility studies for firms involved in U.S.-Soviet trade.

Global Concepts, Inc.
P.O. Box 540007
Dallas, TX 75354-0007
Phone: (214) 351-0001
FAX: (214) 902-9020
Telex: 163410 PROBUS UT

Contact: L. C. Smith
Services: Global Concepts deals with trade and travel between the U.S. and Soviet Union. The firm is also beginning a program to assist companies that wish to start up businesses with the Soviet Union.

Global Trading Associates, Inc.
in Washington:
1155 Connecticut Avenue, NW
Suite 500
Washington, DC 20036
Phone: (202) 467-8589
FAX: (202) 452-8654
Telex: 4933729 WASH UI
Contact: William S. Loiry, Chairman; Terence W. Dittrich, President
in Moscow:
29, Guild 4,
Chekhow str.
103006 Moscow
Phone: 299-84-45
FAX: 200-22-12 (Attn: Anton E. Pronin)
Telex: 411700 VAPRO 0310
Contact: Anton E. Pronin
Services: The company provides feasibility studies, arranges for joint venture partners, and helps to negotiate joint ventures. The firm also develops regional business centers in the Soviet Union and conducts U.S.-Soviet trade conferences in the U.S. and in the Soviet Union. Global Trading is the publisher of the *U.S.-Soviet Trade Alert.*

Hazard, John
435 W. 116th Street
New York, NY 10027
Phone: (212) 854-2646
FAX: (212) 854-7946
Contact: John Hazard
Services: Hazard consults on aspects of Soviet law with particular reference to formation of contracts. He is the revisor of the *U.S.S.R. Law Digest* in the *Martindale Hubble Law Directory.*

Henry A. Raab Consulting
10 Shore Boulevard
Manhattan Beach, NY 11235-4056
Phone: (718) 648-7570, (212) 691-3666
FAX: (718) 934-8392
Telex: 423029 SHRAZ
Contact: Henry A. Raab, President
Services: The company performs consulting and feasibility studies in the Soviet Union and Eastern Europe. The firm's other activities include: industrial developments, hotels, motels, office buildings, residential complexes, rehabilitation and preservation of regional identity, department stores, hospitals, sports facilities, recreational grounds, manufacturing facilities, joint ventures, countertrade, turnkey operations, and trading in consumer-oriented commodities.

Inform-Pravo
Ul. Druzhby, 10/32
Phone: 117330 Moscow

143-17-95, 143-67-70, 938-21-20
Telex: 411734 INF SU
Services: Inform-Pravo is a Soviet-multinational joint venture that specializes in industrial trade and consumer research and provides economic, legal and technical assistance in foreign trade operations.

Jarrett International, Inc.
P.O. Box 132
Weston, MA 02193
Phone: (617) 893-5406
FAX: (617) 891-9316
Contact: Derek Jarrett
Services: The firm offers consulting services for U.S.-Soviet trade and joint ventures.

Kent Group International
131 State Street
Boston, MA 02109
Phone: (617) 232-8008
FAX: (617) 730-6485
Telex: 8100071150
Contact: George Cuker, President
Services: Kent Group International specializes in project management and construction, and constructs office buildings, industrial plants, and other sophisticated projects for its clients. The firm is developing a chain of business centers and hotels throughout the Soviet Union and is training Soviet general contractors in "Fast Track Construction" and quality control.

KRI, Kiser Research, Inc.
1233 20th Street, NW
Suite 505
Washington, DC 20036
Phone: (202) 223-5806
FAX: (202) 452-9571
Telex: 499160 (ITT)
Contact: John W. Kiser
Services: KRI provides a range of approaches to industry for acquiring knowledge of, and rights to, proprietary Soviet technology, including licensing, co-venturing, investment in new start-ups, task research agreements, R&D partnering, and special reports.

Madsen Marketing Strategies
31 Kidder Avenue
Somerville, MA 02144
Phone: (617) 628-9297
Contact: Carol J. Madsen, Principal
Services: Madsen Marketing Strategies supports international businesses and programs which promote trade between the U.S. and the Soviet Union and have U.S. businesses and business people among their target markets. Services include market research, marketing plans, and plan emplementation with special emphasis on marketing communications, public relations, direct mail, lead generation, sales coaching, and networking

26

Malmgren Group
2001 L Street, NW
Suite 1040
Washington, DC 20036
Phone: (202) 466-8740
FAX: (202) 872-1529
Telex: 440555
Contact: Harald B. Malmgren
Services: The Malmgren Group provides consulting services for large banks and corporations on overseas investment and joint ventures with special expertise in the Baltic Republics. The firm has offices in London, Brussels and Washington, DC.

MK Technology*Deltac
1920 N Street, NW
Suite 650
Washington, DC 20036
Phone: (202) 463 0904
FAX: (202) 429-9812
Contact: Mitchell Eisen
Services: MK Technology*Deltac is an international market research consulting firm specializing in assisting companies enter difficult foreign markets, including the Soviet Union. The firm identifies potential distributors, agents, and foreign distributors for the Soviet Union and Eastern Europe. The company also provides a monthly clipping service on Western business activity in these areas. MK Technology publishes *Export Control News,* focusing on U.S. government and COCOM export regulations and policies.

Moscow Boston International, Ltd.
P.O. Box 1327
Cambridge, MA 02238 U.S.A.
Phone: (617) 868-2080
FAX: (617) 864-8002
Contact: John K. Garrity, Chairman of the Board; Yuri A. Brazhenko, President
Services: An American-style joint-venture company providing marketing and sales services to firms transacting business with the Soviet Union. Consultations on taking advantage of business opportunities in the U.S.S.R.

Moscow Project Management
131 State Street
Boston, MA 02109
Phone: (617) 720-2000
FAX: (617) 720-3909
Telex: 8100071150
Contact: Rita Cuker
Services: The company provides services, including joint venture assistance, business development, and business seminars in the U.S. and U.S.S.R. The company is currently developing the first institute for hotel management in the U.S.S.R. in conjunction with a leading U.S. university.

Phargo Information, Inc.
369 Wayside Rd.
Portola Valley, CA 94028
Phone: (415) 851-2102
FAX: (415) 851-2353
Contact: Donna Carano, Project Director

27

Services: Phargo provides information and consulting services for companies involved in trade with the U.S.S.R.. The firm also provides communications and translation services.

PlanEcon, Inc.
1111 14th Street, NW
Suite 801
Washington, DC 20005-5603
Phone: (202) 898-0471
FAX: (202) 898-0445
Contact: Dr. Jan Vanous
Services: PlanEcon is a research and consulting firm in Washington, DC specializing in information on the economies of the Soviet Union and Eastern Europe. The firm provides economic analysis and data, specialized research on a contract basis, and business consulting on investment in the region.

Premier Global Group, Ltd.
The Toomey Building
47 South Hamilton Street
Poughkeepsie, NY 12601
Phone: (914) 454-4111
FAX: (914) 473-0305
Contact: Lev Fedyniak, President
Services: Premier Global Group, Ltd. is an international business consulting firm active in the Soviet Union as a whole and in the Ukraine in particular. It is the Western partner of the joint venture UkrNOVATSIA, which provides language and translation services, as well as a database of projects both in the Soviet Union and in the West. The database is designed to introduce potential partners, provide market research and industry profiles, assist in negotiations, and in the final formation of joint ventures and other enterprises, provide U.S. and Soviet legal counsel, accounting specialists, etc.

Price Waterhouse
in London:
Southwark Towers
32 London Bridge Street
London SE1 9SY
United Kingdom
Phone: (1) 407-8989
FAX: (1) 378-0647
Telex: 884657/8
Contact: Bruce Edwards
in Moscow:
Kursovoy Pereulok
Office 4
119034 Moscow
Phone: 202-17-17
FAX: 200-12-34
Telex: 413526 SUL SU
Contact: Susan Shale
Services: Price Waterhouse provides accounting and consulting services to firms involved in U.S.-Soviet trade and joint ventures. The services for U.S.-Soviet trade are headquartered in the London office.

Prometey
29, building 4

Checkhow str.
103006 Moscow
Phone: 299-84-45
FAX: 200-22-12 (Attn: Anton E. Pronin)
Telex: 411700 VAPRO 0310
Contact: Anton E. Pronin
Services: Prometey is an umbrella consulting and trading organization, with numerous members in all business sectors throughout the Republic of Russia and the Ukraine. It is the Soviet partner of Global Trading Associates, Inc.

RHA Group
in the U.S.:
2182 Dupont Drive
Suite 23
Irvine, CA 92715
Phone: (714) 851-0623
FAX: (714) 851-0837
Contact: Paul Armstrong, President
in Moscow:
1st Krasnopresnenskaya Nab., 224
123100 Moscow
Phone: 205-75-32
FAX: 971-56-56
Contact: Andrei Lefebvre
Services: RHA provides a range of business consulting and support services, including seminars, marketing, communications, advertising, distribution, representation, public relations, market research, hotel arrangements, and business development. RH also carries out countertrade projects.

Riga-American, Ltd.
in the U.S.:
1201 West Main Street
Waterbury, CT 06708
Phone: (203) 757-5052
FAX: (203) 596-8073
Telex: 62806768
Contact: Baxter K. Walsh
in Riga:
Latvian Orthopaedic Institute
Duntes Ul. 12/22
226005 Riga
Latvian S.S.R.
Phone: 39-26-23, 39-30-00
FAX: 39-26-23
Contact: Maris O. Toms
Services: Riga American, Ltd. was founded in 1987 to form a joint venture in the Soviet medical community to produce and distribute modern orthopedic equipment and technology throughout the U.S.S.R..

ROI Research & Analysis, Inc.
39C1 Roswell Road
Suite 133
Marietta, GA 30062
Phone: (404) 578-0474
FAX: (404) 578-0527
Contact: Alan Urech
Services: The firm specializes in business intelligence, including competitive analysis, target market analysis, focus groups and surveys, marketing and business plans, sales force productivity studies, marketing audits, sales territory and distribution analysis, site selection, sales and marketing systems, and more.

Silliman, Emily
2434 Rock Street, #1
Mountain View, CA 94043
Phone: (415) 968-9099
FAX: (415) 968-7423
Contact: Emily Silliman
Services: Silliman is an independent consultant specializing in joint ventures and other business relationships with Soviet organizations. In particular, she negotiates agreements, provides information on the U.S.S.R. legal system and recent developments in the legal regulation of the Soviet economy and trade, and offers strategic planning assistance to Western firms. Silliman has experience negotiating agreements for a range of projects including consumer products, small surgical equipment, oil and gas equipment, and other manufacturing-oriented projects.

Soviet Business Center
Yaroslavskaya Ulitsa, 13
Moscow 129366
Phone: 282-42-07
FAX: 200-22-16, 200-22-17
Telex: (095) 2889587 ECHO
Contact: Dr. Vladimir S. Shustikov, President; Yuri V. Korkin, Vice President
Services: The Center provides support services to companies pursuing trade in the U.S.S.R.

Soviet Business Connections
P.O. Box 925
Oneonta, NY 13820
Phone: (607) 433-2654
FAX: (607) 433-2654
Contact: Tom Scholet, President
Services: The firm handles business arrangements between the U.S. and U.S.S.R. including travel services, office space procurement, people-to-people connections, and communications within the U.S.S.R..

SOVUS
40 West 67 Street
Suite 7C
New York, NY 10023
Phone: (212) 580-4973
FAX: (212) 580-4990
Contact: Grace Kennan Warnecke, President
Services: SOVUS is a consulting firm advising Western companies that are or wish to do business in the Soviet Union. The firm offers feasibility studies, location surveys, negotiations, marketing, and information exchange.

Stafford Holding Company
P.O. Box 175
Colfax, NC 27235
Phone: (919) 996-4087
FAX: (919) 996-3225
Telex: 62034336
Contact: Suzanne Beane Stafford
Services: Stafford provides services

to U.S. companies setting up joint ventures in the U.S.S.R..

Summit Limited
The Omaha Building
1650 Farnam Street
Omaha, NE 68102
Phone: (402) 346-5151
FAX: (402) 346-1148
Telex: 484415
Contact: Wallace Johnson, President
Services: Summit Limited has been engaged in Soviet trade for over ten years, carrying out a wide range of transactions both in its own name and on behalf of its clients. While Summit specializes in the fields of agriculture and food processing, the company has also assisted in many other areas of Soviet trade. Summit has carried out demonstration and pilot agricultural projects in the Soviet Union, is a partner in the designing and equipping of a factory in the Ukraine to produce drip irrigation equipment, and has been instrumental in the establishment of the Food Industries International Trade Council (FIITC), a joint Soviet-American trade group representing the interests of food processing companies in both the U.S. and Soviet Union. Summit is currently assisting several major American companies in the establishment of joint ventures and other commercial relationships in the Soviet Union.

The Delphi International Group
1019 19th Street, NW
Suite 900
Washington, DC 20036
Phone: (202) 466-7951
FAX: (202) 466-4113
Telex: 989989
Contact: Sam A. Mariam, Project Specialist
Services: The company provides support services for U.S. firms seeking to develop markets in the Soviet Union, including: identifying new markets and sales opportunities, supporting communications and negotiations across national frontiers, developing marketing materials, and providing logistical support for all aspects of the business and trade venture. Professional training programs, consultation, and observation.

The Phargo Group
33 Young Street, Suite 1150
Toronto, Ontario
M5E 1G4 CANADA
Phone: (416) 360-6003
FAX: (416) 360-7942
Contact: VP, Business Development
Services: Involved in several joint ventures: AlphaGraphics Printshops of the Future in Moscow; printing and publishing; Kniga Bookstores; two MicroAge Computer Centres in Moscow.

Publishes the weekly *U.S.S.R. Business Reports* distributed in North America. Phargo is the international master licensee for the Soviet Union for AlphaGraphics and MicroAge and offers full consulting and advisory services to Western organizations interested in penetrating Soviet and East European markets.

Twain Trading Company
2 W. End Avenue
Suite 4D
Brooklyn, NY 11235
Phone: (718) 236-8308
(718) 891-3922
FAX: (718) 645-9596
Telex: 178-384 or 289-793
Contact: Edward Dubrovsky, President
in Moscow:
8/4 Ulitsa Svoboda
Moscow 123362
Phone: 491-06-77
Services: Twain Trading Company offers market research, sales representation, and support services to American companies interested in doing business in the Soviet Union. Twain is the American partner in the U.S.-Soviet joint venture IMC Corporation. IMC has offices and affiliates in New York, Moscow, Vladivostok, and Ashkhabad. The staff has many years of business, scientific research, and legal expertise in the U.S. and U.S.S.R..

Union of the World Advisory Companies
50 Milk Street
Boston, MA 02109
Phone: (617) 426-7671
FAX: (617) 451-2589
Telex: 951-131 HQ-BSN
Contact: J. Michael Any, President
Services: The firm offers trade representation and assistance in arranging joint ventures in the manufacturing, housing, and food processing industries.

Vencor
1001 3rd Avenue, West
Suite 350
Bradenton, FL 22505
Phone: (813) 747-5700
FAX: (813) 748-1049
Contact: Michael T. Ligett
Services: Vencor provides office service in Moscow, technical translation in Russian, commercial services (negotiations, contracts, licenses, trade documents), duty-free zones for exports, travel assistance to the U.S.S.R., and lead generation and screening.

V/O Vnesheconomservice
12, 1-ST Krasnogvardejskc Proezd
123100 Moscow
Phone: 259-37-53
FAX: 921-53-97
Telex: 412138 VES SU

Services: The firm provides a range of consulting services, including partner identification, joint venture structuring, drafting of documentation, and more.

V/O Vneshekonomservice
Ul. Kuybysheva, 6
6103684 Moscow
Phone: 925-35-29
Telex: 411431 A, 411431 B TPP SU
Services: The firm provides a range of consulting services, including partner
identification, joint venture structuring, drafting of documentation, and more.

Washington Researchers, Ltd.
2612 P Street, NW
Washington, DC 20007
Phone: (202) 333-3533
Contact: Leila Kight, President
Services: Washington Researchers, a firm specializing in competitive intelligence, can provide corporate firms with information on markets and the activities of corporate competitors in the Soviet Union and Eastern Europe. The firm also publishes a variety of directories, handbooks, and newsletters.

Washington Resources International
2101 Wilson Boulevard
Suite 900
Arlington, VA 22202

Phone: (703) 522-6900
Telex: 4933729 WASH UI
Contact: William Chastka, President
Services: WRI provides services in international trade, government affairs, international marketing, operations, and regulatory advice, specializing in computer exports.

TRADING COMPANIES

Argus Trading Ltd.
in the U.S.:
6110 Executive Boulevard
Suite 502
Rockville, MD 20852
Phone: (301) 984-4244
FAX: (301) 984-4247
Telex: 248209 ARGS UR
Contact: Michael Rae, President
in Moscow:
Per. Sadovskikh 4, kv. 12
103001 Moscow
Phone: 209-7071, 209-7843
FAX: 200-02-07
Telex: 413376 CIMOS SU
Contact: David Cant
Services: Argus is an established supplier of electronic products, industrial machinery, and chemicals, and an innovator in export financing, buyback, and countertrade. Offices are maintained in Moscow, U.S.S.R. and Sofia, Bulgaria.

Auriema International Group, Inc.
747 Middleneck Rd.
Great Neck, NY 11024

Phone: (516) 487-0700
FAX: (516) 487-0719
Telex: 62402 17505
Contact: Robert Auriema, President
Services: The company is involved in import/export and publishing.

Belarus, Inc.
7075 W. Parkland Ct.
P.O. Box 23608
Milwaukee, WI 53223
Phone: (414) 355-2000
Telex: 177050 BELARUSNYK
Contact: Edward Ossinski, President
Services: The corporate headquarters for Belarus Inc., manages distribution and sales of Belarus farm equipment.

BERUSA Corporation
in New York:
5411 Queens Boulevard
Woodside, NY 11377
Phone: (718) 779-0500
Contact: Tom Aman
in Milwaukee:
7075 W. Parklawn Ct.
Box 23608
Milwaukee, WI 53223
Phone: (414) 355-2000
Services: The company is involved in commodities trade, including wood products, cement, glass materials, etc. The corporation is willing to represent all industries.

BET Trading Associates
in the U.S.:

P.O. Box 771909
Houston, TX 77215-1909
Phone: (713) 266-5881
FAX: (713) 266-5985
Telex: 774697
in Moscow:
Hotel National, Rm. 315
103001 Moscow
Phone: 203-5303, 203-5335
Contact: Bobby E. Taylor, President
Services: The company is involved in equipment sales for the oil, gas, and mining industry, and is willing to represent companies in most industries.

CAMCO Trading Co.
in the U.S.:
P.O. Box 14484
Houston, TX 77221
Phone: (713) 747-4000
FAX: (713) 747-6751
Contact: Roger Parrish
Services: CAMCO is a major manufacturer and also represents firms in the area of oil and gas production and drilling equipment.
in Moscow:
CAMCO
Hotel Mezhdunarodnaya
Krasnopresnenskaya Nab., 12
Room 1340
123610 Moscow
Phone: 253-15-75
FAX: 253-13-40
Telex: 413205 U.S.CO

Chilewich International Corp.
in the U.S.:

12 Water Street
White Plains, NY 10601
Phone: (914) 997-2000
FAX: (914) 997-2122
Telex: 232088 CSC
Contact: Simon Chilewich, President
in Moscow:
Kursovoy Pereulok #9
Phone: 119034 Moscow
203-51-92
FAX: 200-12-15
Telex: 413211 CHILWSU
Services: Chilewich International
Corporation is an export trading
company that primarily handles foods,
animal by-products and consumer
goods.

Construction, Marketing, & Trading, Inc.
8150 Leesburg Pike
Suite 1200
Vienna, VA 22180
Phone: (703) 761-3188
FAX: (703) 790-5933
Telex: 3792650 COMCORTY 1200
Contact: Eric Crabtree
Services: The company provides
services for U.S. firms involved in any
aspect of construction and that wish
to enter the Soviet market.

DRG International, Inc.
in the U.S.:
1167 Route 22 East
P.O. Box 1178
Mountainside, NJ 07092
Phone: (201) 233-2075

FAX: (201) 233-0758
Telex: 178110 DRG INTL
in Moscow:
Inpred
Krasnopresnenskaya Nab., 12
123610 Moscow
Telex: 411813 REPR SU
Contact: Cyril Geacintov, President
Services: The company markets
diagnostic products and equipment,
biotechnology, chemicals, and hospital
disposable supplies.

Global Trading Associates, Inc.
in the U.S.:
1155 Connecticut Avenue, NW
Suite 500
Washington, DC 20036
Phone: (202) 467-8589
FAX: (202) 452-8654
Telex: 4933729 WASH UI
Contact: William S. Loiry,
Chairman; Terence W. Dittrich,
President
in Moscow:
29, Guild 4,
Chekhow str.
103006 Moscow
Phone: 299-84-45
FAX: 200-22-12 (Attn: Anton E.
Pronin)
Telex: 411700 VAPRO 0310
Contact: Anton E. Pronin
Services: Working with a top Soviet
foreign trade organization, the firm
trades products in a variety of fields
and arranges unique financing
methods.

Intertorg, Inc.
in the U.S.:
940 Sagamore Way
Sacramento, CA 95822
Phone: (916) 443-2981
FAX: (914) 443-2991
Telex: 176834
in Moscow:
Gruzinskiy Pereulok 3, kv. 63
123056 Moscow
Phone: 253-97-71, 254-31-62
Services: Intertorg provides a complete capability in traditional representation and sales support. The company is involved in marketing, promotion, and sales support and is willing to represent companies selectively.

Laurel Industries
in the U.S.
280 Laurel Avenue
Highland Park, IL 60035
Phone: (708) 432-8204
FAX: (708) 432-8243
Telex: 720457 CRL INC HLPK
Contact: Catherine Lambrecht
in Moscow:
Hotel Mezhdunarodnaya 2
Krasnopresnenskaya Nab., 12
123610 Moscow
Phone: 437-54-64
FAX: 437-54-64
Services: Laurel Industries is a trading company specializing in lasers, analytical instrumentation, machine tools and commodities, and is willing to represent firms in most industries.

LIC-CON Technologies, Inc.
655 3rd Avenue
Suite 1620
New York, NY 10017
Phone: (212) 818-9010
FAX: (212) 818-0463
Telex: CMC 66403 UW
Contact: Peter Walsh
Services: LIC-CON is a U.S. company jointly owned and managed by Soviet and U.S. partners, and was established to market Soviet technologies and products to American industry.

Louis & Johnson, Chartered
7611 Lexington Avenue
Laurel, MD 02707
Phone: (301) 498-9404
FAX: (301) 604-7348
Telex: 6504339454
Contact: Zakhar Matlin
Services: Market analyses; export and joint-venture opportunities and formation; and development of industrial projects, construction, architectural, and engineering support services.

Midwest Enterprises, Inc.
8493 16th Road
Almond, WI 54909
Phone: (715) 366-8800
FAX: (715) 366-4400
Contact: Mark Dzulynsky, President
Services: The firm offers engineering and manufacturing assistance in joint venture development and

import/export assistance.

P.D.I.-Barcon Inc.
25 W. 43rd Street
New York, NY 10036
Phone: (212) 764-8800
FAX: (212) 764-8850
Telex: 6790550
Contact: Joseph H. Filner, CEO;
Jacob Pollock, Chairman
in Ohio:
3200 W. Market Street
Akron, OH 44313
Phone: (216) 869-8734
FAX: (216) 869-8726
Telex: 205938 BARMET
Services: PDI-Barcon Inc.
specializes in commodity trade,
countertrade of all goods and
equipment, organization of industrial
projects within the U.S.S.R., and
technology transfer in both directions.

Philipp Brothers, Ltd.
1221 Avenue of the Americas
New York, NY 10020
Phone: (212) 575-5900
FAX: (212) 790-6810
Telex: 233031
Contact: Gary Marcus
Services: The company specializes
in countertrade.

Polmark, Inc.
150 West 56th Street, Suite 4101
New York, NY 10019
Phone: (212) 262-1212

FAX: (212) 956-5022
Telex: 650 379 6500 MCI UW
Contact: George M. J. Meller,
President
Services: The firm offers
international trade and countertrade,
consulting, and financial services.
Polmark participates in joint ventures
in U.S.S.R. in the areas of market
research, medical equipment supply,
and technology transfer.

Potomac Group International, Ltd.
P.O. Box 18226
Washington, DC 20036
Phone: (703) 538-4553
FAX: (703) 538-6007
Telex: 510 601 7467
Contact: Scott M. Blacklin
Services: This firm primarily
represents American companies in
the Soviet market; establishes repeat
exports of Soviet products into the
U.S. market; sources at low-cost from
the U.S. and Far East for Soviet
cooperatives and foreign trade
enterprises; and offers
nontraditional financing for Soviet
customers through its office and
commercial relations in Yugoslavia.

**Project Development International,
Inc.**
25 W. 43rd Street
New York, NY 10036
Phone: (212) 764-8800
FAX: (212) 764-8850
Telex: 6790550

Contact: Joseph H. Filner, CEO
Services: PDI specializes in commodity trade, countertrade of all goods and equipment, organization of industrial projects within the U.S.S.R., and technology transfer in both directions.

Satra Corp.
in the U.S.:
645 Madison Avenue
New York, NY 10022
Phone: (212) 355-3030
FAX: (212) 758-6366
Telex: 225747
Contact: Ara Oztemal, President
in Moscow:
11/13 Tryekhprudnyy Per.
103001 Moscow
Phone: 299-9164
Telex: 413129 SATRA SU
Services: The firm is involved in extraction industries, i.e. ores, raw materials, oils, rubber products, synthetic rubber, cars and auto products, oil drilling equipment on- and offshore, computers, and other electronic materials.

Scott European Corp.
in the U.S.:
58 E. State Street
Montpelier, VT 05602
Phone: (802) 223-0262
FAX: (802) 223-0265
Telex: 5101011983
Contact: Robert L. Krattli

in Moscow:
Inpred
Krasnopresnenskaya Nab., 12/501
123610 Moscow
Phone: 253-10-94
FAX: 253-93-82
Telex: 411813 REPR SU
Contact: Andrei Zelenov
Services: SEC provides sales representation and services in Eastern Europe and in the U.S.S.R.; imports industrial, mineral, and consumer products from the socialist countries for its own and its clients' accounts; assists in the conceptualization, negotiation, and organization of joint ventures in the socialist countries; organizes and negotiates countertrade and compensation agreements; and arranges and conducts seminars and exhibitions which facilitate East-West trade.

Technology Contact International
758 Lowell Street
Peabody, MA 01960
Phone: (617) 598-1753
Contact: Vladimir L. Tsivkin, President
Services: The firm provides identification of new business opportunities; searches for prospective business partners in the Soviet Union; participates in business negotiations with a Soviet counterpart; refines technical details of joint-venture or technology transfer agreements; and compiles presentation materials.

The Russian Business Center
P.O. Box 2332
Cambridge, MA 02238
Phone: (617) 492-1558
FAX: (617) 577-1209
Telex: 324168 OAKS CAMB
Contact: John Garrity
Services: The firm provides consulting services to U.S. firms wishing to do business in the Soviet Union. It provides legal consultation on Soviet and U.S. law. The principals are fluent in Russian and also provide legal translations. Services are also offered to Soviet companies wishing to do business in the U.S.

The Stern Group, Inc.
1133 Connecticut Avenue, NW
Suite 1000
Washington, DC 20036
Phone: (202) 775-2379
FAX: (202) 833-8491
Contact: Paula Stern
Services: The Stern Group provides a broad range of services to companies investigating U.S.-Soviet trade prospects. The firm specializes in analyzing policy trends in Washington and overseas and assisting firms impacted by U.S. trade regulations.

U.S.-U.S.S.R. Marine Resources Company
in the U.S.:

192 Nickerson
Suite 307
Seattle, WA 98109
Phone: (206) 285-6424
FAX: (206) 282-9414
Telex: 277115MCR UR
Contact: James Talbot, President
in Moscow:
SOVAM
National Hotel, kv. 450
Moscow
Phone: 230-2214
Telex: 413052 SOVAM
Contact: Paul Iremonger
Services: Marine Resources is a fifty-fifty joint venture between Bellingham Cold Storage, WA and the Soviet Ministry of the Fishing Industry. The firm specializes in fisheries and oceanographic equipment, timber equipment, trucks, packaging materials
and equipment, buying/selling fish, and is willing to represent companies on a case-by-case basis. The firm prefers to focus on areas linked to natural resource development. MRCI has a subsidiary trading company, SOVAM, with offices in Moscow.

Welt International, Inc.
1413 K Street, NW
Suite 800
Washington, DC 20005
Phone: (202) 371-0555
FAX: (202) 862-5833
Telex: 248599
Contact: Leo Welt, President
Services: The firm is involved with

unconventional forms of financing, countertrade, various industries and electronics. Willing to represent companies in all areas.

SECTION 2

U.S. LAW FIRMS, ATTORNEYS & LEGAL ORGANIZATIONS

Listed in this section are law firms and individual attorneys who have indicated experience in law pertaining to U.S.-Soviet trade and/or the formation of joint ventures. In selecting legal representation, consider the firm's past experience in U.S.-Soviet trade, their client list, and their access to the Soviet Union.

Legal organizations are involved in U.S.-Soviet trade as well. For example, the American Bar Association's Section of International Law and Practice sponsors an annual Soviet Lawyer Internship Program for Soviet attorneys to receive practical training in U.S. law firms and corporations. The New York State Bar Association has a Committee on Soviet and East European Law, which has co-sponsored a workshop on the practice of law in the Soviet Union and a welcoming reception for visiting Soviet lawyers.

Akin, Gump, Strauss, Hauer & Feld
1333 New Hampshire Avenue, NW
Suite 400
Washington, DC 20036
Phone: (202) 887-4000
FAX: (202) 887-4288
Contact: Daniel Spiegel
Services: Through its U.S. offices, as well as its 25-lawyer Brussels office, the firm assists clients with a variety of transactional and policy matters relating to trade with the Soviet Union and East European countries. Ambassador Robert S. Strauss, former U.S. Special Trade Representative, is a partner with the firm.

American Bar Association
Soviet Lawyer Internship Program
1800 M Street, NW
Washington, DC 20036
Phone: (202) 331-2280
FAX: (202) 331-2220
Contact: Steven G. Raikin, Esq., Program Director
Services: ABA sponsors a Soviet Lawyer Internship Program founded by the Soros Foundation Soviet Union for outstanding young Soviet lawyers with a variety of specialties who have distinguished themselves as practitioners or scholars and speak excellent English. They receive practical training and experience by working in U.S. law firms, corporations, and law schools. ABA

41

also sponsors a comparable Central and East European Lawyer Internship Project. All interns are selected via an unprecedented open competition which includes personal interviews and English proficiency examinations. All American lawyers interested in serving as hosts are encouraged to contact the ABA.

Arnold & Porter
1200 New Hampshire Avenue, NW
Washington, DC 20036
Phone: (202) 872-6929
FAX: (202) 331-9832
Telex: 89-2733
Contact: Jeffrey A. Burt
Services: Represents numerous clients and foreign government officials in commercial transactions in Eastern Europe and the Soviet Union in the areas of hotels, office buildings, health care, chemicals, the pulp and paper industry, oil and gas, food processing, technology transfers, and various manufacturing activities. In 1989, the firm successfully completed the negotiation of the largest U.S.-Soviet joint venture in the health care field, and the firm recently finalized the largest U.S.-Soviet joint venture in the publishing industry.

Baker & Botts
555 13th Street, NW
Suite 500 East
Washington, DC 20004-1109
Phone: (202) 639-7700
FAX: (202) 639-7832, 639-7993
Telex: 6974881, 6502067689
BAKERBOTTS WAS
Contact: Paul Freedenberg
Services: Baker & Botts provides advice and representation for U.S. export control regulations, and assistance in structuring deals and obtaining financing, assistance in barter and countertrade arrangements, assistance in structuring joint ventures and technology licensing. Paul Freedenberg specializes in international trade issues, export financing, technology transfer, and export licensing. Dr. Freedenburg formerly served in the Department of Commerce as Under Secretary for Export Administration (1987-1989) and as Assistant Secretary for Trade Administration (1985-1987).

Baker & McKenzie
in Washington:
815 Connecticut Avenue, NW
Washington, DC 20006-4078
Phone: (202) 452-7012
FAX: (202) 452-7074
Telex: 89552
Contact: Eugene Theroux
in Chicago:
One Prudential Plaza
130 East Randolph Drive
Chicago, IL 60601
Phone: (312) 861-8179
FAX: (312) 861-2899
Telex: 25-4425

Contact: Preston M. Torbert
in Moscow:
"Pushkin Plaza"
Bolshoy Gnezdnykovskiy Pereulok, 7
103009 Moscow
Phone: 200-61-67, 200-49-06, 200-61-86
FAX: 200-02-03
Telex: 413671 BAKER SU
Contact: Paul J. Melling, Arthur L. George, John P. Hewko
Services: The international law firm of Baker & McKenzie provides services to foreign and Soviet enterprises on all legal aspects of investment projects in the Soviet Union and abroad. Theroux is the Co-Chair of the Committee on Soviet and East European Law of the American Bar Association.

Bryan, Cave, McPheeters & McRoberts
700 13th Street, NW
Washington, DC 20005-3960
Phone: (202) 508-6000
FAX: (202) 508-6200
Telex: 440321 BCMM UI
Contact: Peter D. Ehrenhaft, Anita C. Esslinger
Services: The firm has approximately 350 lawyers and nine offices. Peter Ehrenhaft, Vice Chairman of Bryan Cave's Corporate Department, has been the registered agent of the Commercial Counselors of Poland and Czechoslovakia, has represented numerous East European Foreign Trade Organiza-

tions and enterprises in U.S. administrative proceedings and litigation, and has assisted U.S. firms in the establishment of joint ventures in Eastern Europe. He is presently advising government ministries in the U.S.S.R. and Hungary on foreign investment laws and privatization issues.

Chadbourne, Hedman & Raabe & Advocates CCCP
International Lawyers
123610 Krasnopresnenskaya Nab. 12.
Mezhdunarodnaya-2, Kv. 1421
Moscow
Phone: 253-14-21
FAX: 253-16-51
Contact: Robert E. Langer, Resident Attorney
Services: Chadbourne & Parke is a partner in the multinational joint venture law office in the Soviet Union, Chadbourne, Hedman & Raabe/Advocates CCCP. The joint venture provides legal services to facilitate international trade and project development in the Soviet Union and provides ongoing training programs, including an international exchange of lawyers among the venture's member firms.

Chadbourne & Parke
30 Rockefeller Plaza
New York, NY 10112
Phone: (212) 408-5100
FAX: (212) 541-5406
Telex: 620520

43

Contact: William E. Holland and Eugene R. Sullivan, Jr.
Services: Active in Soviet transactions for over 12 years. Has advised clients with respect to joint ventures, technology transfers, purchases and sales of goods, and financing of transactions, and has also represented Soviet companies with respect to activities in the United States.

Cole Corette & Abrutyn
in the U.S.:
1110 Vermont Avenue, NW
Washington, DC 20005
Phone: (202) 872-1414
FAX: (202) 296-8238; (202) 872-1396
Telex: 64391
Contact: Edward H. Lieberman
in London:
21 Upper Broot Street
London W1Y 1PD
Phone: 44 71 491-3735
FAX: 408-0843
Telex: 264598
Contact: Robert Stan
Services: Cole Corette & Abrutyn advises clients from North America and Europe on Soviet projects and is the principal external advisor to Moscow Narodnyy Bank on trade, investment, and finance matters. Sectors in which the firm has experience in the Soviet Union include financial management, consumer goods, pharmaceutical production in the Georgian republic, computer equipment and software, publishing, real estate development, metals, minerals, timber, mining and production equipment, foodstuffs and food processing, timber, energy, transportation equipment, countertrade in the Uzbek Republic and Siberia, construction in the Baltics, and oil exploration and development projects. Professor William Butler, of counsel to the firm, is an advisor to Mr. Leonid Abalkin on Soviet legal reforms and the firm enjoys a unique cooperation with the Soviet Institute of State and Law.

Coudert Brothers
in the U.S.:
200 Park Avenue,
New York, NY 10166
Phone: (212) 880-4400
FAX: (212) 557-8137, 557-8136
Telex: 666764
Contact: Douglas R. Aden
in Moscow:
Ulitsa Petrovka, 15
Second Floor
Phone: 230-2547, 928-7838
FAX: 200-1228, 200-0268
Telex: 413-310; 413-329, 413-267 IPATC-SU
Contact: Richard N. Dean
Services: Coudert Brothers maintains a Moscow office and offers services in planning and negotiating transactions and preparing English- and Russian-language documents. In the past

three years, Coudert's Moscow office has advised on over 150 projects, including joint ventures, turnkey projects, licensing, compensation trade arrangements, tax questions, and establishing foreign business offices in Moscow.

Covington & Burling
1201 Pennsylvania Avenue, NW
Washington, DC 20044
Phone: (202) 662-5172
FAX: (202) 662-6288
Telex: 89593 COVLANG WSH
Contact: Russell H. Carpenter
Services: The firm has counseled a number of corporations concerning the possibility of their entering into joint ventures with various entities in the Soviet Union. This work is performed principally by Russell Carpenter, who speaks Russian fluently and travels frequently to the Soviet Union.

Debevoise & Plimpton
875 Third Avenue
New York, NY 10022
Phone: (212) 909-6421
FAX: (212) 909-6836
Telex: (RCA) 234400 DEBS UR
Contact: Roswell Perkins, Jonathan H. Hines
Services: Debevoise & Plimpton has been involved in the negotiations of joint ventures in the Soviet Union and Hungary on behalf of a large U.S. advertising agency.

It has also provided counsel to leading U.S. and Western European food processing, clothing, cosmetics, and health care companies on the establishment of joint venture production facilities in the Soviet Union. The firm participated in negotiations in 1989 of a Soviet joint venture in Tobolsk (Siberia, U.S.S.R.) involving a prospective $2.2 billion plant construction for petrochemical production.

Dilworth, Paxson, Kalish & Kauffman
1001 Pennsylvania Avenue, NW
Suite 275 North
Washington, DC 20004
Phone: (202) 624-5900
FAX: (202) 624 -5904
Contact: Martin Mendelsohn
Services: Martin Mendelsohn, is a former official with the U.S. Department of Justice. He has had extensive contact with legal authorities in the Soviet Union concerning violations of Soviet criminal law. Mendelsohn also has experience in trade and countertrade, including the cosmetics, heavy and light machinery, and engine parts industries.

The Florida Bar
Soviet and Eastern European Law Committee

c/o Maureen O'Brien
1380 N.E. Miami Gardens Drive
Suite 200
North Miami Beach, FL 33179
Phone: (305) 949-0093
FAX: (305) 949-9325
Services: The Soviet and Eastern European Law Committee of the International Section of The Florida Bar was organized in 1990. It is a cosponsor of The Florida Conference On Trade And Investment With The Soviet Union and Eastern Europe.

Foley & Lardner
in Milwaukee:
First Wisconsin Center
777 East Wisconsin Avenue
Milwaukee, WI 53202-5367
Phone: (414) 289-3586
FAX: (414) 289-3791
Telex: 26819 FOLEY LARD MIL
Contact: John W. Brahm
in Washington:
1775 Pennsylvania Avenue
Washington, DC 20006-4680
Phone: (202) 862-5300
FAX: (202) 862-5339
Telex: 904136 (FOLEY LARD WASH)
Contact: Peter C. Linzmeyer
Services: Foley and Lardner's International Business Group provides legal counsel in all facets of international business transactions in the Soviet Union and Eastern Europe. Included among the areas in which the firm provides assistance

are import/export transactions, customs and import regulation, licensing and technology transfers, direct foreign investment and joint ventures, international dispute resolution, international tax planning, and immigration matters. Among its projects, the firm has negotiated a U.S.-Soviet joint venture involving tractor assembly and distribution. For more than a decade, Foley & Lardner has represented Soviet organizations in their business relations with the United States.

Fried, Frank, Harris, Shriver & Jacobson
1001 Pennsylvania Avenue
Suite 800
Washington, DC 20036
Phone: (202) 639-7000
FAX: (202) 639-7003, 639-7004, 639-7008
Contact: David Birenbaum

Garrity, John K.
36 Linnaean Street
Suite 12A
Cambridge, MA 02138
Phone: (617) 868-2080
FAX: (617) 864-8002
Telex: 324168 OAKS CAMB
Contact: John K. Garrity
Services: Russian-speaking attorney providing legal services to clients doing business with the Soviet Union. In cooperation with

46

corresponding Moscow attorney, specializing in consultations on Soviet commercial law. Member of the U.S.S.R. Committee of the International Business Center of New England.

Gaston and Snow
1511 K Street, NW
Suite 1200
Washington DC 20005
Phone: (202) 347-230
FAX: (202) 347-4819
Telex: 3725451 COMCOR WASH DC
Contact: James Gallatin

Gibson, Dunn and Crutcher
in the U.S.:
1050 Connecticut Avenue, NW
Washington, DC 20036
Phone: (202) 955-8500
FAX: (202) 467-0539
Telex: 197659 GIBTRASK WSH
Contact: Paul R. Harter
in London:
30/35 Pall Mall
London SW1Y 5LP
Phone: (071) 925-0440
FAX: (071) 925-2465
Telex: 27731 GIBTRK G
Services: With attorneys fluent in Russian, Gibson, Dunn & Crutcher provides a broad range of services in connection with trade and investment activities in the Soviet Union. The firm combines prudent legal advice, creative approaches to solving problems, and linguistic and cultural expertise to bridge the gap between West and East. In addition to services in connection with trade and finance, the firm has served as counsel to U.S. and other Western clients in the successful establishment of joint ventures pursuing a wide range of activities in the Soviet Union.

Goodwin & Soble
1300 19th Street, NW
Suite 350
Washington, DC 20036
Phone: (202) 223-8282
FAX: (202) 223-8560
Telex: 272691 GOSO UR
Contact: Steve Soble
Services: Goodwin & Soble is a small law firm which specializes in international commercial transactions. Attorneys at the firm have had extensive experience in negotiation, drafting, and concluding major transactions in the Soviet Union in diverse fields. The areas of the firm's experience include energy industries, heavy machinery, infrastructure development, transportation, and construction, including turnkey factory contracting and multiple-party transactions, in geographic regions ranging from the Baltic States to major cities to Siberia. The firm has additional expertise in international financing and dispute resolution.

Hall, Dickler, Lawler, Kent & Friedman
460 Park Avenue
New York, NY 10022
Phone: (212) 838-4600
FAX: (212) 935-3121
Telex: 239857 GONY UR
Contact: Mark A. Meyer
Services: The firm provides services directed to the middle-market business man. The firm's activity has been concentrated in the republics, especially Georgia, Belorussia, and the Ukraine. Projects have included shoe factory and brewery set-ups.

Henson & Efron
1200 Title Insurance Bldg.
Minneapolis, MN 55401
Phone: (612) 339-2500
FAX: (612) 339-6364
Contact: Robert Bayer
Services: Henson & Efron is a 19-person law firm with experience in international law. Robert Bayer has been an IREX-fellow studying Soviet law in Moscow and teaches a Soviet law course on an adjunct basis.

Hogan & Hartson
555 13th Street, NW
Washington, DC 20004
Phone: (202) 637-5964
FAX: (202) 637-5910
Telex: 248370 (RCA)
Contact: Alex Frishberg
Services: Hogan & Hartson has affiliations in the Russian and Ukrainian republics, among others. The firm structures and negotiates transactions, including joint ventures, contractual, and licensing arrangements. The firm advises clients in all aspects of Soviet intellectual property law, including patents, trademarks, copyrights, authors' rights, and commercial secrets. The firm also has a substantial practice in Eastern Europe, including Poland and Hungary.

Jones, Day, Reavis, & Pogue
Metropolitan Square
1450 G Street, NW
Washington, DC 20005-2088
Phone: (202) 879-3939
FAX: (202) 737-2832
Telex: 892410 - Domestic, 64363 - International
Contact: Michael R. Silverman or Charles Mathias, Jr.
Services: Jones, Day, Reavis & Pogue has represented clients in dealings with the Soviet Union since the early 1970s. Recent matters include joint ventures in such areas as oil exploration and refining, consumer electronics, cosmetics and household goods, hotel construction, agribusiness, and the manufacture of heavy industrial equipment and agricultural machinery. Mathias is a former U.S. Senator from Maryland.

Jurjans, Peteris
38021 Euclid Avenue
Cleveland, OH 44094
Phone: (216) 951-6665
FAX: (216) 951-4797
Telex: 7101109209
Contact: Peteris Jurjans [Yuryans]
Services: The firm's services include legal expertise for U.S.-Baltic joint ventures, denationalization of properties in Latvia, and inheritance matters. The firm has on-going joint venture projects for farm equipment, ceramic tiles, brick production, computer software, shoe factories, paper mills, and fine art exchanges. Fluent in Latvian language.

Karl, Ann Marie
2880 N. Meridian Rd.
Tallahassee, FL 32312
Phone: (904) 385-9747
Contact: Ann Marie Karl
Services: Referral services.

KFC Corporation
1441 Gardiner Lane
Louisville, KY 40213
Phone: (502) 454-2169
FAX: (502) 456-8323
Contact: R. Scott Toop
Services: Toop is counsel to PepsiCo, Inc.

Kutak, Rock & Campbell
The Omaha Building

1650 Farnam Street
Omaha, NE 68102
Phone: (402) 346-6000
FAX: (402) 346-1148
Telex: 484 415 Kuroc
Contact: William E. Holland
Services: The firm has been continuously active in Soviet transactions for over 12 years. Its lawyers have advised clients with respect to joint ventures, technology transfers, purchases and sales of goods, and financing of transactions, and have also represented Soviet companies with respect to activities in the United States. As a member of the Legal Committee of the U.S.-U.S.S.R. Trade and Economic Council, a firm attorney commented on the drafts of the original Soviet joint venture decree. The firm has special expertise in technology transfers and in the areas of agriculture and food processing.

LeBoeuf, Lamb, Leiby & MacRae
520 Madison Avenue
New York, NY 10022
Phone: (212) 715-8000
FAX: (212) 371-4840
Telex: 423416
Contact: John I. Huhs

Licata, Arthur F., P.C.
20 Custom House Street
Suite 1010
Boston, MA 02110
Phone: (617) 345-9588, (800) 777-0899

FAX: (617) 345-9787
Contact: Arthur F. Licata
Services: Arthur Licata represents U.S. businesses in the Soviet Union and Eastern Europe. He is also serving as a representative of a U.S. company to identify and market consumer products from the East to retailers in the United States. Licata has assembled a national sales force for this purpose in the U.S.

Lord Day & Lord, Barrett Smith
1675 Broadway
New York, NY 10019-5874
Phone: (212) 969-6000
FAX: (212) 969-6100
Telex: 62589
Contact: Peter Pettibone, Polina Smith, Jonathan Pavluk
Services: This firm has served as the counsel to the U.S.-U.S.S.R. Trade and Economic Council since the mid-1970s. It assists clients in export licensing issues, establishing joint ventures, negotiating licenses of technology and sales of equipment, and other commercial transactions.

Mayer, Brown & Platt
787 7th Avenue
New York, NY 10019
Phone: (212) 554-3000
FAX: (212) 262-1910
Telex: 701842
Contact: Michael G. Capatides
Services: Mayer, Brown & Platt initiated its involvement in the Soviet Union with its representation of the Bank of Foreign Economic Affairs of the U.S.S.R. (Vneshekonombank) in the U.S. Several months ago, the firm completed the process of establishing a Vneshekonombank representative office in New York. Presently, the firm's attorneys are engaged in a variety of matters for Vneshekonombank, including trade-related financing issues. In addition, Mayer, Brown & Platt's Chicago office has participated in a recent joint venture involving the sale of Soviet film rights to a U.S. company.

McAulay Fisher Nissen & Goldberg
261 Madison Avenue
New York, NY 10016
Phone: (212) 986-4090
FAX: (212) 818-9479
Telex: 427294
Contact: J. Harold Nissen, international patent and trademark attorney
Services: The firm has offered protection of intellectual property matters, including preparation and prosecution, in the U.S. and the Soviet Union for over thirty years. Patents have been granted in various areas of Soviet technology. The firm is also involved in the licensing and sale of technology into and out of the Soviet Union. The firm is a member of various bar associations throughout the world.

Milbank, Tweed, Hadley & McCloy
International Square Building
1825 Eye Street, NW, Suite 900
Washington DC 20006
Phone: (202) 835-7500
FAX: (202) 835-7586
Telex: 440887
Contact: Stanley J. Marcus/Fred W. Reinke
Services: Milbank represents a number of U.S. and international companies and financial institutions actively exploring new business opportunities in the Soviet Union. Milbank has traditional strengths in joint ventures, trade transactions, leasing and capital markets, which has resulted in the firms's recent involvement in a number of manufacturing, energy, and service industry projects in the Soviet Union. Moreover, the firm's leading reputation in project finance has resulted in its involvement in some of the largest and most complex projects in Eastern Europe and the Soviet Union. Milbank also has extensive experience in advising clients on U.S. export controls as well as on U.S. lending and financing restrictions applicable to trade transactions with the Soviet Union.

Morrison & Foerster
1290 Avenue of the Americas
New York, NY 10104
Phone: (212) 468-8057
FAX: (212) 468-7900

Contact: James R. Silkenat
Services: The firm specializes in licensing, bank loans, technology transfers, international trade, and intellectual property.

Miller & Chevalier
655 15th Street, NW
Washington DC 20005
Phone: (202) 626-5800
FAX: (202) 628-0859
Telex: 440250
Contact: Homer E. Moyer, Jr.
Services: Homer Moyer, Jr. is Chairman of the Section of International Law and Practice of the American Bar Association (ABA). He is also former Chairman of the Trade Committee of the ABA and former General Counsel of the U.S. Department of Commerce. Moyer was a participant in the first U.S.-U.S.S.R. Legal Seminar, is Chairman of the Executive Committee of the 1990 Moscow Conference on Law and Bilateral Economic Relations, and is Chairman of the Executive Board of the ABA's Central and East European Initiative.

New York State Bar Association
Committee on Soviet and Eastern European Law
c/o Brian G. Hart
Simpson, Thacher & Bartlett
425 Lexington Avenue
New York, NY 10017

51

Phone: (212) 455-2000
FAX: (212) 455-2502
Telex: 4552500
Contact: Brian G. Hart
Services: This committee co-sponsored a workshop on the practice of law in the Soviet Union and a welcoming reception with visiting Soviet lawyers in January of 1990. Its parent section, the International Law and Practice Section, co-sponsored a conference on U.S.-Soviet trade in April of 1990.

O'Brien, Maureen
1380 N.E. Miami Gardens Drive
Suite 220
North Miami Beach, FL 33179
Phone: (305) 949-0093
FAX: (305) 949-9325
Services: Specializes in the area of international investment, business and corporate law, and heads the firm's Soviet and Eastern European Practice Group with a primary emphasis on doing business in Ukraine. She is Chairman of the International Law Section of The Florida Bar, a member of the Executive Council of the International Law Section, and Chairman of its Soviet and Eastern European Law Committee. O'Brien is also a member of the Board of Directors of the Ukrainian American Bar Association.

Paul, Hastings, Janofsky & Walker
1050 Connecticut Avenue, NW
Twelfth Floor
Washington, DC 20036
Phone: (202) 223-9000
FAX: (202) 452-8149
Telex: 710-822-9062
Contact: G. Hamilton Loeb
Services: The firm has direct experience in handling import and export matters in Eastern Europe, setting up joint ventures in Eastern Europe, and assisting individuals' emigration from the Soviet Union and their immigration to the U.S.

Pepper, Hamilton & Scheetz
1300 19th Street, NW
Suite 700
Washington, DC 20036
Phone: (202) 828-1200
FAX: (202) 828-1665
Telex: 1240653 ITT
Contact: Stephen B. Ives, Jr.
Services: The firm is active in joint ventures, technology transfers, and trade with the Soviet Union. It represented Carlisle SynTec Systems in negotiating its joint venture, K r o v t e x ,   w i t h Soyuzpromstroykomplekt to produce 30 million square meters per year of modern roofing material and is working on other ventures. The firm has a long history of involvement in the Soviet Union and East European countries, including Yugoslavia.

Salans, Hertzfeld & Heilbronn
in the U.S.:
1270 Avenue of the Americas
New York, NY 10020
Phone: (212) 974-8400
FAX: (212) 974-8318
Telex: RCA 839554
in Paris:
9 rue Boissy d'Anglas
Paris 75008
Phone: (1) 42-68-48-00
Telex: 280 990 Parilex
Contact: Jim Hogan or Jeff Hertzfeld
Services: Salans Hertzfeld & Heilbronn is a French-American law firm, with offices in Paris and New York. Founded in 1978, the firm has twenty-nine attorneys and is one of the biggest international law firms in Paris. The firm is very active in representing Western companies in sales, technology transfers, commercial transactions, and industrial projects, including joint-ventures, cooperation agreements, and countertrade in the Soviet Union and Eastern Europe. The firm has participated or is participating in the negotiation of over 50 joint-ventures in the Soviet Union alone.

Shaw, Pittman, Potts & Trowbridge
2300 N Street, NW
Washington DC 20037
Phone: (202) 663-8136
FAX: (202) 663-8007
Telex: 892693 SHAWLAW WSH

Contact: Robert B. Robbins
Services: The firm is involved in the representation of Eastern European countries in the West. It also represents U.S. entities in joint-venture transactions with the Soviet Union and other East European countries.

Sherr, Alan B.
39 Blaney Street
Swampscott, MA 01907
Phone: (617) 581-7651, (401) 863-3465
FAX: (617) 581-7651, (401) 274-8440
Contact: Alan B. Sherr
Services: Alan B. Sherr, lawyer and electrical engineer, is Director of the Project on Soviet Foreign Economic Policy and International Security at Brown University where he leads a team of researchers working on Soviet trade. He works independently, or with major law firms, banks, and others, to assist in the negotiation and operation of joint ventures, sales, and other transactions between U.S. and Soviet entities.

Shillinglaw, Thomas
Division Counsel
Corning Inc.
Corning, NY 14830
Phone: (607) 974-8164
FAX: (607) 974-6135

Telex: 192809010
Contact: Thomas Shillinglaw
Services: Shillinglaw is Co-chairman of the ABA Committee on Soviet and East European Law and a member of the Legal Committee of the U.S.-U.S.S.R. Trade and Economic Council.

Sidley & Austin
1722 I Street, NW
Washington, DC 20006
Phone: (202) 429-4101
FAX: (202) 429-6144
Telex: 8-9463 (SIDLEY AUS WSH)
Contact: Robert B. Shanks

Simpson, Thacher & Bartlett
425 Lexington Ave
New York, NY 10017
Phone: (212) 455-2000
FAX: (212) 455-2502
Telex: 4552500
Contact: Brian G. Hart

Smith & Williams, P.A.
712 South Oregon Avenue
Tampa, Florida 33606
Phone: (813) 253-5400
FAX: (813) 254-3459
Contact: Sam Mandelbaum
Highlights: The firm has eleven lawyers, with offices in Tampa and Orlando, Florida, specializing in commercial, banking, insurance and real estate law. Representing both national and international clients, the firm has clientele which include manufacturing companies, banks, hotel and office development companies, and insurance companies throughout the United States and Europe. The firm handles joint ventures, international business transactions and commercial agreements. Mandelbaum is the Co-Chair of the Committee on Soviet and East European Law of the Hillsborough County Bar Association (Tampa), and speaks Russian and German.

Spindler, James W.
66 Weston Road
Lincoln, MA 01773
Phone: (617) 275-1269
FAX: (508) 658-2492
Contact: James Spindler
Services: Spindler provides general corporate and international legal services, with special emphasis on the Soviet Union and Central Europe.

Squire, Sanders & Dempsey
1201 Pennsylvania Avenue, NW
Washington, DC 20004
Phone: (202) 626-6600
FAX: (202) 626-6780
Contact: Charles A. Vanik, Stephen Bell
Services: Former Congressman Charles A. Vanik was co-author of the Jackson-Vanik Amendment.

54

Steptoe & Johnson
in Washington:
1330 Connecticut Avenue, NW
Washington, DC 20036
Phone: (202) 429-3000
FAX: (202) 429-3000
Telex: 98-2503
Contact: Sarah Carey
in Moscow:
26 Rublevskoye Shosse
Moscow, U.S.S.R.
Phone: 415-42-49
FAX: 415-29-20
Contact: Alexander Papachristou
Services: Steptoe and Johnson
attorneys have helped dozens of U.S.
companies plan, negotiate, and form
joint ventures in the Soviet Union
and Eastern Europe. The Moscow
office offers on-site expertise, advice,
and introductions to relevant
officials and business opportunities.
In addition to investment advice, the
firm's extensive East-West trade
practice includes advice to clients
regarding U.S. export controls,
import restrictions, and tax
considerations. Several Steptoe &
Johnson attorneys and staff members
speak Russian.

Stroock & Stroock & Lavan
1150 Seventeenth Street, NW
Washington, DC 20036
Phone: (202) 452-9250
FAX: (202) 293-2293
Telex: 84238 STROOCK DC; 89401
STROOCK DC
Contact: George G. Lorinczi or

Michael H. Mobbs
Services: Stroock & Stroock &
Lavan has represented a major U.S.
manufacturing company in the
negotiation and documentation of a
contract involving machinery and
equipment for the KAMA River
Truck Manufacturing Complex.
Stroock has also advised U.S. and
French clients concerning businesses
and joint-venture transactions in the
Soviet Union in such fields as
textiles, glassware, barter and
countertrade transactions, and joint
ventures involving the tire
vulcanizing and recapping industry.
Michael H. Mobbs, a partner in the
firm, speaks fluent Russian and has
had substantial experience in U.S.-
Soviet negotiations at senior levels
of government (international security
policy) and in private practice
(various commercial matters).

Swacker & Associates, P.C.
15950 Bay Vista Drive, Suite 240
Clearwater, FL 34620
Phone: (813) 530-0800
FAX: (813) 538-2080
Contact: Drucilla E. Bell
Services: The firm offers
counseling in investment, trade, and
commercial joint ventures involving
the Soviet Union. Particular areas of
expertise include factory automation,
food processing, and computer
software and hardware development.
Drucilla E. Bell served on the Board
of Directors of the Tallahassee-

Krasnodar Sister City Program during the late 1980s.

Thelen, Marrin, Johnson, & Bridges
One Kaiser Plaza
Suite 1950
Oakland, CA 94612
Phone: (415) 893-5195
FAX: (415) 891-9086
Contact: Richard N. Gary
Services: Thelen, Marrin, Johnson & Bridges was organized as a partnership in 1924 in San Francisco. It now has more than 300 lawyers at nine offices throughout the United States and in Hong Kong. The firm has negotiated contracts for an engineering client covering the design and construction management of the Moscow World Trade Center and has recently completed two major sales contracts for an industrial client with V/O Raznoimport, Moscow. It currently represents a client in negotiations with representatives of the Soviet nonferrous metals industry. These negotiations are expected to result in the formation of a joint venture for the construction of a major industrial facility in Siberia.

Trenan, Simmons, Kemker, Scharf, Barkin, Frye & O'Neill
2700 Barnett Plaza
Tampa, FL 33602
Phone: (813) 223-7474
FAX: (813) 229-6553

Telex: 6502251910 MCI UW
Contact: Richard A. Jacobson
Services: Richard A. Jacobson heads the International Practice Group of this firm and was a speaker at The Florida Conference on Trade & Investment with the Soviet Union And Eastern Europe. He is Chairman of the International Law Section of the Hillsborough County Bar Association and is Editor of *Tradeline,* the newsletter of the Tampa Bay International Trade Council.

Vorys, Sater, Seymour and Pease
Suite 1111
1828 L Street, NW
Washington, DC 20036-5104
Phone: (202) 822-8200
FAX: (202) 835-0699
Telex: 440693
Contact: Randal C. Teague
Services: The firm has been actively involved in the Soviet Union since 1984. The firm has handled negotiations and agreements for Smith Corona, W.K. Kellogg Foundation, and ABX Air, Inc., among others.

Walter, Conston, Alexander & Green, P.C.
90 Park Avenue
New York, NY 10018-1387
Phone: (212) 210-9400
FAX: (212) 210-9444
Telex: INTL 234435 RCA,

DOM/INTL 125410 WU
Contact: Henry S. Conston
Services: The firm represents a variety of East and West European clients. The firm's clients include large multinational corporations in the U.S. and Europe as well as small U.S. and foreign businesses. Areas of firm specialization include international taxation, joint ventures, licensing, mergers and acquisitions, and litigation.

Weadon, Rehm, Thomsen, Scott
1301 Pennsylvania Avenue
Suite 500
Washington, DC 20004
Phone: (202) 783-9200
FAX: (202) 783-9071
Telex: 6971742 WRTS UW
Contact: George Rehm

Weil, Gotshal & Manges
in Washington:
1615 L Street, NW
Suite 700
Washington, DC 20036
Phone: (202) 682-7000
FAX: (202) 857-0167, (202) 857-0930, (202)857-0940
Telex: ITT 440045
Contact: M. Jean Anderson
in New York:
767 Fifth Avenue
New York, NY 10153
Phone: (212) 310-8000
FAX: (212) 310-8007
Telex: ITT 424281

Contact: Robert Todd Lang
in London:
50 Stratton Street
London W1X 5FL
Phone: 1-493-9933
FAX: 1-629-7900
Contact: Peter D. Standish
Services: Weil, Gotshal and Manges has broad experience in international and East-West trade matters, including import/export issues, U.S. and CoCom controls on technology transfer, structuring and financing joint ventures and other business arrangements, countertrade, intellectual property rights, arbitration, state enterprises and state trading, and international environmental issues.

White & Case
1155 Avenue of the Americas
New York, NY 10036
Phone: (212) 819-8200
FAX: (212) 354-8113
Telex: 126201
Contact: Daniel J. Arbess

Williams, Kastner & Gibbs
Two Union Square
601 Union Street
Suite 4100
Seattle, WA 98111-0040
Phone: (206) 628-6600
FAX: (206) 628-6611
Telex: 6286611
Contact: Michael Jay Brown
Services: Williams, Kastner &

Gibbs provides a comprehensive range of legal services and has 120 attorneys in five offices in the Pacific northwest. The firm is engaged in representation of clients in the Soviet Union, China, South Korea, and Eastern Europe. The firm's special expertise lies in tax and business, including corporate and securities matters and cross-border transactions.

Womble, Carlyle, Sandridge & Rice
Charlotte Office
3300 One First Union Center
301 South College Street
Charlotte, NC 28202
Phone: (704) 331-4900
FAX: (704) 331-4955
Telex: 853609
Contact: Larry B. Coffey

SECTION 3

U.S. GOVERNMENT RESOURCES

This section includes U.S. agencies involved in the promotion, monitoring, or restriction of U.S.-Soviet trade. For the fledgling exporter, a good place to begin is with the nearest Department of Commerce International Trade Administration office, which should be able to provide relevant information on resources available at the local, state, and national level.

U.S. DEPARTMENT OF AGRICULTURE

Foreign Agricultural Service
U.S. Department of Agriculture
14th & Independence Avenue, SW
Washington DC, 20250-1000
Phone: (202) 447-6219
FAX: (202) 382-6140
Contact: Margie Bauer
Services: The organization oversees the Export Enhancement Program (EEP) and other programs for U.S. exporters. The agency includes commodity and marketing programs for: Dairy, Livestock, Poultry: (202) 447-8031
Export Programs: (202) 447-3031
Forestry Products: (202) 382-8138
Grain and Feed: (202) 447-6219
High-Value Products: (202) 447-7103
Horticulture, Tropical Plants: (202) 447- 6590
Oilseeds and Oilseed Products: (202) 447-7037
Tobacco, Cotton, and Seeds: (202) 382-9516
Agricultural Information and

Marketing Services: (202) 447-7103
Export Programs Division: (202) 477-3031

Commodity Credit Corporation
Foreign Agricultural Service
U.S. Department of Agriculture
14th & Independence Avenue, SW
Rm. 4509
Washington DC, 20250
Phone: (202) 447-3224
FAX: (202) 447-2949
Contact: Richard Godsey

Centrally Planned Economics Branch
Economic Research Service
U.S. Department of Agriculture
1301 New York Avenue, NW
Washington, DC 20005-4788
Phone: (202) 786-1620
Contact: Ed Cook

Office of Foreign Agricultural Affairs
U.S. Department of Agriculture
14th Street & Independence Avenue, SW
Washington, DC 20250

Phone: (202) 447-6138
Contact: Wayne Sharp

Office of International Trade Policy
U.S. Department of Agriculture
Foreign Agricultural Service
Washington, DC 20250-1000
Phone: (202) 382-1289
Contact: Scott Bleggi

U.S. DEPARTMENT OF COMMERCE

Herbert Hoover Bldg.
14th and Constitution Avenue
Washington, DC 20230
Phone: (202) 377-2000

Bureau of Export Administration (BXA)
U.S. Department of Commerce
Washington, DC 20230
Phone: (202) 377-2000
Contact: Quincy M. Krosby
Services: The bureau administers federal export controls.

International Trade Administration (ITA)
U.S. Department of Commerce
Room 1015
Washington, DC 20230
Phone: (202) 377-0550
Contact: J. Michael Farren, Under Secretary for International Trade

DISTRICT OFFICES OF THE ITA

Alabama
2015 2nd Avenue, N.
Berry Building, 3rd Floor
Birmingham, Alabama 35203
Phone: (205) 264-1331

Alaska
U.S. & FCS, ITA, Anchorage DO
222 N. 7th Avenue, Box 32
Anchorage, AK 99513-7591
Phone: (907) 271-5041
FAX: (907) 271-5173
Contact: Charles F. Becker, Director

Arizona
Federal Building and U.S. Courthouse
230 N. 1st Avenue
Room 3412
Phoenix, AZ 85025
Phone: (602) 254-3285

Arkansas
Savers Federal Building
Suite 635
320 W. Capitol Avenue
Little Rock, AR 72201
Phone: (501) 378-5794

California
Room 9200
11000 Wilshire Boulevard
Los Angeles, CA 90024
Phone: (213) 575-7103
116-A, W. 4th Street

Suite 1
Santa Ana, CA 92701
Phone: (714) 836-2461
P.O. Box 81404
San Diego, CA 91238
Phone: (619) 557-5395
Federal Building
Box 36013
450 Golden Gate Avenue
San Francisco, CA 94102
Phone: (415) 556-5860

Colorado
Room 119
U.S. Customhouse
721 19th Street
Denver, CO 80202
Phone: (303) 844-3246

Connecticut
Federal Building
Room 610-B
450 Main Street.
Hartford, CT 06103
Phone: (203) 722-3530

Delaware
Serviced by Philadelphia office.

District of Columbia
Serviced by Baltimore office.

Florida
224 Federal Building
51 SW 1st Avenue
Miami, FL 33130

Phone: (305) 536-5267
128 N. Osceola Avenue
Clearwater, FL 33515
Phone: (813) 461-0011

3 Independent Drive
Jacksonville, FL 32202
Phone: (904) 791-2796

75 E. Ivanhoe Boulevard
Orlando, FL 32802
Phone: (305) 425-1247

107 W. Gaines Street
Room G-20
Tallahassee, FL 32304
Phone: (904) 488-6469

Georgia
Suite 504
1365 Peachtree Street, NE
Atlanta, GA 30309
Phone: (404) 881-7000

Federal Building
Room A-107
120 Bernard Street
Savannah, GA 31404
Phone: (912) 944-4204

Hawaii
4106 Federal Building
P.O. Box 50026
300 Ala Moana Boulevard
Honolulu, HI 96850
Phone: (808) 546-8694

Idaho
Statehouse
Room 113
Boise, Idaho 83720
Phone: (208) 334-2470

Illinois
1406 Mid Continental Plaza Bldg.
55 East Monroe Street
Chicago, IL 60603
Phone: (312) 353-4450

Harper College
Algonquin and Roselle Rd.
Palatine, IL 60067
Phone: (312) 397-3000

515 N. Court Street
P.O. Box 1747
Rockford, IL 61110-0247

Indiana
357 U.S. Courthouse & Federal Bldg.
46 E. Ohio Street
Indianapolis, IN 46204
Phone: (317) 269-6214

Iowa
817 Federal Bldg.
210 Walnut Street
Des Moines, IA 50309
Phone: (515) 284-4222

Kansas
727 N. River Park Pl.
Suite 565,
Waco, KS 67203

Phone: (316) 259-6160

Kentucky
Rm 636B
U.S. Post Office and Courthouse Bldg.
Louisville, KY 40202
Phone: (502) 582-5066

Louisiana
432 International Trade Mart
No. 2 Canal Street
New Orleans, LA 70130
Phone: (504) 589-6546

Maine
Memorial Circle, Casco Bank Bldg.
Augusta, ME 04330
Phone: (207) 622-8249

Maryland
415 U.S. Custom House
Gay & Lombard Streets
Baltimore, MD 21202
Phone: (301) 962-3560

101 Monroe Street
15th Floor
Rockville, MD 20850

Massachusetts
10th Fl.
441 Stuart Street
Boston, MA 02116
Phone: (617) 223-2312

Michigan
445 Federal Bldg.
231 W. Lafayette
Detroit, MI 48226
Phone: (313) 226-3650

Minnesota
108 Federal Bldg.
110 S. 4th Street
Minneapolis, MN 55401
Phone: (612) 349-3338

Missouri
120 S. Central Avenue
Street Louis, MO 63105
Phone: (314) 425-3302

Room 635
601 E. 12th Street
Kansas City, MO 64106
Phone: (816) 374-3142

Montana
Phone: Serviced by Denver, CO
office.

Nebraska
1st Fl.
300 S. 19th Street
Omaha, NE 68102
Phone: (402) 221-3664

1755 E. Plumb Lane, #152
Reno, NV 89502
Phone: (702) 784-5203

New Hampshire
Serviced by Boston office.

New Jersey
3131 Princeton Pike
4-D Suite 211
New Jersey, Trenton 08648
Phone: (609) 989-2100

New Mexico
517 Gold SW, Suite 4303
Albuquerque, NM 87102
Phone: (505) 766-2386

New York
1312 Federal Bldg.
111 W. Huron Street
Buffalo, NY 14202
Phone: (716) 846-4191

121 E. Avenue
Rochester, NY 14606
Phone: (716) 263-6480

Federal Bldg.
26 Federal Plaza
Foley Pl.
New York, NY 10278
Phone: (212) 264-0634

North Carolina
203 Federal Bldg.
324 W. Market Street
P.O. Box 1950
Greensboro, NC 27402
Phone: (919) 378-5354

63

North Dakota
Serviced by Omaha, NB office.

Ohio
9504 Federal Bldg.
550 Main Street,
Cincinnati, OH 45202
Phone: (513) 684-2944

Room 600
666 Euclid Avenue
Cleveland, OH 44114
Phone: (216) 522-4750

Oklahoma
6601 Broadway Ext., Suite 200
Oklahoma City, OK 73116
Phone: (405) 231-5302

440 S. Houston Street
Tulsa, OK 74127
Phone: (918) 581-7650

Oregon
Room 618, 1220 SW, 3rd Avenue
Portland, OR 97204
Phone: (503) 221-3001

Pennsylvania
9448 Federal Bldg.
600 Arch Street
Philadelphia, PA 19106
Phone: (215) 597-2866

2002 Fed Bldg.
1000 Liberty Avenue
Pittsburgh, PA 15222
Phone: (412) 644-2850

Puerto Rico
Rm. 659 Federal Bldg.
(Hato Rey) San Jan, PR 00918
Phone: (809) 753-4555

Rhode Island
7 Jackson Walkway
Providence, RI 02903
Phone: (401) 528-5104

South Carolina
Federal Bldg. Suite 172
1835 Assembly Street
Columbia, SC 29201
Phone: (803) 765-5345

9 Liberty Street, Room 128
Charleston, SC 29424
Phone: (803) 724-4361

South Dakota
Serviced by Omaha

Tennessee
1114 Parkway Towers
404 Jas. Roberston Pkwy.
Nashville, TN 37219-1505
Phone: (615) 736-5161

3876 Central Avenue
Memphis, TN 38111
Phone: (901) 521-4826

Texas
Room 7A5
1100 Commerce Street,
Dallas, TX 75242
Phone: (214) 767-0542

P.O. Box 12728
Capitol Station
Austin, TX 78711
Phone: (512) 472-5059

2625 Federal Courthouse
515 Rusk Street
Houston, TX 77002
Phone: (713) 229-2578

Utah
Room 340 U.S. Courthouse
350 S. Main Street
Salt Lake City, UT 84101
Phone: (801) 524-5116

Vermont
Serviced by the Boston office

Virginia
8010 Federal Bldg.
400 N. 8th Street
Richmond, VA 23240
Phone: (804) 771-2246

Washington
Rm 706
Lake Union Bldg.
1700 West Lake Avenue, N.
Seattle, WA 98109
Phone: (206) 442-5616

P.O. Box 2170
Spokane, WA 99210
Phone: (509) 838-8202

West Virginia
3402 Federal Building

500 Quarrier Street
Charleston, WV 25301
Phone: (304) 347-5123
Contact: James Pittard, Trade
Specialist

Wisconsin
Federal Bldg.,
U.S. Courthouse
517 E. Wisc. Avenue,
Milwaukee, WI 53202
Phone: (414) 291-3473

Wyoming
Serviced by Denver

Office of Eastern Europe and Soviet Affairs
U.S. Department of Commerce
Room 3413, Main Commerce Bldg.
Washington, DC 20230
Phone: (202) 377-1104, 377-4655
FAX: (202) 377-2155
Telex: 892536
Contact: Jack Brougher, Leslie
Brown, Susan Lewenz
Services: The Office of Eastern
Europe and Soviet Affairs is involved
in policy formulation and heads up
the U.S. side in the Joint U.S.-
U.S.S.R. Commercial Commission--
the official bilateral trade dialogue
between the U.S. and the Soviet
Ministry of Foreign Economic
Relations. The U.S.S.R. "trade desk"
also provides policy guidance, current
information, and analysis on
economic developments to the private
sector to facilitate U.S.-Soviet trade.

Office of Import Investigations
U.S. Department of Commerce
Room 3047
Washington DC 20230
Phone: (202) 377-5497
Services: A unit of the U.S. Department of Commerce, this office identifies restrictions on imports from the Soviet Union and has current information on the status of dumping and countervailing duty investigations.

Office of Joint Ventures
U.S. Department of Commerce
Room 4060, Main Commerce Bldg.
14th Street and Constitution Ave, NW
Washington DC 20230
Phone: (202) 377-5695
FAX: (202) 377-0937
Contact: Surendra K. Dhir

Office of Technology and Policy Analysis
U.S. Department of Commerce
Rm 4061
14th Street and Constitution Ave, NW,
Washington DC 20230
Phone: (202) 377-4516

U.S. DEPARTMENT OF STATE

Office of Soviet Union Affairs, Economic Section
U.S. Department of State
EUR/SOV Room 4229
2201 C Street, NW
Washington DC, 20520

Phone: (202) 647-8920
Contact: Edward J. Salazar
Services: The office participates in the formulation and implementation of U.S. economic policies regarding the Soviet Union.

International Trade Controls
U.S. Department of State
Room 3529, 2201 C Street, NW
Washington DC, 20520
Phone: (202) 647-1625
Contact: Mike Zacharia, Deputy Assistant Secretary

Office of East-West Trade
U.S. Department of State
Bureau of Economic Affairs, Room 3529
2201 C Street, NW
Washington DC, 20520
Phone: (202) 647-2875
Contact: Patrick Nichols, Director of East-West Trade
Services: The office participates in the formulation and implementation of U.S. trade policies regarding the Soviet Union.

U.S. DEPARTMENT OF TRANSPORTATION

Office of East-West Economic Policy
U.S. Department of Transportation
1550 Pennsylvania Ave, NW
Room 444
Washington DC 20220
Phone: (202) 556-5637

Office of International Transportation and Trade
U.S. Department of Transportation
400 7th Street, SW, Room 10300
Washington DC 20590
Phone: (202) 366-4368
FAX: (202) 366-7483
Contact: Arnold Levine
Services: Develops policies and programs regarding all forms of international transportation-related trade issues.

ENVIRONMENTAL PROTECTION AGENCY

Office of International Activities
Environmental Protection Agency
401 M Street, SW
Mail Code A106
Washington, DC 20460
Phone: (202) 475-8597
FAX: (202) 382-4470
Contact: Gary Waxmonsky
Services: The agency serves on the U.S.-U.S.S.R. Joint Committee in the Field of Environmental Protection. Its activity centers primarily on research cooperation, but it supports the trade programs conducted by the Department of Commerce.

OTHER FEDERAL AGENCIES IN THE U.S.

Office of European Affairs, Soviet Desk
U.S. Information Agency
301 4th Street SW
Washington DC 20547
Phone: (202) 485-8857
Services: The agency conducts various programs dealing with the Soviet Union, including trade exhibitions and exchanges.

President's U.S.-Soviet Exchange Initiative
United States Information Agency
Office of the Coordinator,
Room 751, 301 4th Street SW
Washington DC 20547
Phone: (202) 619-4548
FAX: (202) 619-5958
Contact: Gregory Guroff, Coordinator
Services: The coordinator's office gives guidance and assistance to U.S. citizens and organizations wishing to establish cultural, educational, and private-sector exchanges with organizations in the Soviet Union.

Agency for International Development (AID)
Office of Business Relations
Department of State Building
320 21st Street, NW
Washington, DC 20523-1414
Phone: (202) 647-1850; (703) 875-1551
FAX: (703) 875-1498
Contact: John Wilkinson, Director
Services: AID is the government agency which administers the majority of the U.S. government's foreign economic assistance programs. It

maintains a database of U.S. companies that can provide goods or services to foreign countries and offers U.S. exporters opportunities to compete for sales to AID recipient countries.

Center for International Research
Bureau of the Census
Scuderi Bldg., Room 710
Washington DC 20233
Phone: (202) 763-4020
FAX: (301) 763-7610
Contact: Matthew Sagers, Branch Chief; Jeanine Braithwaite
Services: The center conducts long-term research on the economy and demographics of the Soviet Union.

National Institute of Standards and Technologies
108 Bureau Drive
Gaithersburg, MD 20899
Phone: (301) 975-2000
FAX: (301) 975-2128

Nuclear Regulatory Commission
Public Document Room
Washington, DC 20555
Phone: (202) 634-3273
Services: The commission implements the U.S.-Soviet exchange agreement on nuclear reactor safety. All non-classified information related to this agreement can be accessed through the Public Document Room.

Office for Europe
Office of International Health
Parklawn Bldg. Rm 18-75
5600 Fishers Lane
Rockville, MD 20857
Phone: (301) 443-4010

Office of International Activities
U.S. Department of Housing and Urban Development
451 7th Street, SW, Room 7114
Washington, DC 20410
Phone: (202) 755-6422

Office of the United States Trade Representative
East-West and Non-Market Economies Division
Winder Bldg.
600 17th Street, NW
Washington, DC 20506
Phone: (202) 395-3074; (202) 395-3211
Contact: Gordana Earp, Michael Brownrigg
Services: The organization provides input into the formulation of the United States' trade policy.

Small Business Administration (SBA)
Office of International Trade
1441 L Street,, NW
Washington, DC 20416
Phone: (202) 653-7794
Services: The Small Business Association provides educational, training, and counseling programs

and seminars for small U.S. businesses. The SBA's export assistance programs are conducted primarily by the SBA Field Offices.

U.S. Trade and Development Program
Room 309 SA-16
Washington, DC 20523-1602
Phone: (703) 875-4357
FAX: (703) 875-4009
Contact: Barbara Bradford, private sector
Fred Eberhard, public sector
Services: The program funds feasibility studies for government projects and awards contracts to U.S. bidders. It also provides four-year interest-free loans for up to half the costs of feasibility studies.

U.S. International Trade Commission
500 E Street, SW
Room 602
Washington DC 20436
Phone: (202) 252-1263
FAX: (202) 252-1789
Contact: Constance Hamilton, Chief, East-West Branch
Services: The ITC is an independent government agency that advises the administration, Congress and other government agencies on international affairs and issues.

STATE AGENCIES

New York/New Jersey Port Authority
1 World Trade Center
Room 63 East
New York, NY 10048
Phone: (212) 466-8499
Services: The organization occasionally sponsors seminars related to U.S-Soviet trade.

Massachusetts Port Authority
Trade Development Unit
World Trade Center
Suite 321
Boston, MA 02210
Phone: (617) 439-5560
Services: Massport has a recently established program aimed at promoting exports to the U.S.S.R..

U.S. FEDERAL GOVERNMENT AGENCIES IN THE SOVIET UNION

American Embassy, Moscow
Mailing address:
APO New York, NY, 09862-5438
Street address:
Ul. Chaykovskogo, 19/23
Moscow
Phone: 252-24-51 through 252-24-59; 230-20-01
Telex: 143160 USGSO SU
Services: The following embassy departments may be of assistance to the US businessman:

Office of Economic Affairs
The office assists business travelers with travel-related problems in the Soviet Union, facilitates contacts with Soviet authorities, and provides briefings.

Agricultural Section
A unit of the U.S. Department of Agriculture, this office assists in identification of trade opportunities, current market analysis, and crop reports.

U.S. Commercial Office (USCO)
Ulitsa Chaikovskogo 15, Moscow
Phone: 255-4848, 255-4660
or 252-2451, x. 276, 277, 278
Telex: 413205 USCO SU
FAX: 230-2101
Contact: Maria Aronson

U.S. Consulate General
Ul. Pyetra-Lavrova, 15
Leningrad
Phone: 292-45-48
Telex: 64121527 AMCONSUL
Services: Consular services

SECTION 4

SOVIET GOVERNMENT AND OTHER RESOURCES

This section includes key Soviet government and non-government organizations that are involved in trade, including ministries, state committees, foreign trade organizations, chambers of commerce, and other pertinent agencies. Unlike U.S. government agencies, most Soviet government organizations are direct participants in foreign trade activities.

Recently, Soviet ministries have undergone considerable reorganization. In an effort to streamline administrative activities, several ministries have been dissolved and their responsibilities turned over to umbrella organizations. These new organizations have been described as "superministries," even though some of them are state committees. The immediate impact of this restructuring on trade has been limited, since even after a ministry has been dissolved, it may be months before personnel and offices are transferred.

Bank for Foreign Economic Affairs of the U.S.S.R.
Vneshekonombank
37 Plyuschikha Ul.
119121 Moscow
Phone: 256-67-80, 246-67-88, 246-67-98, 246-67-70
Telex: Telex 411174
Contact: Yuriy S. Moskovskiy, Chairman of the Board
Services: The bank handles all foreign currency transactions between Western companies and Soviet agencies.

Expocenter
1a Sokolnicheskiy Val
107113 Moscow
Phone: 268-5874
Telex: 411185 EXPO SU

Services: Expocenter organizes and sponsors many of the trade exhibitions in the Soviet Union. It also offers publicity, service facilities, and hotel accommodations.

Main Customs Administration
9 Komsomolskaya Ploshchad 1a
107140 Moscow
Phone: Protocol 208-24-41; Information 208-44-62
Services: This organization verifies that all shipments entering the Soviet Union comply with customs regulations.

Moscow City Council (Mossoviet)
13 Ul. Gorkogo

103789 Moscow
Phone: 229-79-51
Contact: S. I. Dolgoshljbov, Director of Foreign Relations Department
Services: Mossoviet is Moscow's government administrative organ, and is involved in several joint ventures with Western companies.

V/O Vneshekonomservice
12, 1-ST Krasnogvardejskc Proezd
123100 Moscow
Phone: 259-37-53
FAX: 921-53-97
Telex: 412138 VES SU
Contact: Valeriy Glazunov
Services: The company provides market research, finance and accounting advice, economic analytic services, cost effectiveness studies, and legal consultation for joint ventures.

ALL-UNION MINISTRIES1

Ministry of the Atomic Energy Industry
Services: Created shortly after the Chernobyl accident, the Ministry maintains responsibility for all nuclear energy in the Soviet Union. The control of individual atomic stations now lies with the State Committee for Supervision of Safety in Industry and Atomic Energy.

Ministry of Automotive and Agricultural Machine Building (Minavtoselkhozmash)
Kuznetskiy Most, 21-5
100031 Moscow
Services: Created in December 1988, this ministry incorporates the former Ministry of the Automobile Industry and the Ministry of Tractor and Agricultural Machine Building.

Ministry of Aviation (Minaviaprom)
16 Ulanskiy Per.
101849 Moscow
Phone: Foreign Relations Department 207-02-73
Services: The organization is responsible for production of aircraft, guidance systems, and light-weight alloys.

Ministry of the Chemical and Petroleum Machine Building (Minkhimmash)
25 Bezbozhnyy Per.
129833 Moscow
Phone: Foreign Relations Department 288-64-33; Protocol 288-40-10

Ministry of Civil Aviation (MGA)
37 Leningradskiy Prosp.
125167 Moscow
Phone: Foreign Relations Department 155-57-28; Protocol Section 155-54-94

Services: The ministry provides commercial passenger service and agricultural, general aviation, and industrial support, using the name Aeroflot.

Ministry of the Coal Industry (Minugleprom)
23 Kalinina Prosp.
121910 Moscow
Phone: Foreign Relations Department 202-87-67, 202-87-58; Protocol Section 202-26-94
Services: This ministry was formerly the State Committee for the fuel industry. It became an All-Union Ministry in 1987, and became responsible for the coal industry.

Ministry of Defense (Minoborony)
37 Ul. Kirova
103160 Moscow
Phone: 223-61-08
Telex: The Ministry is concerned with the defense of the Soviet Union.

Ministry of the Defense Industry (Minoboronprom)
35 Ul. Gorkogo
Moscow
Phone: 209-85-87
Services: Minoboronprom is responsible for conventional ground forces weapons, solid propellant missiles, and optical systems.

Ministry of the Electronics Industry (Minelektronprom)
7 Kitayskiy Proyezd
103074 Moscow
Phone: Foreign Relations Department and Protocol Section 155-40-35
Telex: 411390 METP SU
Services: Primary responsibilities of this ministry include research and development, and the production of electronic and electrical devices, such as solid-state and miniature electronic components and devices.

Ministry of the Fishing Industry (Minrybkhoz)
12 Rozhdestvenskiy Bulvar
103031 Moscow
Phone: Foreign Relations Department 228-28-73, 228-12-96
Telex: 411208, 411210 SRF SU
Services: The organization handles all matters pertaining to the Soviet fishing industry.

Ministry of Foreign Economic Relations (MVES)
32/34 Smolenskaya-Sennaya Ploshchad
121200 Moscow
Phone: Protocol Section 244-34-83, 244-34-80
Telex: 411931 TIOJP SU
Services: The ministry is responsible for administering foreign trade policy and foreign aid agreements.

Ministry of General Machine Building (Minobshchemash)
3 Miusskaya Pl.
125833 Moscow
Phone: Foreign Relations Department 251-68-50
Services: The ministry is responsible for strategic ballistic missiles, spacecraft, and space launch systems, as well as many types of nondefense related machinery. Many of the plants under the supervision of the Ministry are now involved in the production of medical equipment.

Ministry of Geology (Mingeo)
4/6 Bolshaya Gruzinskaya Ul.
123242 Moscow
Phone: Foreign Relations Department 254-11-33
Services: Mingeo is responsible for the exploration and surveying of the geological resources of the Soviet Union, the expansion of proven mineral reserves, and the development of new technology. The Ministry is also very active in seismic studies.

Ministry of Heavy, Power and Transport Machine Building (Mintyazhmash)
5 Nizhne-Kislovskiy Per.
103906 Moscow
Phone: Foreign Economic Relations Administration 291-09-70;
Protocol Section 291-27-52
Telex: 411337

Services: This ministry was established in 1987 and is responsible for a wide range of machine building tasks. Some of its subordinate factories and plants are part of the on-going conversion process and are beginning to produce consumer goods.

Ministry of Land Reclamation and Water Conservation (Minvodkhoz)
10 Novobasmannaya Ul.
107803 Moscow
Phone: Foreign Relations Department 267-34-71;
Protocol Section 265-91-87
Telex: 411857 WODA SU
Services: The ministry supervises the country's water resources and its management.

Ministry of the Machine Tool and Instrument Building Industry (Minstankoprom)
20 Ul. Gorkogo
103789 Moscow GSP-3
Phone: Foreign Relations Department 209-79-65;
Protocol Section 209-55-17, 209-23-86
Telex: 411053 MINST SU
Services: Minstankoprom is in charge of machine tool R&D as well as production.

Ministry of the Medical Industry (Minmedprom)
Prospekt Khudozhestvennogo Teatra, 2

103823 Moscow GSP
Services: The ministry is responsible for the production of pharmaceuticals and other health care products

Ministry of Metallurgy (Minmet)
27 Prosp. Kalinina
121911 Moscow
Services: The ministry is responsible for ferrous and nonferrous metallurgical production in the Soviet Union.

Ministry of the Maritime Fleet (Minmorflot)
Ul. Zhdanova, 1/4
103759 Moscow GSP
Phone: 226-10-00
Services: This ministry oversees the Soviet merchant shipping industry.

Ministry of the Oil and Gas Construction Industry (Minneftegazstroy)
Services: Minneftegazstroy overseas the development of industry related equipment and resource development in the Soviet Union.

Ministry of the Radio Industry (Minradioprom)
7 Kitaysky Proyezd
103074 Moscow
Phone: Main Administration for Economic, Scientific, and Technical Cooperation with Foreign Countries 925-24-21; Protocol Section 207-96-27
Services: Minradioprom is involved in research and production of television sets, radios, tape recorders, computers, radio instruments, and other electronic gear.

Ministry of the Railways (MPS)
2 Novobasmannaya Ul.
107174 Moscow
Phone: Foreign Relations Department 262-16-28
Telex: 411 832 CIMPS
Services: MPS oversees the Soviet railway industry.

Ministry of the Shipbuilding Industry (Minsudprom)
11 Sadovo-Kudrinskaya Ul.
123231 Moscow
Phone: Foreign Relations Department 252-07-40
V/O Sudozagranpostavka 254-98-29
Telex: 411116 KURS SU
Services: The organization is responsible for production of naval vessels, naval fire-control systems, mines and torpedoes, as well as merchant vessels.

Ministry of Transport Construction (Mintransstroy)
21 Sadovaya-Spasskaya Ul.
107217 Moscow
Services: Mintransstroy supervises

the construction of railroads, large bridges, tunnels, and subways in seaports and river ports, construction of national highways, and airfields.

UNION REPUBLIC MINISTRIES2

Ministry of Communications (Minsvyaz)
7 Ul. Gorkogo
103375 Moscow
Phone: Foreign Relations Department 295-51-08;
Protocol Section 229-98-78, 292-25-58
Services: Minsvyaz is responsible for radio, telegraph, telephone transmissions, postal service, and publication dissemination.

Ministry of Culture (Minkultury)
35 Ul. Arbat
121835 Moscow
Phone: Foreign Relations Department 248-12-80;
Protocol Section 248-10-26, 248-10-14
FAX: 411290 MUZA SU
Services: Minkultury directs theater, dance, music, fine arts, circuses, and other cultural events in the country.

Ministry of Energy and Electrification(Minelektrotekhprom)
19 Prospekt Kalinina
121908 Moscow G-19

Phone: Foreign Relations Department 291-50-48;
Protocol Section 291-50-45
Telex: 411390 METR SU

Ministry of Finance (Minfin)
9 Ul. Kuybysheva
103097 Moscow
Phone: Foreign Relations Division 298-51-88;
Protocol Section 298-51-45
Telex: 411144 INGS SU
Services: Minfin develops and implements Soviet financial policies. It is also the organization that provides final approval and registers all Soviet joint ventures with foreign partners.

Ministry of Foreign Affairs (MID)
32/34 Smolenskaya-Sennaya Ploshchad
121200 Moscow
Phone: Information Department 244-41-19;
Protocol Department 244-43-03
Telex: 411458 OPMID S
Services: MID oversees the administrative apparatus for the conduct of Soviet foreign policy.

Ministry of the Forestry Industry (Minlesbumprom)
1 Telegraphnyy Per.
101934 Moscow-Centre
Phone: Foreign Relations Department and Protocol Section 207-96-43, 208-02-57

Services: The Ministry oversees Soviet lumber, paper, and pulp production.

Ministry of Health (Minzdrav)
Rakhmanovskyy Per., 3
101431 Moscow
Phone: Protocol Section 921-46-72; Information 228-44-78
Telex: 411355
Services: Minzdrav oversees the Soviet health care industry.

Ministry of Internal Affairs (MVD)
6 Ul. Ogareva
103009 Moscow
Phone: Foreign Relations Division 222-68-20
Services: MVD regulates internal commerce, including the conduct of customs operations.

Ministry of Justice
4 Ul. Obukhova
129028 Moscow
Services: The Ministry provides guidance to the courts of the Union Republics and military tribunals and formulates proposals on the codification of legislation.

Ministry of Installation and Special Construction (Minmotazhspetsstroi)
B. Sadovaya 8
103379 Moscow
Phone: 209-10-09

Services: The Ministry carries out special construction projects throughout the Soviet Union.

Ministry of Trade (Mintorg)
14 Ul. Razina
103688 Moscow-Centre
Phone: Foreign Relations Department 298-39-34; Protocol Section 298-47-76
Telex: 411424 BAM SU

ALL-UNION STATE COMMITTEES3

State Committee for Computer Technology and Information Science (GKVTI)
Services: The GKVTI is responsible for coordinating all work in the creation, production, utilization, and service of computational technology in the economy.

State Committee for Hydrometerology(Goskomhydromet)
12 Per. Pavlika Morozova
123376 Moscow
Phone: Foreign Relations Department 252-08-08; Protocol Section 255-52-26
Services: This committee monitors and reports on meteorological conditions throughout the Soviet Union.

State Committee for Production Quality and Standards (Gosstandart)
9 Leninskiy Prosp.
117049 Moscow G-49
Phone: Foreign Relations Department 236-40-44, 236-71-03
Services: Gosstandart establishes the technical standards for production, output, and for output quality.

State Committee for Science and Technology (GKNT)
11 Ul. Gorkogo
103095 Moscow
Phone: Protocol Section 229-20-00, 229-20-39, 229-22-36
FAX: 229-47-30
Telex: 411241 GKNT SU, 411 354 DMNTS SU
Services: The GKNT ensures a unified state policy for science and technology. It is also active in Soviet R&D in a broad range of technologies.

U N I O N   R E P U B L I C
COMMITTEES4

State Committee for Cinematography (Goskino)
7 Malyy Gnezdikovskiy Per.
103877 Moscow
Phone: Foreign Relations Department 229-13-30;
Protocol Section 229-04-74
Telex: 411417 KINO SU
Services: The committee oversees the Soviet film industry.

State Committee for Construction (Goskomstroy)
26 Pushkinskaya Ul.
103828 Moscow
Phone: Foreign Relations Department 292-75-87;
Protocol Section 292-69-74
Services: Goskomstroy implements a unified technical policy, effectiveness in capital construction, technical progress, quality, and construction periods, development of construction industry, city planning and architectural design, improved planning and estimates; does state appraisals of plans and estimates; establishes norms and technical conditions for construction planning, length of construction period, and estimate, appraisals and prices.

State Committee for Environmental Protection (Goskompriroda)
Ulitsa Nezhdanovoy, 11
Moscow
Services: Goskompriroda was established to devise, coordinate, and direct national environmental protection efforts and the rational use of natural resources until the year 2005.

State Committee for the Forestry (Goskomles)
18 Ul. Lesteva
113808 Moscow GSP-230
Phone: Foreign Relations Department 236-83-03
Services: The committee manages Soviet forests and game.

78

State Committee for Labor and Social Affairs (Goskomtrud)
1 Ul. Kuybysheva
103706 Moscow K-12
Phone: Foreign Relations Department and Protocol Section 298-39-24
Services: The committee establishes Soviet labor policies.

State Committee for Material and Technical Supply (Gossnab)
5 Orlikov Per.
107801 Moscow
Phone: Foreign Relations Department 208-33-18, 208-02-17
Services: Gossnab coordinates the supply and distribution of materials for most Soviet industries.

State Committee for Physical Culture and Sports (Goskomsport)
8 Luzhnetskaya Nab.
119270 Moscow
Phone: Protocol Section 201-14-10, 201-06-01
Telex: 411287

State Committee for Planning (Gosplan)
12 Prosp. Marksa
103009 Moscow
Services: Gosplan is responsible for formulating and monitoring the implementation of national economic plans.

State Committee for Prices (Goskomtsen)
20 Bersenevskaya Nab.
109072 Moscow ZH-72
Phone: Inquiries 231-02-45
Services: The committee establishes and approves prices for most products.

State Committee for Publications (Goskomizdat)
5 Strastnoi Bulv.
101409 Moscow K-6
Phone: Foreign Relations Department 295-58-42
Telex: 113428 CHTENIE
Services: Goskomizdat supervises the publishing and printing industry and exercises national control over the thematic content of literature.

State Committee for Public Education
51 Ul. Lyusinovskaya
Moscow
Phone: 237-77-95
Services: The Committee was created in 1988 to take over the function of the Ministry of Education and the State Committee for Vocational and Technical Education.

State Committee for Statistics (Goskomstat)
39 Ul. Kirova

103450 Moscow
Phone: Foreign Relations Division
207-49-17
(new office at Izmaylovskoye Shosse,
Moscow)
Services: Goskomstat maintains all
statistical records of the Soviet
Union.

**State Committee for Supervision of
Safety in Industry and Atomic
Energy (Gospromatomnadzor)**
Taganskaya Ul., 34
109147 Moscow
Services: Controls the construction
and operation of nuclear power and
heat-supply stations.

**State Committee for Television and
Radio Broadcasting (Gosteleradio)**
25 Pyatnitskaya Ul.
Moscow
Phone: Main Administration for
External Relations 217-78-48,
217-70-09, 233-60-60
Telex: 411130 RADIO SU

**State Committee for the Utilization
of Atomic Energy (GKAE)**
Staromonetnyy Per., 26
109180 Moscow
Services: Controls the construction
and operation of nuclear power and
heat-supply stations.

State Security Committee (KGB)
2 Ul. Dzerzhinskogo

101000 Moscow
Services: The KGB ensures the
security of the country.

CHAMBERS OF COMMERCE AND RELATED ORGANIZATIONS

Armenian Chamber of Commerce
24 Kutuzov Ul.
375033 Yerevan
Phone: (885) 27-73-90
Services: The organization provides
information and assistance in
establishing contact with Armenian
businesses.

Belorussian Chamber of Commerce
65 Ya. Kolasa
220843 Minsk
Phone: (017) 66-04-60
Services: This organization will
provide information and assistance
in arranging contact with
Belorussian businesses.

Estonian Chamber of Commerce
17 Toomkooli Ul.
200001 Tallinn
Phone: (014) 44-49-29
Services: The Chamber will provide
information and aid in arranging
contact with Estonian businesses.

Georgian Chamber of Commerce
1 I. Chavchavadze Prospect
380079 Tbilisi
Phone: (883) 22-25-54

Kirgiz Chamber of Commerce
435 Frunze Ul.
720345 Frunze
Phone: (331) 26-49-42
Services: The Chamber will provide information and assistance in arranging contact with Kirgiz businesses.

Latvian Chamber of Commerce
21 Ul. Lenina
226189 Riga
Phone: (013) 33-22-05
Services: The Chamber will provide information and assistance in arranging contact with Latvian businesses.

Leningrad Chamber of Commerce
10 Krasnyy Flot Embankment
190000 Leningrad
Phone: (812) 314-99-53

Lithuanian Chamber of Commerce
31 Algirdo St.
232600 Vilnius
Phone: (012) 66-15-50
Services: This organization will provide information and aid in arranging contact with Lithuanian businesses.

Ministry of Local Industries, Uzbek S.S.R.
Department of International Economic Relations
5 Alleya Paradov

700017 Tashkent
Phone: (371) 33-62-44
Contact: U. K. Ismailov
Services: The Department provides information and assistance in establishing contacts with Uzbek businesses.

Moscow Chamber of Commerce
13-17 Ul. Chekova
103050 Moscow
Phone: 299-76-12
Services: The Chamber will provide information and assistance in arranging contact with businesses in the Moscow area.

V/O Sovincentr
12 Krasnopresnenskaya Nab.
123610 Moscow
Phone: 256-63-03, 255-64-01
Telex: 411486 SOVIN SU
Services: Sovincenter operates the World Trade Center in Moscow and is a division of the Chamber of Commerce and Industry of the U.S.S.R.

Tadzhik Chamber of Commerce
31 Sh. Rustaveli Ul.
734025 Dushanbe
Phone: (377) 22-69-68
Services: This organization will provide information and aid in arranging contacts with Tadzhik businesses.

Ukrainian Chamber of Commerce
33 Zhitomirskaya Ul.
252625 Kiev
Phone: (044) 22-29-11
Services: This organization will provide information and assistance in arranging contacts with Ukrainian businesses.

U.S.S.R. Chamber of Commerce and Industry
Ul. Kuybysheva, 6
101000 Moscow
Phone: 298-3231, 223-4323
Telex: 411126 TPP SU
Contact: Victor Mishchenko
Services: The organization acts to develop Soviet exports and new forms of economic cooperation. Its subsidiary firms include Sovincenter, Expocenter, Vneshtorgreklama, and Soyuzpatent.

Uzbek Chamber of Commerce
16 Leninskiy Prospekt
700017 Tashkent
Phone: (371) 33-62-82
Services: The Chamber will provide information and aid in arranging contacts with Uzbek businesses.

SOVIET GOVERNMENT AGENCIES WITH U.S. LOCATIONS

Aeroflot
630 Fifth Ave., Suite 241
New York, NY 10111

Phone: (212) 397-1660 through - 1664
FAX: (212) 397-1667
Telex: (212) 495-0721
Services: Aeroflot is the official Soviet government airline.

Amtorg Trading Company
in the U.S.:
1755 Broadway
New York, NY 10019
Phone: (212) 956-3010
FAX: (212) 856-2995
Telex: 422400
Contact: Yuri Mashkin, President
in Moscow:
General Representative of Amtorg in the Soviet Union
Trubnikovskiy Pereulok, dom 19
121069 Moscow, U.S.S.R.
Phone: 202-57-49
FAX: 871-411-257
Services: The firm provides assistance to U.S. companies pursuing trade opportunities in the Soviet Union.

Belarus Machinery, Inc.
115 East 57th St.
Suite 1450
New York, NY 10022
Phone: (212) 751-8550
FAX: (212) 371-4587
Telex: 177050 BELARUSNYK
and
Rt. 7 Box 7438R
Slidell, LA 70461
Phone: (504) 649-3000
Contact: Edward Ossinski, President

Services: The corporate headquarters for Belarus Inc., manages distribution and sales of Belarus farm equipment.

Embassy of the U.S.S.R.
1125 Sixteenth Street, NW
Washington, DC 20036
Phone: (202) 628-7551
Contact: Alexander Kluyev
Services: The Embassy facilitates diplomatic relations between the U.S. and Soviet Union. For visa services, see separate listing for the Soviet Consular Office.

Intourist
630 Fifth Ave., Suite 868
New York, NY 10111
Phone: (212) 757-3884
Contact: Yuri Bagrov, General Manager
Services: Intourist is the official Soviet travel agency.

Soviet Consular Office
1852 Phelps Place, NW
Washington, DC 20009
Phone: (202) 939-8916
FAX: (202) 483-7579
Services: This Soviet office processes visas. Visa applications must include three identical photographs (matt finish) 1 1/2 x 1 3/4, signed on the back; an official invitation (letter or cable) from the Soviet Union, confirming the trip; passports of non-U.S.A. citizens and photocopies of the photograph and signature page of U.S. citizens' passports (all passports must be valid at least one month after the departure date from the Soviet Union), a cover letter from the organization requesting the visa, and an address label or self-addressed envelope.

Soviet Information Department
1706 18th St., NW
Washington, DC 20009
Phone: (202) 328-3234
Contact: Oleg Benyukh, Head
Services: This agency is more involved with collecting information than it is disseminating it.

Soviet Mission to the UN
136 E. 67th St.
New York, NY 10021
Phone: (212) 861-4900

TASS News Agency
50 Rockefeller Plaza
New York, NY 10020
Phone: (212) 245-4250
Contact: I. Makhurin, Editor
Services: TASS is the official Soviet news agency.

Trade Representation of the U.S.S.R. in the U.S.A.
2001 Connecticut Avenue, NW
Washington, DC 20008
Phone: (202) 232-5988

Contact: Valeriy Ponomarev, Senior Economist
Services: The Trade Representation provides some assistance to U.S. organizations pursuing trade opportunities in the Soviet Union.

U.S.S.R.-U.S. Fisheries Claims Board
1609 Decatur Street, NW
Washington, DC
Phone: (202) 726-3838
Contact: Gennady Chursin, Attache

SOVIET FOREIGN TRADE ORGANIZATIONS & FIRMS

Despite decentralization of Soviet foreign trade, less than 15 percent of Soviet imports are purchased directly by end-users with hard currency retention accounts. Foreign trade organizations (FTOs) and foreign trade firms subordinate to ministries are still responsible for over 80 percent of Soviet hard currency import/export transactions.

Of the roughly 100 organizations presented in the following list, the handful of FTOs subordinate to the USSR Ministry of Foreign Economic Relations (MVES) still manage roughly 40 percent of Soviet imports, according to Soviet estimates. These 24 agencies, identified in the following list by (*) have greater access to hard currency because they administer the country's top exports, such as petroleum products, fertilizers and minerals, nonferrous metals and lumber.

Agropromservice
Per. Chernyshevskovo, 1
103030 Moscow
Phone: 281-22-01
Telex: 411624

V/O Almazyuvelirexport
25/1 Zubovskiy Bulvar
119021 Moscow
Cable: Almazyuvelirexport Moscow
Telex: 411115
Phone: 245-02-59; 245-34-10; 245-34-20
General Director: I. S. Alekseev
Imports: natural quartz, tools for diamond mining, gem cutting, and jewelry making industries.
Exports: jewelry, cut diamonds, pearls, gold and silver with precious stones, platinum, semi-precious metals, synthetic optical quartz, and synthetic crystals.

V/O Atomenergoexport
32/34 Smolenskaya-Sennaya Pl.
121200 Moscow
Phone: 220-14-36
Director: Vladimir D. Gulko
Imports: nuclear power generating equipment, materials, plants, and instruments.
Exports: technical assistance in constructing nuclear power plants.

V/O Aviaexport
19 Trubnikovskiy Per.
121817 Moscow
Cable: Aviaexport Moscow
Telex: 411257
Phone: 290-01-71
General Director: V. S. Studenikin
Imports: aviation technology, airport equipment, and furnishings.
Exports: aircraft, helicopters, engines, and aircraft equipment.

V/O Avtoexport
8 Ul. Marksa-Engelsa
119902 Moscow
Cable: Avtoexport Moscow
Telex: 411135; 411253
Phone: 202-83-37; 202-85-35
General Director: E. N. Lyubinskiy
Imports: special purpose vehicles, trailers, bicycles, and spare parts.
Exports: cars, trucks, trailers and associated parts.

V/O Avtopromimport
50/2 Ul. Pyatnitskaya
109017 Moscow
Cable: Avtopromimport Moscow
Telex: 411961A API; 411961B API; 411961C API; 411961D API
Phone: 231-81-26
General Director: Yu. V. Kalashnikov
Imports: turnkey plants, tools, spare parts for work shops, manufacturing technology, and machine building equipment for automobiles, aircraft, power and tractor and agricultural machine building.

Bashneftekhimexport
14 Ul. Mira
450064 Ufa
Cable: Bashneftekimzavody Ufa
Telex: 21429 Bonex SU
Phone: 43-25-14
General Director: L. G. Sushko
Imports: technology and equipment for oil refineries and petrochemical plants.
Exports: petroorganic synthetic products (fatty alcohols, petroleum solvents, petroleum slag).

Belavtomaz
3 Ul. Sotsialisticheskaya
220831 Minsk
Cable: TF Belavtomaz Minsk
Telex: 252160 Maz
Phone: 46-96-08
General Director: A. N. Apukhtin
Imports: assemblies and materials for automotive production.
Exports: chassis, dump trucks, saddle tractors, trailers, coupling, and towing devices.

Biokard
15/1 Tretya Cherepkovskaya Ul.
121552 Moscow
Cable: Biokard Moscow
Telex: 411355 EKE
Phone: 499-61-37
General Director: Yu. N. Chernikov
Exports: biotechnology (drugs, preparations, chemicals).

Bobruiskshinaexport
Minskoye Shosse
213824 Bobruisk

Mogilevskaya oblast
Cable: Bobruiskshinaexport
Bobruisk Mogilevskoi
Telex: 252167 Wheel SU
Phone: 3-50-65
General Director: V. V. Alekseyev
Imports: rubber and accelerators for the production of rubber mixers.
Exports: tires for trucks, tractors and other farm vehicles, inner tubes.

Burevestnik
68 Malookhotinskiy Prosp.
195272 Leningrad
Cable: FTF Burevestnik Leningrad
Phone: 528-11-23
General Director: Ye. P. Sharanov
Imports: spare   parts   for instrumentation.
Exports: X-ray and diagnostic equipment for structural and spectral analysis,   signal   measuring instrumentation, consumer products.

V/O Chimmashexport
35 Mosfilmovskaya Ul.
114330 Moscow
Telex: 411068 Tehex SU; 411228 Tehex SU
Phone: 143-86-63; 288-36-90
General Director: A. I. Burgazliyev
Imports: components for exports, industrial fittings, Christmas trees.
Exports: geological prospecting equipment,   pipeline   construction equipment, equipment for chemical and petroleum processing and pulp and   paper   industries,   rubber processing and plastics production.

Elektron
68-A Komsomolskaya Ul.
244030 Sumy
Cable: Spektr Sumy
Telex: 131473 KRON
Phone: 2-14-14
Director: V. N. Kaplichnyy
Exports: electron   microscopes, m a s s - s p e c t r o m e t e r s , spectrophotometers, electron welding instrumentation.

Elektronintorg
Ul. Usiyevicha 24/2
125315 Moscow
Telex: 411362 EZP SU
Phone: 155-40-26, 155-40-38

Vum E/I Elektronmash
4 Bolshaya Okruzhnaya Ul.
252180 Kiev
Cable: Elektronmash Kiev
Phone: 487-06-28
Director: V. G. Sirota
Exports: computers and spare parts.

V/O Elektronorgtechnika
32/34 Smolenskaya-Sennaya Pl.
121200 Moscow
Telex: 411385; 411386
Phone: 205-00-33
General Director: V. F. Beresnev
Imports: computers, peripherals, and software.
Exports: computers, peripherals, and software.

Elektrosila
139 Moskovskiy Prosp.
196105 Leningrad
Cable: TF Elektrosila Leningrad
Telex: 121588 Motor
Phone: 298-2075
Director: N. B. Filippov
Imports: spare parts and materials for metal working.
Exports: electric machines, steam generators, gas turbines, circuit breakers.

MPO Elektrozavod
21 Ul. Elektrozavodskaya
105023 Moscow
Telex: 411589 Mez SU
Phone: 369-30-78
Director: S. L. Ponamaryov
Exports: power transformers, high tension equipment, consumer goods.

Elmashintorg
73 Petergofskoye Shosse
198206 Leningrad
Cable: Elmashintorg Leningrad
Phone: 130-80-77
Director: O. E. Rumyantsev
Exports: N/C systems, electrical meters, computer software, fishing equipment.

Energomashexport
19 Prosp. Kalinina
121019 Moscow
Telex: 411965
Phone: 203-15-71
General Director: V. I. Filimonov

Exports: equipment for thermal and hydraulic power stations, power turbines, gas turbo drives, hot water boilers, diesel engines, welding equipment, and spare parts.

V/O Expocentr
Sokolnicheskiy Val, 1a
107113 Moscow
Telex: 411185 EXPO SU
Phone: 268-70-83, 268-63-52

*Exportkhleb
32/34 Smolenskaya-Sennaya Pl.
121200 Moscow
Cable: Exportkhleb Moscow
Telex: 411145 E-KHLEB; 411146 E-KHLEB; 411147 E-KHLEB
General Director: O. A. Klimov
Imports: Cereals, beans, grain, bread products, malt, flowers.
Exports: malt, hops, flour, grain.

V/O Exportljon
33 Ul. Arkhitektora Vlasova
117393 Moscow
Cable: Exportljon Moscow
Telex: 411204
Phone: 128-07-86; 128-18-24
General Director: I. N. Gorokhov
Imports: raw materials for textiles industry.
Exports: textiles.

Exportles
19 Trubnikovskiy Pereulok
121803 GSP Moscow

Cable: Exportles Moscow G-69
Telex: 411229 Eles SU
Phone: 291-58-15; 291-61-16
General Director: Yu. V.
Vardashkin
Imports: timber, woodpulp, paper
products and technology for paper
production.
Exports: lumber, woodpulp.

Impuls
2 Pl. Pobedy
349940 Severodonetsk
Voroshilovgradskaya oblast
Cable: FTF Impuls Severodonetsk
Phone: 4-13-23
Director: V. I. Smolin
Exports: computers and associated
spare parts.

Internauchpribor
26 Prospekt Ogorodnikova
198103 Leningrad
Telex: 121549 NTO AN
Phone: 251-88-89; 135-50-38
Director: Yu. A. Konopaltsev
Imports: instrumentation for
automation.
Exports: machine tools.

V/O Intourservice
16 Prosp. Marksa
Moscow
Telex: 411211 INTOU SU
FAX: 200-12-43
Phone: 203-31-91
General Director: I. A. Feodorov
Activity: official Soviet tourist
agency.

ISPO
1 Ul. Stankostroiteley
153009 Ivanovo
Cable: Granit Ivanovo
Telex: 412687
Phone: 3-37-24
Director: A. V. Mayerov
Exports: machine tools for metal
working, spare parts.

Kirishinefteorgsintez
187110 Kirishi
Leningradskoy oblasti
Cable: Kirishinedteorgsintez Kirishi
Leningradskaya FTF
Phone: 2-11-90; 9-12-30
Director: A. P. Smirnov
Exports: petrochemical products.

Krasitel
2 Prospekt Khimikov
3 4 9 8 7 0   R u b e z h n o y e
Voroshilovgradskoy oblasti
Cable: Rubezhnoye   70
Voroshilovgradskoy Rubin
Director: S. P. Pushkin
Imports: raw materials for the
production of dyes.
Exports: dyes.

Krayan
2 Ul. Yanvarskogo Vosstaniya
270017 Odessa
Cable: Podem Odessa
Telex: 232714 Kran
Phone: 66-01-03
Director: V. V. Larionov
Exports: 25-250 ton heavy-duty self-

propelled cranes on pneumatic wheels, spare parts, and maintenance packages.

V/O Legpromexport
Prosp. Kalinina 29, Kor. 4
121905 Moscow
Telex: 411859 NORD SU
Phone: 291-94-96, 259-99-79

Lenfintorg
98 Moskovskiy Prosp.
196084 Leningrad
Cable: Lefintorg Leningrad M-84
Telex: 122724 Lenfin
Phone: 292-56-33; 296-1165
General Director: V. N. Gladkov
Imports: finished wood products, clothing, yarn, perfume, cosmetics, commodities.
Exports: timber, musical instruments, construction materials.

LMZ
18 Sverdlovskaya Naberezhnaya
195108 Leningrad
Cable: Leningrad 108 Turbina
Phone: 248-70-19
Director: A. I. Burgazliyev
Exports: equipment for thermal and hydraulic power stations and associated spare parts.

*Licensintorg
11 Minskaya Ul.
Moscow 121108
Cable: Licensintorg Moscow

Telex: 145-27-00; 145-29-00
General Director: V. V. Ignatov
Activity: sells and buys patents, technology licenses, know-how.

LTZ
2 Krasnogvardeyskaya Ul.
Lipetsk
Cable: Lipetsk 30 Proton
Phone: 23-74-64
Director: V. V. Antonov
Exports: tractors.

*V/O Mashinoexport
32/34 Smolenskaya-Sennaya Pl.
121200 Moscow
Phone: 147-15-42
Director: Vladimir V. Zasedatelev
Imports: power-generating, lifting and conveying, pumping and compressing equipment.

*V/O Mashinoimport
32/34 Smolenskaya-Sennaya Pl.
121200 Moscow
Cable: Mashinoimport Moscow
Telex: 411231
Phone: 244-33-09
General Director: A. G. Yushkin
Imports: equipment for power plants, hoisting and conveyer machines, pumps, compressors, excavators, trenching machines, refinery equipment, spare parts, steam generators, gas turbines, technical assistance for construction and surveying for oil and gas industries.

Exports: parts for rolling stock, cranes, pile drives, revolving wheel loaders.

Mashpriborintorg
32/34 Smolenskaya-Sennaya Pl.
121200 Moscow
Cable: Mashpribor Moscow
Telex: 411235; 411236
Phone: 244-27-75
General Director: V. F. Klimov
Imports: radio communications equipment, TV studio equipment, telephone and telex exchanges, equipment for communication, and facsimile equipment.
Exports: geophysical survey equipment, testing machinery, electron microscopes.

V/O Mebelintorg
35 Bolshaya Filyovskaya Ul.
121433 Moscow
Cable: Mebelintorg Moscow
Telex: 411282
Phone: 146-36-72
General Director: A. P. Grachev
Imports: household furniture, special-purpose furniture for offices, metal hardware, semi-finished wood products.

V/O Medexport
Ul. Kakhovka 31, Kor. 2
113461 Moscow
Telex: 411247 MEDEX SU
Phone: 331-82-00, 321-85-22

V/O Metallurgimport
33, Ul. Arkhitektora Vlassova
117393 Moscow
Cable: Metallurgimport Moscow
Telex: 411388
Phone: 128-09-32
Acting General Director: A. V. Tverdokhlebov
Imports: mining, drilling, crushing, grinding and dressing equipment, turnkey plants for rolling mills, coke, blast-furnaces, steel-smelting, and other metallurgical equipment.

Meta-Filtr
77 Ul. Frunze
600016 Frunze
Cable: Poisk SU
Telex: 218291 Poisk SU
Phone: 1-56-74
Director: V. B. Kryukovskiy
Exports: membrane technology, laboratory equipment.

Mezhdunarodnaya kniga
39 Ul. Dmitrova
113095 Moscow
Cable: Mezhkniga Moscow
Telex: 411160
Phone: 238-46-00
General Director: S. V. Ostapishin
Imports: periodicals, books, records, compact disks, cassettes, art, films, postcards, posters.
Exports: periodicals, books, records, compact disks, cassettes, art, films, postcards, posters.

V/O Morsvyazsputnik
Ul. Rozhdestvenka 1/4
103759 Moscow
Telex: 411197 MMF SU
Phone: 258-70-45

Mortekhinformreklama
Ul. Rozhdestvenka 1/4
103759 Moscow
Telex: 411197 MMF SU
Phone: 158-2553

V/O Mosinter
Ul. Gorkogo 13
103032 Moscow
Phone: 229-58-27

Moskvitch
46-A Volgogradskiy Prosp.
109316 Moscow
Cable: FTF Moskvitch Moscow
Phone: 276-87-32
Director: V. K. Fedulov
Imports: spare parts for automobiles.
Exports: cars and spare parts, maintenance packages.

MSPO
16 Oktyabraskaya Ul.
220801 Minsk
Cable: Minsk Koltso
Phone: 22-00-32
Director: D. I. Karzov
Exports: machine tools.

PO MTZ V.I. Lenin
61 Ul. Dolgobrodskaya

220668 Minsk-GSP
Cable: Nord Minsk
Phone: 44-12-64
Director: P. Ya. Lyubchevskiy
Exports: tractors through the U.S.-based Belarus Machinery.

V/O Neftekhimexport
Ul. Gilyarovskogo 31
129832 Moscow
Telex: 411615 NEXT
Phone: 284-8768, 284-8855

Nevmashexport
52 Prosp. Obukhovskoy Oborony
193029 Leningrad
Cable: Kit Leningrad 29
Telex: 121574
Phone: 221-04-85; 567-69-42
Director: V. I. Savoshchev
Imports: materials and equipment for heavy power and transport engineering.
Exports: gas pumping plants, heavy-duty stationary compressors, steam turbines, air blowers for metallurgy, steel forgings.

*V/O Novoexport
32/34 Smolenskaya-Sennaya Pl.
SU-121200 Moscow
Phone: 128-68-59
Telex: 411204 NOVEX SU
Director: Igor N. Gorokhov
Exports: secondary raw materials and industrial wastes, peat and peat products, cotton, wool, flax.

Obshchemashexport
Ul. Krasnoproletarskaya, 9
101444 Moscow
Telex: 411836
Phone: 258-19-70, 258-66-56

Osporad
6 Ul. Lomonosova
302018 Oryel
Cable: Rele Oryol
Telex: 412505 Prima
Phone: 22-13-54; 22-10-86
Director: K. M. Manenkov
Exports: radial drilling machines, boring machines, flexible, production units.
Imports: N/C machine tools.

Polimir
Vitebskoy oblasti
211440 Novopolotsk
Phone: 5-73-38; 5-11-05
Director: N. N. Markovich
Imports: Rhizella oil, toponal M, armoslin SP, siloid 385, stearic acid, sorbitol, leomin, titanium dioxide.
Exports: high-pressure polyethylene, acrylic acid nitrile, polyethylene wax, polyacrylnitrile fibre.

Poljot
34 Ul. Marksistkaya
109147 Moscow
Cable: FTF Polyot Moscow 147
Telex: 411989 Polex
Phone: 272-01-08
Director: Yu. N. Nikitin
Exports: wrist watches.

*Prodintorg
32/34 Smolenskaya-Sennaya Pl.
121200 Moscow
Cable: Prodintorg Moscow
Telex: 411206
Phone: 244-26-29
General Director: A. K. Krivenko
Imports: sugar, spices, cocoa, tea, coffee.
Exports: meat and meat by-products, dairy products and tabacco.

Prometey
29, build 4
Checkhow str.
103006 Moscow
Phone: 299-84-45
FAX: 200-22-12 (ATTN: Anton E. Pronin)
Telex: 411700 VAPRO 0310
Contact: Anton E. Pronin
Services: Prometey is an umbrella consulting and trading organization, with numerous members in all business sectors throughout the Republic of Russia and the Ukraine. It is the Soviet partner of Global Trading Associates, Inc.

V/O Promexport
Ul. Gorkogo, 37a
125047 Moscow
Telex: 411045
Phone: 282-20-45

*V/O Promsyrioimport
13 Ul. Chaykovskogo
121834 Moscow
Cable: PSIM Moscow

Telex: 111824
Phone: 203-05-77; 203-05-95; 203-06-46
General Director: G. S Afanasyev
Imports: iron, steel, crude oil, pipes, casings, ferro-alloys.
Exports: steel wire and strips, tin plates.

Raduga
106 Ul. B. Khmelnitskogo
290024 Lvov
Cable: Stroimaterialintorg Moscow
Telex: 411887; 411889
Phone: 269-05-54; 269-05-55
Director: A. I. Burgazliyev
Exports: crystal and glassware.

*Raznoexport
15 Verkhnaya Krasnoselskaya Ul.
107896 Moscow
Cable: Raznoexport Moscow
Telex: 411408
Phone: 264-56-56; 264-01-83; 264-04-83
General Director: Yu. Kostrov
Imports: clothing, footwear, hosiery.
Exports: tobacco products, musical instruments.

Raznoimport
32/34 Smolenskaya-Sennaya Pl.
SU-121200 Moscow
Phone: 220-18-49
Director: Vyacheslav N. Semin
Imports: nonferrous metals, ores, concentrates.
Exports: rare metals.

Red Excavator
83/2 Prosp. Pobedy
252062 Kiev
Cable: Krex Kiev
Phone: 433-69-18
Director: I. K. Gudz
Exports: excavators and spare parts.

Rigaselmash
23-A Daugavrivas
226007 Riga
Cable: Riga TF Rigaselmash
Phone: 246-55-51
Director: S. S. Yatsenko
Imports: farm equipment, feed distributors.

*Selkhozpromsexport
32/34 Smolenskaya-Sennaya Pl.
SU-121200 Moscow
Imports: plants for fisheries, forestry, food, woodworking, flour and grain elevators, and construction industries.

Skotoimport
6 Ul. Makarenko
103062 Moscow
Cable: Skotoimport Moscow
Phone: 221-64-79
General Director: B. F. Chutchev
Imports: livestock, meat products.
Exports: pedigrees, race horses, farm animals.

V/O Sovbunker
10/12 Kaloshin Per.
121002 Moscow
Cable: Sovbunker Moscow
Telex: 411170

Phone: 248-23-40; 248-23-60
General Director: Yu. P. Drobinin
Imports: spare parts for ships, tools, navigational and communication equipment.

V/O Sovelectro
1/4 Deguninskaya Ul.
127486 Moscow
Telex: 410003
Phone: 487-31-82
General Director: V. B. Ulyanov
Imports: electric locomotives, lighting devices, light sources, electric insulation materials, electric appliances.
Exports: transformers, high voltage electric equipment.

V/O Sovfracht
1/4 Ul. Zhdanova
103759 Moscow
Cable: Sovfracht Moscow
Telex: 41168
Phone: 926-11-18
General Director: V. L. Shutov
Activity: charters dry-cargo and tanker tonnage for shipping Soviet exports.

Sovintersport
5 Bolshoy Rzhevskiy Per.
121069 Moscow
Cable: 114108 SPIDV
Telex: 411578 PIK SU
Phone: 291-91-49; 291-98-37

Acting General Director: V. N. Zhukov
Imports: sporting gear.

Sovkabel
5 Shosse Entuziastov
111112 Moscow
Cable: Sovkabel Moscow
Phone: 361-61-82
Director: A. D. Orlov
Imports: cables, cable manufacturing technology, materials for cable production, wires.
Exports: licenses for cable production technology.

Sovkomflot
1/4 Ul. Zhdanova
103759 Moscow
Cable: Sovkomflot Moscow
Telex: 411168
Phone: 926-13-01
Director: I. S. Osminin
Imports: ships, containers.
Exports: scraps, used ships.

Sovryblot
9 Rozhdestvenskiy Bulvar
103045 Moscow
Telex: 411206
Phone: 208-40-57
General Director: G. V. Zhigalov
Imports: fresh and salted fish, canned and preserved fish.
Exports: frozen fish, canned fish, crabmeat, salmon, caviar.

V/O Sovexportkniga
Ul. Gorkogo 50
125047 Moscow
Telex: 411069 SUPER SU
Phone: 251-72-76, 251-63-03

Sovincentr
12 Krasnopresnenskaya Nab.
123610 Moscow
Telex: 411486 SOVIN SU
Phone: 256-63-03, 255-64-01

V/O Soyuzagrokhimexport
Ul. Gritsevetskaya 2/16
119900 Moscow
Telex: 411297 KHIM SU

*Soyuzgazexport
20 Leninskiy Prosp.
117071 Moscow
Cable: Sovgaz Moscow
Telex: 411987 Sgaz SU
Phone: 230-24-10; 230-24-40
General Director: V. N. Mikhaylov
Imports: liquified petroleum, butane.
Exports: natural gas.

Soyuzkarta
45 Volgogradskiy Prosp.
109125 Moscow
Cable: Soyuzkarta Moscow
Telex: 411222 REN
Phone: 177-40-50
General Director: V. A. Piskulin
Imports: geodetic instrumentation.

Exports: maps, aerial surveys.

V/O Soyuzkhimexport
Smolenskaya-Sennaya Pl., 32/34
121200 Moscow
Telex: 411297 KHIM SU
Phone: 244-22-84, 224-41-83

V/O Soyuzkinoservice
Skatertnyy Per., 20
121069 Moscow
Telex: 411114 INFLM SU
Fax: 200-12-86

V/O Sovinteravtoservice Insititutsky
Per. 2/1
Moscow
Telex: 411008
Phone: 299-77-73, 299-59-00;
Protocol Department: 971-03-37;
Moscow-Helsinki Two-Way Courier Service: 299-77-73, 299-59-00
Fax: 230-24-50

V/O Soyuzkoopvneshtorg
15 Bolshoy Cherkasskiy Per.
103626 Moscow
Cable: Soyuzkoopvneshtorg Moscow
Telex: 411127
Phone: 924-81-71; 924-75-37
General Director: A. N. Starykh
Imports: clothing, footwear, fabrics, carpets, furniture, plates, dishes.
Exports: raw materials, preserves, fruits, vegetables, honey, wax, nuts, mushrooms, souvenirs.

V/O Soyuznefteexport
32/34 Smolenskaya-Sennaya Pl.
121200 Moscow
Cable: Nafta Moscow
Telex: 411148, A, B, C, D, E
Phone: 244-40-48; 244-40-49
General Director: V. A. Arutyunyan
Imports: petroleum products.
Exports: crude oil.

V/O Soyuzpatent
Ul. Kuybysheva, 5/2
103684 Moscow
Telex: 411431 ATPP SU
Phone: 925-16-61, 925-68-00

V/O Soyuzplodoimport
32/34 Smolenskaya-Sennaya Pl.
121200 Moscow
Cable: Plodoimport Moscow
Telex: 411262; 411329
Phone: 244-22-58
General Director: L. P. Batov
Imports: processed fruits and vegetables.
Exports: salt, tea, canned fruits and vegetables, seeds.

*V/O Soyuzpromexport
32/34 Smolenskaya-Sennaya Pl.
121200 Moscow
Cable: Promexport Moscow
Telex: 411268
Phone: 244-19-79; 244-47-68
General Director: Ye. F. Manakhov
Imports: ores, fertilizers, raw materials.
Exports: solid fossil fuels, coke,

anthracite, coal coke, coal pitch.

Soyuzpushnina
1-y Krasnogvardeisky Per., 12
103012 Moscow
Cable: Soyuzpushnina Moscow
Telex: 411150
Phone: 259-99-79; 259-99-85
General Director: Yu. M. Mashkin
Exports: pelts, furs, and fur garments.

V/O Soyuzregion
Ul. Kuybysheva, 6
103864 Moscow
Phone: 525-48-73

V/O Soyuztorgoborudovaniye
Ul. Pushkinskaya 9, kor. 8
Telex: 471209
Phone: 229-34-48

*Soyuzvneshtrans
17 Gogolevskiy Bulvar
121019 Moscow
Cable: Vneshtrans Moscow
Telex: 411441
Phone: 203-11-79
General Director: V. I. Aliseichik
Activity: storage, delivery and forwarding services in connection with export and import of commodities carried by sea, rail, motor, or air.

*Soyuzvneshstroyimport
32/34 Smolenskaya-Sennaya Pl.
SU-121200 Moscow
Phone: 290-00-98
Director: Grant G. Grigoryan
Activity: organization and provision
of supplies for projects in designing,
building, renovating and equipping
industrial, civil engineering and
transport construction with Soviet
organizations.

Soyuzzagranpribor
5 Ul. Ogareva
K-9 Moscow 103918
Telex: 411437
Phone: 229-61-10
General Director: Yu. A. Agapov
Exports: computer hardware, office
equipment, software, jewelry, medical
instrumentation, watches, clocks.

V/O Soyuzzdravexport
32/34 Smolenskaya-Sennaya
121200 Moscow
Director: V. Zharikov
Imports: medical equipment and
instrumentation.

Stanimpex
2 Ul. B. Khmelnitskogo
342042 Ulyanovsk
Cable: Granit Ulyanovsk
Telex: 214117
Phone: 6-15-87
Director: O. Ye. Benkovskiy
Exports: heavy duty vertical and
plane-milling machines.

Stankiyev
67 Prosp. Pobedy
252062 Kiev
Cable: Patron Kiev
Telex: 131462
Phone: 442-83-24; 442-83-98
Director: S. A. Vdovichenko
Exports: lathes, automatic and
semiautomatic multispindle turning
machines, single-spindle turning
machines, thread milling machines,
turret lathes, two-speed drills, vices,
spare parts.

Stankoimport
34/63 Ul. Obrucheva
117839 Moscow
Cable: Stankoimport Moscow
Telex: 411991; 411992; 411993
Phone: 333-51-01; 334-83-04
General Director: V. I. Marinin
Imports: N/C machines, casting
machines, thermoplastic casting
machines.
Exports: lathes, screw-cutting lathes,
grinding machines, metal working
equipment, saws.

V/O Stroidormashexport
Suvorovskiy Bulvar 7
Moscow
Telex: 411063 BREIM SU
Phone: 291-49-31

V/O Stroimaterialintorg
2 Sokolnicheskiy Val, korpus 50
107113 Moscow
Cable: Stroimaterialintorg Moscow

Telex: 411887; 411889
Phone: 269-05-54; 269-05-55
General Director: V. V. Devyatov
Imports: linoleum, structural glass, plumbing fixtures, finishing materials.
Exports: cement, crystal, asbestos fiber, soft roofing materials, wool.

Stromavtoliniya
77 Ul. Pervomayskaya
212648 Mogilev
Cable: Press Mogilev 212648, U.S.S.R.
Telex: 252161 Liniya
Phone: 3-44-17
Director: A. A. Usenya
Imports: automated lines, construction materials.
Exports: licenses.

Svetotechnika
5 Shosse Svetotechnikov
430023 Saransk
Cable: FTF Svetotechnikov Saransk
Telex: 412512 Svet
Phone: 4-89-68; 2-22-16
Director: D. S. Sozin
Exports: electric bulbs and light sources.

Sudoexport
Ul. Chaykovskovgo 1
123231 Moscow
Telex: 411116
Phone: 255-18-13, 255-48-04

*Sudoimport
10 Uspenskiy Per.
103006 Moscow
Telex: 411387 Sudo SU; 411443 Sudo SU
Phone: 299-68-49; 299-02-14; 299-58-77;
Acting General Director: B. A. Yakimov
Imports: ships, marine equipment, drilling rigs, equipment for prospecting and production of off-shore oil and gas, navigation equipment.
Exports: fishing vessels, hydrofoils.

Tallex
12 Ul. Mustomayae
200105 Tallinn
Cable: FTF TALLEX Tallinn
Phone: 49-82-20
Director: E. A. Mark
Exports: trenching excavators, land-reclamation drain-laying excavators, spare parts.

*V/O Techmashimport
19 Trubnikovskiy Per.
121819 Moscow
Cable: Techmashimport Moscow
Telex: 411194; 411195; 411306
Phone: 202-48-00; 248-83-00
General Director: V. I. Grib
Imports: turnkey plants for the production of synthetic fibers and raw materials, organic chemicals.

*Technoexport
32/34 Smolenskaya-Sennaya
Su-121200 Moscow

Phone: 233-59-87
Director: Yuri V. Chugunov
Imports: equipment for producing construction materials, glass, pulp, and paper.

*Technointorg
64 Pyatnitskaya Ul.
M-95 113836 Moscow
Telex: 411200
Phone: 231-26-22
General Director: A. A. Vasilyev
Imports: household appliances, refrigerators, TV sets, radios, optical instruments.

*V/O Technopromexport
32/34 Smolenskaya-Sennaya Pl.
SU-121200 Moscow
Phone: 220-15-23
Director: Alexander S. Postovalov
Activity: construction of thermal and diesel power stations, hydro power stations, high voltage transmission lines.

*V/O Technopromimport
35 Mosfilmovskaya Ul.
117330 Moscow
Cable: Technopromimport Moscow
Telex: 411233
Phone: 147-22-85; 147-22-77; 143-87-85
General Director: V. I. Boiko
Imports: equipment for food, dairy, meat and fish processing industries, equipment for grain elevators and animal feed mills, equipment for

light industry and radio engineering.

Techsnabexport
32/34 Smolenskaya-Sennaya Pl.
121200 Moscow
Cable: Techsnabexport Moscow
Telex: 411328 TSE SU
Phone: 244-32-85
General Director: V.I. Zharikov
Imports: hospital equipment, medical instrumentation.
Exports: radioistope instruments, X-ray unit, rare earth metals.

Textilmash
1 Proyezd Mashinostroiteley
428022 Cheboksary
Cable: FTF Tekstilmash
Telex: 512502
Phone: 23-36-37
Director: Yu A. Cherkasov
Exports: nonshuttle looms, ribbon looms.

Traktoroexport
43 Ul. Lesnaya
103055 Moscow
Telex: 411273A TPEX SU; 111456/2 PAXO
Phone: 258-59-34; 258-18-74
General Director: D. N. Monayenkov
Imports: turn-key plants for animal husbandry, equipment for crop cultivation.
Exports: tractors, agricultural machinery, spare parts.

*V/O Tyazhpromexport
32/34 Smolenskaya-Sennaya Pl.

SU-121200 Moscow
Phone: 220-16-10
Director: Valeri A. Yegorov
Imports: metallurgical, miniing, enrichment, and pipe-rolling equipment.

Ukrimpex
22 Ul. Vorovskogo
252054 Kiev
Cable: Ukrimpex Kiev
Telex: 216-21-74; 216-25-13
General Director: S. T. Sokolenko
Imports: vary.
Exports: clothing, surplus agricultural products.

V/O UNEX
Ul. Kosygina 15
117946 Moscow
Telex: 411049 UNEX SU
Phone: 939-88-67

V/O Vneshekonomservice
Ul. Kuybysheva 6
103684 Moscow
Telex: 411126 TPP
Phone: 259-37-53

*Vneshposyltorg
32/34 Smolenskays-Sennaya Pl.
SU-121200 Moscow
Phone: 271-05-05
Director: Vilik V. Khshtoyan
Imports: foodstuffs, durable consumer goods.

Vneshpromtechobmen
9 Per Vasnetsova
129090 Moscow

Cable: Vneshpromtechobmen
Moscow
Telex: 411181
Phone: 284-72-41
General Director: Yu. I. Cherepanov
Exports: ferrous and nonferrous mettalurgical products.

V/O Vneshtechnika
6 Starokonyushennyy Pereulok
119034 Moscow
Cable: Vneshtechnika Moscow
Telex: 411418 MLT
Phone: 201-72-60
General Director: V. I. Rybak
Activity: acquires and sells licenses, know-how, engineering, and consulting services.

V/O Vneshtorgizdat
1 Ul. Fadeyeva
125047 Moscow
Cable: Vneshtorgizdat Moscow
Telex: 411238 VTI
Phone: 250-51-62
Genral Director: Vladimir I. Prokopov
Activity: Publication of foreign-trade advertising literature in Russian and foreign languages.

V/O Vneshtorgreklama
Ul. Kakhovka 31, Kor. 2
113461 Moscow
Telex: 411265 VTR SU
Phone: 331-83-11

*V/O Vostokintorg
32/34 Smilenskaya-Sennaya Pl.
SU-121200 Moscow
Phone: 205-60-70

Director: Vladimir I. Brazhnikov
Imports: vary.
Exports: vary.

Zarubezhgeologiya
10 Kaholshin Pereulok
121002 Moscow
Telex: 411829 OZGEO
Phone: 241-15-15
General Director: M. I. Nikulshin
Imports: geoprospecting equipment and spare parts.
Exports: geological consulting services.

VPO Zarubezhstroi
Ul. Petrovka 14
103031 Moscow
Telex: 411191
Phone: 200-45-25, 200-45-66

SOVIET REPUBLIC FOREIGN TRADE ORGANIZATIONS

Armenian SSR

Atmenintorg
43, Ul. Chiraki
Yerevan 375086 U.S.S.R.
Phone: 46-42-62, 46-41-64, 64-71-72
General Director: R. A. Sarkisyan

Azerbaijan SSR

Azerintorg
4, Ul. Nekrasova
Baku 370004
Phone: 92-68-64, 92-29-40
Telex: 142127
General Director: A. M. Guseynov

Belorussian SSR

Belorusintorg
Dom Pravitelstva
Minsk 20010
Phone: 29-63-08, 29-63-09, 20-81-88
Telex: 252292
General Director: V. V. Andryushin
Exports: art, carpets, clothes, crafts, furniture, kitchenware, peat, pianos, produce, shoes, timber products, and waste.

Estonian SSR

Estimpex
Ul. Tolly 3
200001 Tallinn
Phone: 60-14-62
Telex: 173288 ANTIK
General Director: O. M. Kaldre

Georgian SSR

Gruzimpex
Prospekt Rustaveli 8,
Dom Pravitelstva
Tbilsi 380018
Phone: 93-71-69
General Director: D. A. Veruleishvili

Kazakh SSR

Kazakhintorg
Ul. Gogol 111
480003 Alma-Ata
General Director: S. Zh. Abishev

Kirgi SSR

101

Kirghizvneshtorg
Ul. Kirova 205
Frunze 72000
Phone: 26-63-66
General Director: E. A. Mochayev

Latvian SSR

Inter-Lavia
Ul. Lenina 85
Riga 2260001
Phone: 27-16-62, 33-28-46
General Director: M. A. Lotagr
Activity: tourism and exchanges in science, culture, and the arts.

Lithuanian SSR

Litimpex
Prospekt Lenian 37
Vilnius 232600
Phone: 62-09-96; 62-14-53
Telex: 278128, 261148
General Director: A. A. Smagin

Moldavian SSR

Moldex
Ul. Botanicheskaya 15
277018 Kishinyev
Telex: 163125 KODRU SU
Phone: 55-70-36
General Director: V. D. Volodin

Russian SFSR

Rosmedintorg
Ul. 25 let Oktyabrya 19
Moscow
Phone: 924-49-29
Director: V. E. Schkapkin

Imports: medical and diagnostic equipment.

V/O Rosvneshtorg
8/5 Ul. Barrikadnaya
123242 Moscow
Cable: Rosvneshtorg Moscow
Telex: 411060 ROSST SU
Phone: 254-80-50
Chairman: I. V. Belotserkovskiy

Tadzhik SSR

Tadjikvneshtorg
Pr. Lenina 42
Dushanbe 734051
Telex: 116119 SAWDO
Phone: 23-29-03
General Director: Yu. G. Gaytsgori

Ukrainian SSR

Ukrimpex
Ul. Vorovskogo 22
242054 Kiev
Phone: 216-21-74
131384
General Director: V. A. Vernigoroz

Uzbek SSR

Uzbekintorg
Pr. Uzebkistani 18
700115 Tashkent
Phone: 45-73-13; 45-78-42
Telex: 457313
General Director: A. I. Ikramov

1 All-Union Ministries govern sectors of industry throughout the territory of the Soviet Union. A ministry may administer its tasks either directly or by means of subordinate organizations.

2 Union Republic Ministries carry out administrative duties through the relevant ministries of the Union Republics; they administer directly only a limited number of enterprises assigned to them by the Supreme Soviet to the USSR.

3 All-Union State committees supervises activity in their relevant fields throughout the territory of the Soviet Union. State Committees competencies are generally outside the realm of heavy industry.

4 Union Republic Committees administrate on a by-region basis, but are linked to each other by a national bureau.

SECTION 5

FINANCING, ACCOUNTING & AUDITING

At the time this directory goes to print, the U.S. exporter to the Soviet Union is unlikely to find financial support from U.S. government agencies. Under terms of current legislation, including the Jackson-Vanik Amendment, U.S. agencies are prohibited from offering guarantees or financial assistance for U.S.-Soviet exports. Federally subsidized U.S.-Soviet grain trade is an exception. Additionally, most of the large U.S. banks listed below tend to focus on financing large deals, and are of limited use to medium-or small-size firms. However, there is a good chance that the present situation, including the U.S. government position on U.S.-Soviet trade, will change significantly during 1990, and that more financing options will become available.

Perhaps overlooked until now is U.S. venture capital. Private venture capital groups or venture capital clubs exist in most cities and are usually eager to see innovative proposals. For a list of these groups and clubs in a particular state, contact your state Department of Commerce.

The Soviet banking institutions listed below, with the exception of Vneshekonombank, are primarily of interest as potential sources of information and financing to U.S. businessmen involved in joint ventures with Soviet partners. Although there are many Western banks with offices in Moscow, they tend to be representational. All Western businesses in the Soviet Union must keep their accounts in Vneshekonombank, and all foreign trade transactions are likewise effected through Vneshekonombank. Hard currency export sales to the Soviet Union are ideally concluded via letter of credit, particularly in light of the Soviet Union's shortage of hard currency. Countertrade is also a viable option, although it can be extremely difficult to locate suitable and available Soviet products.

The auditing and accounting services offered in the Soviet Union by Soviet and Western agencies are also a useful resource to joint venture participants. Many of these firms also provide general trade and consulting services.

U.S. AND U.S.-BASED ORGANIZATIONS INVOLVED IN BANKING AND/OR FINANCE[1]

American Trade Consortium
in New York:
375 Park Avenue, Suite 3200
New York, NY 10152
Phone: (212) 751-8066
Contact: Susan Bird
in Moscow:
Sovincentr 1603A
Krasnopresnenskaya Nab. 12
Moscow
Phone: 253-94-96, 255-18-30
Contact: Rick Spooner
Services: The Consortium was formed to develop and finance business ventures between its members and organizations in the Soviet Union.

Bank of New York
One Wall Street
New York, NY 10015
Phone: (212) 635-8130
Contact: Natasha Gurkinfel

Bank of America
555 California Street
San Francisco, CA 94104
Phone: (415) 622-2073

Bankers Trust
280 Park Avenue
New York, NY 10017
Phone: (212) 850-4882
Contact: Prudencio L. Vieira, Vice

President

Barclays Bank PLC
75 Wall Street
New York, NY 10265
Phone: (212) 412-3661
Contact: Gordon Hough

Bear, Stearns and Co., Inc.
245 Park Avenue
New York, NY 10167
Phone: (212) 272-3597
Contact: Brian Murray, Managing Director

Bojes & Bruchs
Financial Services, Ltd.
8000 Towers Crescent Drive
Suite 900
Vienna, VA 22812
Phone: (703) 506-3298
FAX: (703) 506-3291
Contact: Gary Bojes

CAWT
in San Francisco:
4 Embarcadero Center, Suite 2150
San Francisco, CA 94111
Phone: (415) 781-8520
FAX: (415) 781-0622
Telex: 330452
in New York:
245 Park Avenue
New York, NY 10167
Phone: (212) 856-1228
FAX: (212) 856-1694
Telex: 424700
Contact: Donald Asadorian, Manager

---

[1]Some of the material for this section was provided by BLOC Magazine, 350 Broadway, Suite 1250, New York, NY 10013.

Services: CAWT offers trade finance services which include forfaiting and buyer credits. Countertrade services include parallel transactions, product trading, and switch transactions. CAWT's advisory services include market research, representation in Eastern Europe, and Soviet joint venture consulting.

Chase Manhattan
One Chase Manhattan Plaza, 14th Floor
New York, NY 10081
Phone: (212) 552-4676
Contact: Gail Buyske, Vice President

Chemical Bank
277 Park Avenue
New York, NY 10172
Phone: (212) 310-5370
Contact: Mauri Kutila, Vice President

Citibank
399 Park Avenue
New York, NY 10172
Phone: (212) 559-8577
Telex: 235530
Contact: Miljenko Horvat

Citicorp's East-West Services
Vienna, Austria
Phone: 772-1450
Telex: 112105

1st American Bank
740 15th Street, NW
Washington, DC 20005
Phone: (202) 637-4670
FAX: (202) 637-7923

Telex: 197638 ISTAM UT
Contact: Marilyn Sohl Labriny

First National Bank of Chicago
One First National Plaza
Mail Suite 0040
Chicago, IL 60670
Phone: (312) 732-6796
Contact: Robert L. Thomas, Assistant Vice President, International Structured Finance Group

ICD
641 Lexington Avenue, 11th Floor
New York, NY 10022
Phone: (212) 644-1509
Contact: Daniel Kazdan, Product Manager Eastern Europe

Kiser Research, Inc.
1233 20th Street, NW, Suite 505
Washington, DC 20036
Phone: (202) 223-5806
FAX: (202) 452-9571
Telex: 4991601 ITT
Contact: John Kiser
Services: Provides seed capital for projects acquiring the rights to Soviet technology.

MG Trade Finance Corporation
520 Madison Avenue
New York, NY 10016
Phone: (212) 826-5506
Contact: Huang Hung, Vice President

Manufacturer's Hanover
270 Park Avenue
New York, NY 10022

Phone: (212) 286-3314
Contact: Roger Codat, Vice President

Medical Consortium
1055 Washington Boulevard
Stamford, CT 06901
Phone: (203) 327-0900
FAX: (203) 325-3127
Contact: Dennis A. Sokol, President
Services: The Consortium was formed to develop and finance business ventures between its members and organizations in the Soviet Union.

Morgan Grenfell & Co. Limited
USSR Team, Banking Division
23 Great Winchester Street
London EC2P 2AX, UK
Phone: 588-4545
FAX: 1-826-7130
Telex: 896106 MG BFI G
Contact: Olimpia Cuomo
in Moscow:
USSR Representative Office,
Morgan Grenfell & Co. Limited
Pokrovsky, Bulvar 4/17, kv. 34
Phone: 230-23-86; 207-59-98
FAX: 230-23-86
Telex: 413121 MINBRO SU
Contact: Neil Jenkins
Services: Morgan Grenfell has a record of experience in joint ventures in the Soviet Union, including project finance, arranging loans, and export ·credit schemes.

National Westminster
175 Water Street, 28th Floor
New York, NY 10038

Phone: (212) 602-2120
Contact: Donna Gravier, Assistant Treasurer

Philadelphia National Bank
Offshore Banking Division/Trade Finance and Advisory
P.O. Box 7618
Philadelphia, PA
Phone: (215) 973-7336
Contact: Gerald F. Rama

Philipp Brothers, Inc.
1221 Avenue of the Americas
New York, NY 10020
Phone: (212) 790-5127, 575-5900
FAX: (212) 790-6810
Telex: 233031, 420808
Contact: Gary Marcus, Managing Director
Services: Phibro offers services in trade finance and countertrade.

Riggs National Bank of Washington, DC
International Division
1913 Massachusetts Avenue, NW
Washington, DC 20036
Phone: (202) 835-5391
Telex: 897455, 197660
Contact: Paul Cushman, III, Vice President

Security Pacific Trade Finance
595 Madison Avenue, 12th Floor
New York, NY 10022
Phone: (212) 644-0020
Contact: Jeffrey Malakoff, Sr., Vice President

U.S. GOVERNMENT PROGRAMS

(The following agencies offer financial and insurance programs covering several East European countries. At present, the Soviet Union is not included among them.)

Export-Import Bank of the United States
811 Vermont Avenue, NW
Washington, DC 20571
Phone: (202) 566-8898

Commodity Credit Corporation
Foreign Agricultural Service
U.S. Department of Agriculture,
14th & Independence Avenue, SW
Room 4509
Washington, DC 20250
Phone: (202) 447-3224
FAX: (202) 447-2949
Contact: Richard Godsey

Overseas Private Investment Corporation (OPIC)
1615 M Street
Washington, DC 20527
Phone: (202) 457-7093

Small Business Administration (SBA)
Office of International Trade
1441 L Street, NW
Washington, DC 20416
Phone: (202) 653-7794
Services: The Administration guarantees term loans for U.S. companies exporting to foreign markets and offers an export revolving line of credit (ERLC) program.

ACCOUNTING & AUDITING SERVICES

Arthur Anderson
in New York:
1345 Avenue of the Americas
New York, NY 10105
Phone: (212) 708-4125
FAX: (212) 708-3630
Contact: Paul W. Hoffman
in Moscow:
Leninskaya Sloboda 26
109068 Moscow
Phone: (095) 275-2126
FAX: (095) 275-2126
Contact: Hans Jochum Horn

Ernst & Young
in New York:
East European Division
787 7th Avenue
New York, NY 10019
Phone: (212) 830-6000
FAX: (212) 977-9358
Telex: 7607796
Contact: Stan Polovets, Manager
in Moscow:
119034 Moscow
Kursovoy Pereulok 9
Services: The firm's East European Division helps Western companies assess business opportunities and assists in implementing business strategies in Eastern Europe and the Soviet Union. The firm also provides services to Soviet organizations such as the Academy for Foreign Trade in Moscow. They advise on all issues related to joint ventures, and also on turn-key projects, compensation

arrangements, and countertrade.

Peat Marwick
559 52nd Street
New York, NY 10055
Phone: (212) 909-5596
FAX: (212) 751-1760
Contact: Aidan Walsh

Price Waterhouse
in London:
Southwark Towers
32 London Bridge Street
London SE1 9SY
Phone: (1) 407-8989
FAX: (1) 378-0647
Telex: 884657/8
Contact: Bruce Edwards, Allan
Cooper, Bridget Gough
in Moscow:
Kursovoy Per. 9
119304 Moscow
Services: Price Waterhouse has a
cooperation agreement with
Vneshekonomservice (VES), an
organization directly affiliated with
the USSR Chamber of Commerce
and with the Ministry of Foreign
Economic and Industry Affairs. The
firm is providing assistance to
companies in the area of joint
ventures concerning tax matters and
other regulations.

S O V I E T   F I N A N C I A L INSTITUTIONS

Commercial Bank for Railway Transport
Moscow
Phone: 258-48-93

Commercial Bank for Innovation
5 Khashirskoye Shosse
Moscow
Phone: 393-73-64

East-West Development Corporation
Minsk, Belorussian SSR
Phone: 23-34-27
Contact: V. Semyonov, President
Services: The EWDC is a 50-50 joint
venture between Belorussian
organizations and Lurvink and Co..
LTD. (The shareholders of Lurvink
and Co. are two individuals and
seven investment banking and trading
groups from Western Europe, the
U.S., and Japan.) The EWDC is a
Western-style financial service
company which will promote joint
ventures with and direct trade to the
West. For further information,
contact Franz Lurvink, France, Tel.
93-76-14-65.

Moscow Narodnyy Bank
Pokrovskyy Bulvar 4/17 Suite 34,
Moscow
Phone: 230-2386
Telex: 413121 MNBRO SU
Services: Moscow Narodnyy Bank is
a wholly-owned Soviet bank
incorporated in the United Kingdom.
The bank is an important actor in
the international monetary, foreign
exchange, and bond markets, and also
Eurocurrency markets. Moscow
Narodnyy Bank is one of several
Soviet banks incorporated in the
West, including the Ost-West
Handelsbank and the Wozchod
Handelsbank.

110

**Neftekhimbank
(Commercial Bank for the Petroleum
and Chemical Production Sector)**
Ul. Gilyarskogo 31
129832 Moscow
Phone: 284-81-22

State Bank of the USSR (GOSBANK)
Ul. 12, Neglinnaya
Moscow
Phone: 923-20-38, 925-29-19
Service: Gosbank acts as the Soviet Union's central bank. It regulates the activities of specialized commercial, joint stock, and cooperative banks, implements a unified state monetary policy, regulates national credit resources, analyzes and forecasts domestic and international monetary relations, etc. Prior to the current reform period, Gosbank dominated almost all aspects of Soviet finance; however, as of October 1987, many of its former functions have been assigned to five sector banks; Vneshekonombank (foreign trade), the Sberegatelny Bank (savings), the Agroprombank (agriculture), th Promstroybank (long term investment credits), and the Zhilsotsank (housing and social welfare).

Vneshekonombank
Ul. Pushkinskaya 4/2
103810 Moscos
Phone: Main Office 246-67-80
Moscow World Trade Center address:
Krasnopresnenskaya Nab. 12
Moscow

Phone: 246-67-88
World Trade Center, 253-17-90; 253-81-82
Telex: 411174 (cable address: Vneshbank Moscow), 253-23-49
Services: The bank engages in arranging and effecting settlements under export-import and noncommercial transactions, and granting credits to associations, enterprises, and organizations involved in foreign economic relations. The bank supervises rational and economical utilization of foreign exchange resources of the country, and carries out transactions in international foreign exchange and capital markets, as well as operations connected with cash currency and foreign exchange valuables. Another function of the bank is to promote the creation of joint ventures, international associations and organizations, and direct cooperative ties.

The following are branches of Vneshekonombank in the U.S.S.R.:

Republic Banks

The Ukrainian Republic Bank
8 Ul. Kreshchatnik
252001 Kiev
Cable address: Vneshbank Kiev

The Byelorussian Republican Bank
10 Ul. Zaslavskaya,
220035 Minsk.
Cable address: Vneshbank Minsk

111

The Luthuanian Republican Bank
10/1 Gediminas Prospekt
232629 Vilnius
Cable address: Vneshbank Vilnius

The Estonian Republican Bank
7 Narvskoye Schosse
200001 Tallinn.
Cable address: Vneshbank Tallinn
911

Territorial Offices

15 Ul. Kim Yu-Chena
680000 Khabarovsk
Cable address: Vneshbank
Khabarovsk

Regional Offices

29 Ul. Gertsena
190000 Leningrad
Cable address: Vneshbank
Leningrad

8 Ul. Chernyakhovskogo
270009 Odessa
Cable address: Vneshbank Odessa

1 Ul. Dovganika
290058 Lvov-58
Cable address: Vneshbank Lvov

19 Pl. Vossoedineniya
292000 Uzhgorod
Cable address: Vneshbank Uzhgorod

City Offices

6 Pr. Lenina
277001 Kishenev
Cable address: Vneshbank Kishenev

2 Ul. Nalbandyana
375010 Yerevan
Cable address: Vneshbank Yerevan

Branches

14 Leningradskiy Pr.,
188900 Vyborg
Cable address: Vneshbank Vyborg

34 Ul. Vorovskogo
35400 Sochi
Cable address: Vneshbank Sochi

47 Ul. Sovetov
353900 Novorossisk
Cable address: Vneshbank
Novorossisk

22 Nakhodkinsky Pr
692900 Nakhodka-4
Cable address: Vneshbank
Nakhodka-4

68 Ul. Geroyev Stalingrad
272630 Izmail
Cable address: Vneshbank Izmail

3 Ul. Lenina
334200 Yalta
Cable address: Vneshbank Yalta
Railway Station, 279100 Ungeny
Cable address: Vneshbank Ungeny

AUDITING AND ACCOUNTING SERVICES

Inaudit
Konushkovskaya 28
123242 Moscow
Phone: 921-03-25 (Moscow)
(212) 708-4803 (for information -- New York)
Contact: J. Kenneth Hickman (in New York)
Services: Inaudit is a Soviet joint-stock company created specifically to provide auditing services to joint ventures between Soviet entities and foreign partners.

Vneshaudit
Vneshaudit can be contacted through Ernst and Young's New York office
Phone: (212) 830-6000
Services: The firm is a USSR-based joint venture between Ernst & Young and Vneshconsult which provides auditing and accounting services.

Price Waterhouse
in Moscow:
Kursovoy Pereulok 9
Office 4
119304 Moscow
Phone: 202-17-17, 202-17-29
FAX: 200-12-34
Telex: 413526 SULSU
Contact: Susan Shale

113

SECTION 6

ADVERTISING & PROMOTIONS

This section lists firms specializing in advertising and promoting products and services in the Soviet Union. There are only a handful of advertising agencies that are active in this area since the Western concept of advertising is still quite new to the Soviet Union.

In addition to the U.S. and Soviet agencies offering advertising services, there is a broad array of journals, newspapers, and periodicals that sell advertising space to Western organizations.

Most journals published by Soviet organizations that have foreign trade rights can accept Western advertising.   There are hundreds of Soviet industry-specific journals, as well as general economic publications, such as *Ekonomika i zhizn,* that can now accept advertising. For additional information about these journals, check with the official Soviet advertising agency Vneshtorgreklama or an experienced consultant.

Several Western publications distributed in the Soviet Union also accept advertising. A selected list of these Western publications is included in this section.

BBDO Worldwide
in New York:
1285 Sixth Ave.
New York, NY 10019
Phone: (212) 459-5000
FAX: (212) 459-6645
Contact: Sam Johnson
in Moscow:
c/o VTI Ad Center
1, Ul. Fadeyeva
125047 Moscow
Phone: 250-51-62
FAX: 253-97-94
Telex: 411-238 VTI SU
Contact: Bruce Macdonald

Services: The firm provides marketing and advertising services.

BRM International Division
U.S. Advertising
2700 Rt. 22
Union NJ 07083
Contact: George Black

Catskills Agency
Box 484
Rt. 28
Arkville, NY 12406
Phone: (914) 586-2900,
(800) 537-7265

Contact: David Zeiset
Services: The firm specializes in international marketing in advertisement placement.

Design Dynamics
5525 Twin Knolls Road
Suite 323
Columbia, MD 21045
Phone: (301) 995-3022
FAX: (301) 995-0805
Contact: Alex Koorbanoff
Services: The firm offers complete international and domestic advertising services, public relations, Russian and Eastern Europe language graphic design and production of promotional services, business cards, brochures, and packaging. Translation services available.

Interconcepts
10 E. 21st Street
New York, NY
Phone: (212) 254-8271
Services: The firm's Moscow-based joint venture, Intermedbio, markets, advertises, and conducts trade in scientific, industrial, and agricultural goods and services. The joint venture is also active in the import and leasing of personal computer and markets and develops software products.

Parsons Friedmann Stephan & Rose
418 Commonwealth Ave.

Boston, MA 02215
Contact: John M. Rose, Jr., President
Services: The firm offers complete international and domestic advertising, marketing, and public relations services for broadcast, print, and outdoor advertising, and trade show materials, and incentive programs. The firm also provides Russian translation services available via the Moscow office.

Rossa
Reklamo-KommercheskoyeAgentstvo
Dmitrovskiy Proezd 4
Moscow
Phone: 216-34-18
Services: Rossa is a full-service Soviet commercial advertising agency.

Saatchi & Saatchi
375 Hudson St.
New York, NY 10014-3620
Phone: (212) 463-2000
Services: The firm provides assistance to Western companies in the area of advertising and promotions.

Tisza, Ogilvy & Mather
309 West 49th St.
New York, NY 10019
Phone: (212) 237-5813
FAX: (212) 237-5123
Contact: Deroy Murdock
in Moscow:
Ul. Vernadskogo 33
Moscow

116

Phone: 131-5743
FAX: 237-5123
Telex: 414511
Services: The U.S.-Soviet joint venture provides advertising, public relations, and business consulting from its Moscow and New York offices.

V/O Vneshtorgreklama
31, Ul. Kakhovka
113461 Moscow
Phone: 331-8311, 331-8801
FAX: 310-7005
Telex: 411625 VTR SU
Services: The firm provides a complete package of PR and advertising services in the Soviet Union, including mass media, direct mail, promotional events, symposia, and seminars and exhibits.

Young and Rubicam/Sovero
in Chicago:
C/O Burson Marsteller
1 East Wacker Dr.
Chicago, IL 60601-1854
Phone: (312) 329-9292
FAX: (312) 329-7583
Telex: 6871 401
In Moscow:
1404 Sovincentr,
12 Krasnopolskaya Nab.
123610 Moscow
Phone: 253-1347
FAX: 253-1348
Telex: 412199 ADPR
Contact: Michael Adams, Chief Executive Officer; Vladimir Vlasov, General Manager

Services: The joint venture company, Young & Rubicam/Sovero, provides integrated communications services in the Soviet marketplace to both Soviet and Western clients. The firm has developed a broad portfolio of experience in both U.S. and Soviet markets.

SELECTED PUBLICATIONS OFFERING ADVERTISING IN THE SOVIET UNION

American-Soviet Medical Market Journal
Sales Office, Suite 408
374 Congress St.
Boston, MA 02210
Phone: (617) 451-6633
FAX: (617) 451-6182
Contact: Richard P. Mills
Services: The journal is a Russian-language publication of articles on health care, medical research, and equipment translated from Western sources. The journal is distributed throughout the Soviet Union to a wide range of health care facilities and medical libraries.

Dhalfelt International
in the U.S.:
120 Potter Road
Scarsdale, NY 10583
Phone: (914) 472-2084
Contact: Ulf Nofelt, President
in Moscow:
ICA-Soviet-American Foundation
Moscow 107078, B-87

Phone: 245-02-03
Contact: Alexander Churkin, Associate
Services: Designs and places advertisements in the Soviet mass media.

KOMPASS Intercontinental **Publishing, Inc.**
in Boston:
418 Commonwealth Ave.
Boston, MA 02215
Phone: (617) 266-1214
FAX: (617) 247-3008
in Moscow:
Sovietskaya Hotel
Leningradskiy Prospekt 32
Moscow
Services: KOMPASS provides advertising in its joint publications, *Moscow Business,* and *Music in the USSR.* Additionally, KOMPASS can provide advertising exposure in the Soviet publications *Evening Moscow Supplement, New Times,* and *Echo.*

PC World USSR
International Marketing Services
IDG Communications, Inc.
5 Speen St.
Framingham, MA 01701-9192
Phone: (508) 879-0700
Contact: Frank Cutitta, Managing Director
Services: Advertising space is available in *PC World USSR* magazine.

Science in the USSR
Omni Magazine
1965 Broadway
New York, NY 10133-0116
Phone: (212) 496-6100

USA Today International
Phone: (212) 715-2051
Contact: Barbara Krasne
Services: USA Today International is distributed in Riga, Leningrad, Kiev, and Moscow by Sovaminko, a U.S.-Soviet joint venture based in Moscow.

Ekonomika i zhizn
Bumazhniy proezd, 14
101462, GSP-4, Moscow
Phone: 212-23-89
Telex: 112314 ROGOZA
Services: A weekly Soviet publication focusing on general economics and business issues. The paper includes Western advertising.

SECTION 7

INSURANCE AGENCIES

U.S.-Soviet trade is not without risk. However, potential losses caused by confiscation, expropriation, nationalization, license cancellations, forced withdrawal orders, trade restrictions, ethnic violence, and strikes can now be minimized by obtaining insurance coverage offered by the firms listed in this section.

Government organizations, such as the Overseas Private Investment Corporation and the Export-Import Bank did not provide political risk insurance to support trade with the Soviet Union by the fall of 1990. However, these organizations may be able to write insurance and guarantee loans by the end of the year.

American International Underwriters
(Affiliated with American International Group)
Central and Eastern European Division
70 Pine Street, 16th Floor
New York, NY 10270
Phone: (212) 770-5684, (212) 770-6243
FAX: (212) 809-7642
Contact: Leslie Kerkapoly, Division President, Peter Heimann, Vice President
Services: AIG is a leading U.S. insurance group with over 20 years experience in Eastern Europe. It is involved with a number of joint ventures in Poland, Hungary, and Romania. The firm has an underwriting agency in Vienna, Austria, which in coordination with the New York office, is capable of providing service in all commercial lines for companies engaged in East-West trade.

Chubb and Son
15 Mountain View Road
Warren, NJ 07061-1615
Phone: (201) 580-2000
FAX: (201) 580-2003
Services: Companies of the Chubb Insurance Group have a joint cooperation agreement with the insurance agency of the U.S.S.R., Ingosstrakh. The agreement allows coinsurance of property and casualty exposures of the U.S.-Soviet joint ventures located in the Soviet Union. Subject matters of insurance involve most classes of property and casualty insurance. Premiums and losses may be stated in United States dollars, pound sterling, or other appropriate currencies.

Frank B. Hall & Co of California
Soviet and East European Risk Insurance Facility (SEERIF)

119

One Market Plaza, Spear Street
Tower, Suite 2100
San Francisco, CA 94105-1189
Phone: (415) 543-9360
FAX: (415) 543-5628
Telex: 4937656
Contact: Price G. Lowenstein
Services: SEERIF protects against
U.S. Government trade restrictions,
ethnic violence, strikes, riots,
confiscation, expropriation,
nationalization, and loss of income,
due to interruption of business. The
facility is operated in conjunction
with Lloyd's of London and began
with assets of $400 million.

Ingosstrakh
Insurance Company of the U.S.S.R.
12 Pjatnitskaya Ul.
113184 Moscow
Phone: 231-16-77
Telex: 411144
Contact: Mikhail Safranov
Services: Ingosstrakh is the official
Soviet insurance agency.

Johnson and Higgins
125 Broad Street
New York, NY 10004-2400
Phone: (212) 574-7745
FAX: (212) 574-8993
Telex: 420027
Contact: Ken Horne, Vice President,
Political Risk Unit
Services: Johnson and Higgins is an
insurance broker providing all forms
of political risk insurance.

Marsh and McLennan Worldwide
1221 Avenue of the Americas
New York, NY 10020-1011
Phone: (212) 345-4000
FAX: (212) 345-4054
Contact: Frank Gunderson,
Managing Director
Services: Marsh & McLennan
Companies Inc. is a professional
services firm with insurance and
reinsurance brokering, consulting, and
investment management businesses.
The company has a U.S.S.R. broker
specialization which addresses all
aspects of manufacturing,
construction, export-import, and
distribution. The firm services risks in
all industries, from marine, energy,
health care, financial services, and
farming to electronics and
entertainment.

**Vienna Agency of American
International Underwriters:**
European American Underwriters
Bartensteingasse 2
Vienna, Austria 1010
Phone: 222-402-35560
FAX: 222-402-5160
Telex: 132303
Contact: Gerard Jansen, General
Manager; Mujib Khan, Underwriting
Manager; I. Pollheimer,
Administrative Manager

SECTION 8

COMMUNICATIONS & SHIPPING

Although telephone communications with Moscow have improved significantly over the past several years, the level of service is still far below that taken for granted in the West. The introduction of direct dial service between the U.S. and Soviet Union recently was a major improvement, but the wait for a free line can still be considerable, especially during peak business hours.

And, although most Western businesses in the Soviet Union now have access to fax machines, very few of their Soviet counterparts are equipped with faxes. Thus, telex communications through intermediary organizations for delivery of important communications are still frequently used. This section includes several firms that can facilitate delivery of documents through facsimile or E-mail systems, as well as services which can deliver the original documents or parcels in three or four working days. Any non-document parcel sent to the Soviet Union should absolutely be insured for full value.

It will be a long time before communications between the U.S. and the Soviet Union reach an optimum level. However, it is possible with planning to ensure reasonable contact with your Soviet counterparts.

The export of products to the Soviet Union is best accomplished through an experienced freight forwarder. Freight forwarders handle necessary export documentation and arrange for shipment of the goods to the Soviet Union. The freight forwarders listed below represent only a small fraction of those in operation nationwide. Considerations that should be taken into account when choosing a freight forwarder include:

• Rates -- Are they competitive?
• Warehouse facilities in the U.S. -- Are they appropriate or sufficient for your shipments?
• Experience in shipping to the Soviet Union -- Is there someone on the staff familiar with the documentation and procedures required by Soviet customs?

FREIGHT FORWARDERS

Air-Sea Forwarders, Inc.
P.O. Box 90637
Los Angeles, CA 90009
Phone: (213) 776-1611
FAX: (213) 216-2625
Services: The firm has branches in San Francisco, San Diego, New York, Newark, Boston, Chicago, Atlanta, Houston, London, Munich, and Tokyo.

Aqua Air International
P.O. Box 164
Iselin, NJ 08830
Phone: (201) 283-2150
FAX: (201) 283-2171
Contact: J. Piazza

Business Service Desk
Mezhdunarodnaya Hotel I and II
Krasnopresnenskaya Nab. 12
Moscow
Phone: 253-32-82
Contact: The office provides telex, photocopying, secretarial, translation, and interpretation services.

Columbia Shipping, Inc.
138-01 Springfield Boulevard
Jamaica, NY 11413
Phone: (718) 656-5900
FAX: (718) 712-3622
Telex: 645045
Contact: Loretta Block

Services: The firm has other offices in Los Angeles, Chicago and San Francisco.

Communications House
Prospekt Kalinina 22
Moscow
Phone: 202-03-01
Services: This office provides 24-hour services for telephone and telegraph and provides some postal services during regular business hours.

Danzas Corp.
330 120th Avenue, NE
Bellevue, WA 98005
Phone: (206) 646-7171
FAX: (206) 646-7188

Hudson Shipping Company, Inc.
17 Battery Place
Suite 1230
New York, NY 10004
Phone: (212) 487-2600
Services: Since 1983, the firm has provided import/export and air/ocean services with agents worldwide in all major cities and ports.

International Post Office
Komsomolskaya Pl., 1A
    or
Varshavskoye Shosse, 37A
Moscow

Phone: 111-05-13
Services: The International Post Office provides services including delivery, telegraph, telegram, shipping, and telephone.

Intertrans Corporation
113 Executive Drive
Suite 101
Sterling, VA 22170
Phone: (703) 834-3116
FAX: (703) 834-5786
Contact: Dale Goodson

Kelly International
120-65 168th Street
Jamaica, NY 11434
Phone: (718) 528-0540, (718) 656-5926
FAX: (718) 528-0510
Telex: 427889
Contact: Martin J. Kelly, President
Services: Specializing in clearing New York area ocean and air shipments, as customs brokers/forwarders, consolidators, break-bulk agents, operating their own bonded container freight station, warehouse and trucking operations, distributing throughout U.S.A. and/or exporting worldwide.

Panalpina, Inc
Harborside Financial Center
34 Exchange Place-Plaza II
Jersey City, NJ 07302
Phone: (201) 451-4000

FAX: (201) 451-8572
Telex: 22-2874 PANYC UR

Radix Group International, Inc.
301 East Grand Avenue
South San Francisco, CA 94080
Phone: (415) 742-8231
FAX: (415) 875-3794
Telex: 210620
Contact: Val Anderson
Services: Radix Group International is a customs broker and international freight forwarder "specializing" in trade between U.S.A & U.S.S.R.

Ted L. Rausch Co.
P.O. Box 77147
San Francisco, CA 94107
Phone: (415) 348-5923
Services: The firm, established in 1958, provides brokerage, forwarding, and ocean/air cargo consolidation.

Schenkers International Forwarder
147-29 182nd Street
Jamaica, NY 11413
Phone: Ocean (212) 432-3031
Air (718) 632-7300
FAX: Ocean (718) 432-3092
Air (718) 632-1929

SOVIET SHIPPING COMPANIES

Baltic Shipping Company
U.S. Agent:
Rice, Unruh, Reynolds Co.
232 S. Fourth Street
Philadelphia, PA 19106

123

Phone: (215) 629-1711
FAX: (215) 629-0242
ervices: The Baltic Shipping Company provides the only direct service to Leningrad.

SHIPPING BROKERS

Sovfracht (U.S.A), Inc.
477 Madison Avenue
New York, NY 10022
Phone: (212) 355-6280
Contact: S. Karachkov, President
in Moscow:
1/4 Rozhdestvenka Ul.
103759 Moscow
Phone: 926-11-18
Telex: 411168
Cable: SOVFRACHT MOSCOW
Contact: V. L. Schutov, President
Services: Sovfracht is the sole chartering corporation in the U.S.S.R. and is a general agent for Soviet shipping companies. Sovfracht companies specialized in foreign trade include: Oceanchart, Yuzhchart, Eurochart, Tankerchart, Timechart, and Morpasflot.

TELECOMMUNICATIONS & MAIL SERVICES

DHL Worldwide Express
333 Twin Dolphin Drive
Redwood City, CA 94065
Phone: (800) 225-5345
Services: DHL has been offering air express services to the Soviet Union since 1985. Document delivery to Moscow door-to-door takes four business days. DHL also handles dutiable shipments up to 125 pounds. In addition to Moscow, DHL offers service to 13 other cities in the U.S.S.R.

Emery Worldwide
(A Consolidated Freight Company)
3350 West Bay Shore Road
Palo Alto, CA 94303
Phone: (800) HI-EMERY (Service)
Services: The delivery of urgent letters (one half pound, approximately 20 pages) or urgent packs (up to 2 pounds) takes 3 business days door-to-door. Air cargo freight service is available for large packages, with delivery in five business days door-to-airport.

Moscow Central Post Office
Ul. Kirova, 26A
101000 Moscow
Phone: 228-63-11, 924-02-50, 924-95-29
Services: The Moscow Central Post Office provides 24-hour services such as telex, telegrams, money orders, etc.

Moscow Central Telephone and Telegraph
Ul. Gorkogo, 7
Moscow
Phone: 924-05-20, 924-90-40
Services: This office provides 24-hour services such as telephone,

telegraph, registered mail, shipping, etc.

Telex Service Center
Intourist Hotel
3-5 Ul. Gorkogo
Moscow
Phone: 925-92-681
925-15-88 (Inquiries)
924-47-50 (Telegraph)

TNT SKYPACK
990 Stewart Avenue
Garden City, NY 11530
Phone: (800) 558-5555
Services: Package and document service to all of the Soviet Union and the Eastern bloc. TNT's joint ventures with Aeroflot, Malev and JAT ensure smooth and rapid handling door to door.

United Parcel Service (UPS)
Contact your local UPS office
Phone: (800) 595-9090
Services: Document transit time door-to-door is 3 business days to Moscow, 4 business days to Leningrad. Parcels are accepted up to 70 pounds. Nondocument shipments require additional time for Soviet customs clearance. The shipper must comply with export control laws.

U.S Postal Express Service
Contact your local post office

Services: Documents are delivered in 48 hours.

ELECTRONIC MAIL SERVICES

IDB Communications Group, Inc.
IDB Sales-New York
260 Madison Avenue
New York, NY 10016
Phone: (212) 953-0070
FAX: (212) 986-0132
Telex: 213770
Contact: Dennis Mallon
in Moscow:
CCS Satellite Co.
Phone: 234-28-29
Telex: 411405
Contact: George Korolev
Services: IDB offers a permanent digital telecommunication links to the Soviet Union, assuring reliable, cost-effective transmission of voice, data, facsimile, and compressed video to Moscow or any place in the world.

International Trade and Communications, Inc. (ITC)
1608 Walnut Street
Philadelphia, PA 19103
Phone: (215) 732-2844
FAX: (215) 790-0158
Telex: 4948598
Contact: Richard B. Price, President
Services: ITC recently signed a 15-year contract with a group of five Soviet and East European organizations for the creation and implementation of an electronic, PC-

125

based interactive communications system designed to facilitate East-West trade.

San Francisco/Moscow Teleport
in San Francisco:
3278 Sacramento Street
San Francisco, CA 94115
Phone: (415) 931-8500
FAX: (415) 931-2885
Telex: 9103804097 TELEPORT
in Moscow:
Ul. Nezhdanovoy, 2a
Moscow 103009
Phone: 229-96-63
FAX: 229-41-21
Contact: Deborah L. Miller, Data Communications Manager, SFMT
Services: The firm provides electronic mail service for business, scientific, and educational communities in the U.S. and the Soviet Union.

SECTION 9

TRAVEL ORGANIZATIONS

For American business executives, travel to the Soviet Union is not simple. You need a passport. You need a visa. You need to be invited. You need to know which airline to fly and when to fly to get the best rate. You need to know where to stay when you get to the Soviet Union. And you need to make special arrangements if you're traveling in a group. The various travel agencies, organizations, and offices listed in this section can be helpful.

Special attention should be given to the airline price wars going on this year for travel between the U.S. and the Soviet Union and Eastern Europe. This is an opportunity to cut travel costs. You may want to contact airlines directly to make sure you know who has the best prices.

Academic Travel Abroad, Inc.
3210 Grace Street, NW
Washington, DC 20007
Phone: (202) 333-3355
Telex: 248641
Services: The company primarily conducts tours of an educational nature, often with universities. It also handles professional organizations that need a customized tour.

Aeroflot
630 Fifth Ave, Suite 241
New York, NY, 10111
Phone: (212) 397-1660, (800) 535-9877, (800) 5-FLY-USSR
FAX: (212) 397-1660
Telex: (212) 459-0721
Services: Aeroflot can make all

travel arrangements including flight and hotel.

All World Travel
131 State Street (India Street side)
Boston, MA 02109
Phone: (617) 720-2000, (800) 343-2123
FAX: (617) 720-3909
Telex: 8100071150
Contact: Rita Cuker, President
Services: All World Travel provides full service travel arrangements to the Soviet Union for their clients including: *necessary business invitations and visas,* private hotel accommodations, airline reservations at competitive prices, business meeting arrangements, business introductions to officials and Soviet

business people, and conference center arrangements and reservations. All World Travel packages trade missions as well as tours for business, professional, educational, and *cultural* groups and full service travel arrangements for the individual traveler. All World Travel has a full staff in Moscow to handle interpreting, ground transportation, and business communication needs.

Allied Travel, Inc.
11 E. 44th Street
New York, NY 10017
Phone: (212) 661-7200, (800) 843-2446
Telex: 236098
Services: The firm provides group packages to travel agencies.

American Express Company
Sadovo-Kudrinskaya Ul. 21-A
Moscow
Phone: 254-43-05
Telex: 413075 AMEXM SU
Services: American Express provides a wide range of business travel services.

Anniversary Tours
330 Seventh Avenue, Suite 700
New York, NY 10001
Phone: (212) 465-1200, (800) 366-1336
FAX: (212) 268-4855
Telex: 238608
Services: Anniversary Tours provides

customized business services and can assist in arranging meetings with Soviet officials.

Barry Martin Travel
in New York:
19 West Street, Suite 3401
New York, NY 10004
Phone: (212) 422-0091
FAX: (212) 344-1997
Telex: 4952650
in Moscow:
Hotel Mezhdunarodnaya 2 Kv. 940,
Krasnopresnenskaya Nab., 12
Moscow
Phone: 253-29-40
Services: BMT Travel offers arrangements for business executives in the Soviet Union.

Beverly International Travel, Inc.
4630 Campus Drive, Suite 205
Newport Beach, CA 92660
Phone: (714) 474-7582
FAX: (714) 756-2169
Telex: 4996456

British Airways
in Moscow:
Hotel Mezhdunarodnaya II
Krasnopresnenskaya Nab. 12, Kv. 1905
Moscow
Phone: 253-27-01; (800) 247-9297 (U.S.)
Telex: 413197

Center for International Business and Travel
2185 Wisconsin Avenue, NW
Washington, DC 20001
Phone: (202) 333-5550,
(800) 424-2429
FAX: (202) 333-4753
Services: Business visa services and some consultation services for international travel are offered. The company can also assist in inviting Soviet guests.

Delphi Travel Unlimited
in Washington:
1019 19th Street, NW
Suite 900
Washington, DC 20036
Phone: (202) 466-7951, (800) 826-0196
FAX: (202) 466-4113
Telex: 413931
in Moscow:
Bolshaya Pereyaslavskaya 7-41
Moscow
Phone: 280-5441
Services: The travel agency is part of the Delphi International Group, which is active in a number of trade areas. The firm provides a variety of customized business services.

Finnair
in New York:
10 East 40th Street
New York, NY 10016
Contact: Borje A. Sandberg
Phone: (212) 689-9300, (800) 950-5000

FAX: (212) 481-0569
in Moscow:
Proyezd Khudozhestvennogo, Teatra 6
SU-103009 Moscow
Phone: 292-33-37, 292-87-88
FAX: 230-29-88

Five Star Touring
60 E. 42nd Street
Suite 612
New York, NY 10165
Phone: (212) 818-9140 (in NY); (800) 792-STAR (outside NY)
Telex: 4972143
Services: The firm offers a variety of customized travel services.

General Tours
770 Broadway
New York, NY 10003
Phone: (212) 598-1800, (800) 221-2216
FAX: (212) 598-0117

Global Concepts
2860 Walnut Hill Lane
Suite 104
Dallas, TX 75229
Phone: (214) 351-0001, (800) 322-4552
FAX: (214) 902-9020
Telex: 163410 PROBUS UT
Services: Global Concepts participates in a joint venture with Amtravel, which deals with trade and travel between the U.S. and the

Soviet Union. The firm is also beginning a program to assist companies that wish to start up businesses with the Soviet Union.

Globus-Gateway/Cosmos
150 South Los Robles, Suite 860
Pasadena, CA 91101
Phone: (818) 449-0919, (800) 556-5454
FAX: (818) 584-9857
Telex: 215292
in New York:
95-25 Queens Boulevard
Rego Park, NY 11374
Phone: (718) 268-1700, (800) 221-0090
FAX: (718) 520-1735
Telex: 170903
Services: The company's services are available only to travel agencies.

Inter-Tours Corp.
5458 Wilshire Boulevard
Los Angeles, CA 90036
Phone: (213) 933-7153, (800) 366-5458
FAX: (213) 933-8317
Telex: 691370
Contact: Helen Stein
Services: Inter-Tours conducts a joint venture with the Armenian division of Aeroflot.

Intourist
630 Fifth Avenue, Suite 868
New York, NY, 10111

Contact: Yuri Bagrov, General Manager
Services: Intourist is the official Soviet travel agency.

INTRAVCO Travel Centers, Inc.
211 East 43rd Street
New York, NY 10017
Phone: (212) 972-1155,
(800) ITC-TRVL
FAX: (212) 983-2590
Telex: 201831 ITCNY UR
Contact: Clark Malcom
Services: INTRAVCO provides a wide variety of business travel services.

ITS Tours & Travel
1055 Texas Avenue
Suite 104
College Station, TX 77840
Phone: (409) 764-9400, (800) 533-8688
FAX: (409) 693-9673
Telex: 293148
Services: The firm primarily offers tours of an educational nature, often with universities. It also handles professional organizations that need customized tours. All tours are open to individuals regardless of affiliation.

Klineburger Worldwide Travel
3627 1st Avenue South
Seattle, WA 98134
Phone: (206) 343-9699
FAX: (206) 682-8868
Telex: 185283

Services: The company is a full service travel agency, a travel wholesaler for other agencies and arranges hunting and fishing trips throughout the U.S.S.R.

KLM Royal Dutch Airlines
Hotel Mezhdunarodnaya II
Krasnopresnenskaya Nab. 12, Kv. 1307 Moscow
Phone: 253-21-50-51, 230-23-04; (800) 777-5553 (U.S.)

Lufthansa
in New York:
750 Lexington Avenue
New York, NY 10022-1208
Phone: (212) 745-0701, (800) 645-3880
FAX: (212) 745-0899
in Moscow:
Kuznetskiy Most, 3
Moscow
Phone: 923-04-88

Margo's International Travel Service
1812 Irving Street
San Francisco, CA 94122
Phone: (415) 665-4330; (800) 33 MARGO
FAX: (415) 665-4942
Telex: 340649
Services: In addition to its travel services, the company assists with documentation required for inviting Soviet guests to the United States.

Mir Corporation
3603 S. Hanford
Seattle, WA 98144
Phone: (206) 722-1633
FAX: (206) 624-7360
Services: The firm can provide customized business services, including contacts with Soviet cooperatives.

Organization for American-Soviet Exchanges (OASES-DC)
1430 K Street, NW, Suite 1200
Washington, DC 20005
Phone: (202) 393-0985
FAX: (202) 393-0989
Services: The organization has a number of advocational and professional contacts throughout the Soviet Union and can organize conferences, arrange bilateral exchanges, and provide interpreting and translating services.

Pan American Airways
Mezhdunarodnaya/Sovincenter
Krasnopresnenskaya 12, Kv. 1102A
Moscow
Phone: 253-26-58, 253-26-59
in New York: (800) 221-1111

Percival Tours
Hurst Bldg., Suite 1025
5 Third Street
San Francisco, CA 94103

Phone: (415) 442-1815
(800) 537-8600 (CA); (800) 451-0800
(outside CA)
FAX: (415) 442-1824
Telex: 3717748

Pioneer Travel
203 Allston Street
Cambridge, MA 02139
Contact: Frank "Paco" Norall
Services: Pioneer Travel provides
customized business services.

Rahim Tours, Inc.
12 South Dixie Highway
Lake Worth, FL 33460
Phone: (407) 585-5305
(800) 556-5305
FAX: (407) 582-1353
Services: The company assists
individual business travelers,
international fares, corporate
incentive travel, meetings with Soviet
officials and business people,
expertise on domestic U.S.S.R.
transportation and travel, visa
services.

RHA Group
2182 Dupont Drive
Suite 23
Irvine, CA 92715
Phone: (714) 851-0623
FAX: (714) 851-0623 (auto FAX)
Services: RHA provides a variety of
customized business services and
operates a Moscow office. RHA can
assist in structuring trips for various

kinds of industries. The firm will
arrange to provide interpreters,
chauffeured cars, etc.

Rothschild Travel Consultants
900 West End Avenue
Suite 1B
New York, NY 10025
Contact: Kathy Rothschild
Services: The firm has 18 years
experience in organizing customized
travel planning and cultural
exchanges.

Russart Travel Service
291 Geary Street
Suite 511
San Francisco, CA 94102
Phone: (415) 781-6655
(800) 232-RUSS (CA); (800) 338-
RUSS (outside CA)
FAX: (415) 781-6134
Telex: 255718
Services: The agency operates a
full-service office in Moscow which
provides a variety of business services
such as use of fax and telex machines,
interpreters, guides, rent-a-car, etc.

Russian Travel Bureau, Inc.
225 E. 44th Street
New York, NY 10017
Phone: (212) 986-1500
(800) 847-1800
FAX: (212) 490-1650
Services: The company has
experience with special interest

groups and individual business travel.

SAS Scandinavian Airlines System
in Moscow:
Kuznetskiy Most, 3
Moscow
Phone: 925-47-47
In Washington: (202) 833-3131
Telex: 413077 MOWSK SU

Soviet Consulate
1825 Phelps Place, NW
Washington, DC 20036
Phone: (202) 939-8916
FAX: (202) 483-7579
in San Francisco:
2790 Green Street
San Francisco, CA
Phone: (415) 922-6642
Services: The consulate processes visas for anyone traveling to the Soviet Union. Travelers wishing to obtain visas on their own can do business with the consulate in person or through the mail. Hours are Monday through Friday 9am-12:30pm. Visa applications for business travel should be submitted at least two weeks in advance. The application consists of 3 identical full face photos (1 1/2 by 1 3/4 inches with a matt or dull finish and signed on the back); a typed visa application form; a letter, telex, or fax of invitation from a Soviet organization including each invitee's name, date and place of birth, U.S. passport number, date and place of passport issue, passport expiration date; an address label or self addressed envelope; a cover letter from your firm stating your travel purpose; and a check or money order for $10.00. (For visas issued in five business days or less the fee is $15.00.)

Soviet Business Connections
P.O. Box 925
Oneonta, NY 13820
Contact: Tom Scholet, President
Services: The firm handles Soviet business arrangements between the U.S. and Soviet Union, including travel services, office space procurement, people-to-people connections and communications within the Soviet Union. Can provide travel and other information to individuals interested in having eye surgery done at the Fyodorov Clinic in Moscow.

Swissair
in Moscow:
Sovincenter
Krasnopresnenskaya Nab. 12, Room 2005
Moscow 123100
Phone: 253-89-88, 253-18-59; (800) 221-4750 (U.S.)
FAX: 253-18-52
Telex: 413417

Tour Designs
510 H Street, SW
Washington, DC 20024
Contact: Dan Hays
Services: Tour Designs is

experienced in business and professional travel to the Soviet Union.

Travcoa
P.O. Box 2630
Newport Beach, CA 92658
Phone: (714) 476-2800
(800) 992-2004 (CA); (800) 992-2003 (outside CA)
FAX: (714) 476-2538
Telex: 692483
Services: Travcoa offers deluxe group tours only.

Travel Advisers of America
1413 K Street, NW
Suite 800
Washington, DC 20005
Phone: (202) 371-1440
FAX: (202) 682-5833
Services: The company provides a variety of customized travel services.

Travelling Shoes
P.O. Box 4410
Laguna Beach, CA 92652
Phone: (714) 752-9036
FAX: (714) 752-7105

Troika, Inc.
192 Nickerson Street
Suite 312
Seattle, WA 98109
Phone: (206) 281-9289, (800) 367-9928
FAX: (206) 281-9040
Telex: 256663 TRTR UR

Services: Troika specializes in business and professional groups and individual business travel with particular focus on the Soviet Far East, and serves as exclusive agent for BAM (Baikal-Amur Mainline Railway).

Union Tours, Inc.
79 Madison Avenue, Suite 1104
New York, NY 10016
Phone: (212) 683-9500, (800) 451-9511
FAX: (212) 683-9511

Universal Travel & Tours, Inc.
3495 Thomasville Road
Tallahassee, FL 32308
Contact: Lani Rodgers
Phone: (904) 222-7171,
(800) 524-1524 (in Fla.),
(800) 433-1333 (outside Fla.)
Services: The firm arranges travel to the Soviet Union.

University Travel Services, Inc.
4534 11th Avenue
Seattle, WA 98105
Phone: (206) 296-3080, (800) 426-1419
FAX: (206) 296-3047
Services: The company provides comprehensive visa services.

SECTION 10

TRANSLATORS & INTERPRETERS

Language does not have to be a barrier between the Soviet and American market. This section includes translation and interpretation agencies, as well as individuals, who offer language services. To locate an agency or individual, whose capabilities and experience are commensurate with your company's requirements, you may wish to know the following beforehand:
- Are references available?
- Are they translating into their native language?
- What types of documents do they routinely translate?

Also listed is the American Translators Association, which administers a program to test the translation competence of its members. The accredited services of the individuals listed in this section are denoted by (*).

TRANSLATION AGENCIES

* American Translators Association
109 Croton Avenue
Ossining, NY 10562
Phone: (914) 941-1500

AD-EX Translations
525 Middlefield Road, Suite 250
Menlo Park, CA 94025
Phone: (415) 854-6732
FAX: (415) 325-8428
Telex: 171425
Services: The firm provides Russian-English and English-Russian translation.

Ardis/Russian Literature
2901 Heatherway
Ann Arbor, MI 48104
Phone: (313) 971-2367

Contact: Ellendea Proffer
Services: The firm provides Russian-English translation.

ASET Consultants, Inc.
8350 Greensboro Drive
Suite 805
McLean, VA 22102
Phone: (703) 790-1922
FAX: (703) 883-1305
Telex: TWX 510-660-8023
Contact: Polina Litovaksaya, Coordinator of Translation and Interpretation services.
Services: The firm provides Russian-English and English-Russian translation and interpretation of technical, legal, scientific, and business texts. Arrangements can also be made for any Cyrillic typesetting needs.

Berlitz Translation Services
6415 Independence Avenue
Woodland Hills, CA 91367
Phone: (818) 340-5147
FAX: (818) 340-5425
in Washington:
1050 Connecticut Avenue, NW
Washington, DC 20036
Phone: (202) 331-1163
in New York:
257 Park Avenue, South
New York, NY 10010
Phone: (212) 777-7878

Design Dynamics
5525 Twin Knolls Road
Suite 323
Columbia, MD 21045
Phone: (301) 995-3022
FAX: (301) 995-0805
Contact: Alex Koorbanoff
Services: The firm offers simultaneous and consecutive interpretation in Russian, Ukrainian, Latvian, Lithuanian, Estonian, Polish, Bulgarian, Czech, Romanian, Hungarian, and Serbo-Croat. Rush written translations are available. Translations are done into the native language of the translator and are available for virtually any subject. Other services to be provided are abstracting, word processing, editing, camera-ready art/typesetting, and paste-up mechanicals.

Diplomatic Language Services, Inc.
1111 N. 19th Street, Suite 525
Arlington, VA 22209

Phone: (703) 243-4855
FAX: (703) 358-9189
Services: The firm provides translating and interpreting services for technical, scientific, legal, or business documents and conferences, in any language or dialect, by native speakers with expertise in the corresponding field. The firm also offers editing, proofreading, abstracting, desktop publishing, paste-up, and voice-overs.

East-West Concepts, Inc.
196 Tamarack Circle
Skillman, NJ 08558
Phone: (609) 924-6789, (800) 637-0201
FAX: (609) 466-0864
Telex: 408568 EWC/HVS
Contact: Janos Samu
Services: Translation and interpretation services are provided for Albanian, Armenian, Bulgarian, Czech, Estonian, Georgian, German, Hungarian, Latvian, Lithuanian, Macedonian, Polish, Romanian, Russian, Serbo-Croatian, Slovak, Slovenian, and Ukrainian languages.

FAM Translations
104 E. 40th Street
New York, NY 10016
Phone: (212) 986-5627
Contact: Sally Johns
Services: Services of this firm include Russian-Latvian-Ukrainian translation.

Grimes & Leonard
P.O. Box 55
Hingham, MA 02043
Phone: (617) 749-0772
Contact: William J. Grimes or Isabel A. Leonard
Services: Russian-English* translation services are available, with specialization in technical materials.

Intracom, Inc.
6 New England Executive Park
Burlington, MA 01803
Phone: (617) 229-1685
FAX: (617) 229-1687
Services: The many services offered by this firm include: Russian-English and English-Russian translation, word processing and typesetting, interpretation, audio-video voice over, language instruction, software localization, and business protocol training.

Kniga Printshop
50 Gorky Street
Moscow 125047
Phone: 251-1215
FAX: 230-2207
Services: Kniga owns and operates the AlphaGraphics Printshop on Gorky Street, and this is a convenient place to order translations of written materials while in Moscow.

Linguitronics
P.O. Box 9504
Arlington, VA 22209

Phone: (703) 920-7098
FAX: (703) 979-0467
Contact: Tamara Sherman
Services: Russian-English and English-Russian translation services are available from this firm.

MB International
9704 Burke View Avenue
Burke, VA 22015
Phone: (703) 425-0024
FAX: (703) 425-0025
Services: International services provided by this firm include Russian translation in the U.S. and interpreting services in Moscow.

OASES-DC
1430 K Street, NW, Suite 1200
Washington, DC 20005
Phone: (202) 393-0985
FAX: (202) 393-0989
Contact: Rudy Delassandro
Services: OASES-DC has a pool of professional interpreters and translators who work on high-level exchanges and conferences on a variety of topic areas. OASES can also provide the equipment necessary to support interpreting needs at conferences.

Phargo Information U.S.S.R.
Skorniazhny Pereulok 1
Kvartira 1
Moscow 107078
Phone: 975-3392
Services: This office keeps news clipping files of Soviet press with professional translators.

137

Robert T. Creutz & Co.
P.O. Box 490
S. Weymouth, MA 02190
Phone: (617) 331-8421
FAX: (617) 331-8421
E-mail: MCI mail: CREUTZ;
Compuserve: 70611,3147
Services: The firm specializes in
Russian-English*scientific, technical,
and industrial translations with
special proficiency in computer
science, robotics, communications,
electronics, metallurgy, electrical
engineering, mechanical engineering,
nuclear engineering, and patents.
Abstracting and editing services are
also offered. Full word processing
and telecommunications capabilities.

Rocky Mountain Translators, Inc.
5757 Central Avenue, Suite G
Boulder, CO 80301
Phone: (800) 365-3736, (303) 449-
6954
FAX: (303) 442-6214
Contact: Michael Ferkiss, Marketing
Director
Services: Localization of software
and its accompanying documentation
into all languages of the Soviet
Union. Strict quality control,
integrated team approach and
project management capabilities
make us unique in the industry.

Russian Language Services, Inc.
423 Feather Rock Drive
Rockville, MD 20850
Phone: (301) 424-0158
FAX: (301) 738-9411
Contact: Mark Berkovich

Services: This firm provides
Russian-English and English-Russian
translation and interpretation
services, with special proficiency in
the following areas: aerospace,
automation, civil engineering,
communications, computers,
economics and business, energy,
general engineering, legal affairs,
material science, electronics, military,
medicine, and trade. RLS also
provides Cyrillic typesetting for
business cards, correspondence,
and promotional materials.

Specan International, Inc.
P.O. Box 652
Princeton, NJ 08542-0652
Phone: (609) 683-4900
Services: Translates Russian-
English, English-Russian, and other
East European languages. Also offer
management of interpreting for
conferences, simultaneous and
consecutive interpretation, and
abstracting and editing services.

The Corporate Word, Inc.
18 South, Gateway Center 3
Pittsburgh, PA 15222
Phone: (412) 391-0378
FAX: (412) 391-3935
Services: The firm provides
machine-assisted translation of East
European languages. Has offices in
U.S.S.R. and Poland.

The International Connection
P.O. Box 52332

Atlanta, GA 30344
Phone: (404) 233-8329
FAX: (404) 239-9102
Services: The firm provides translation, interpretation, and consultation services.

Thomas Butler Associates
5A Ellsworth Drive
Cambridge, MA 02139

Transemantics, Inc.
Van Ness Center #147
4301 Connecticut Avenue, NW
Washington, DC 20008
Phone: (202) 686-5600
FAX: (202) 686-5603
Contact: M-L. Wax, Director
Services: The services of Transemantics include all aspects of foreign language communications, for all languages and on all subjects. The firm also provides cultural analysis of promotional materials for foreign audiences, interpreting, audio-visual narration, or subtitling.

Vencor
1001 3rd Avenue, West, Suite 350
Bradenton, FL 33505
Phone: (813) 747-5700
FAX: (813) 748-1049
Contact: Michael T. Ligett
Services: Technical translation is available in the Russian, German, and Hungarian languages.

YAR Communications, Inc.
220 Fifth Avenue
New York, NY 10001

Phone: (212) 447-4000
FAX: (212) 447-4020
Telex: 6504133564
Contacts: Yuri Radzievsky, President; Yakov Menyuk, Director of Marketing and Sales
Services: YAR Communications, Inc. provides full Russian language communications services, including Soviet business consulting, Russian language translations of advertising material, creative services, publicity campaigns in Soviet media, interpreting for conferences and business negotiations, typesetting and graphic design, and audio-visual presentations. It has offices in New York and Moscow.

INDIVIDUAL TRANSLATORS

Adams, Joyce B.
P.O. Box 2893
New Britain, CT 06050
Phone: (203) 232-1248
Services: Russian-English translation. Special proficiency in medical sciences and health care, pharmacy and pharmacology, agriculture, veterinary medicine, religion, and philosophy.

Batki, George
208 Locksley Road
Syracuse, NY 13224
Phone: (315) 446-6451
Services: English-Russian*, Hungarian-English*, English-Hungarian*, and Russian-Hungarian

translation. Areas of special proficiency include art, history, political science, medicine, medical sciences, geography, fiction, and poetry. Abstracting services are also available.

Beerbaum, Mira S.
5881 Roblar Road
Petaluma, CA 94952
Phone: (707) 664-8535
Services: Russian-English* and English-Russian* translation. Special fields: aerospace industry, petroleum, natural gas, fossil fuels, earth sciences, meteorology, oceanography, medicine, medical sciences and nuclear industry.

Bloomstein, Elena
7813 Pickard Avenue, NE
Albuquerque, NM 87110
Phone: (505) 291-9812 (h); (505) 766-4700 (w)
Services: English-Russian* and Russian-English* translation. Special proficiency in geology, mining, waste management, ecology, psychology, medicine, and news media. Also available: abstracting, editing, indexing, proofreading, camera-ready copy and paste-ups, consecutive and escort interpretation. IBM-PC, modem, access to FAX.

Cauvin-Higgins, Catherine Marie
6318 Rutgers
Houston, TX 77005

Phone: (713) 666-5944
Services: English-Russian* and Russian-English translation. Special proficiency in computer science and applications, systems analysis, aerospace and telecommunications industries, petroleum, natural gas, fossil fuels, medical instrumentation, and techniques. Other services include consecutive and escort interpretation for business negotiations, plant tours, etc.

Chestnoy, Vladimir Ivanovich
One Penn Plaza, Suite 100
New York, NY 10119
Phone: (201) 332-8783
or (212) 467-8669
Services: English-Russian*, English-Polish*, Russian-English, Polish-English, and Serbo-Croatian-English* translation services are provided. Special proficiency in advertising, public relations, commerce, finance, marketing, patents, trademarks, copyrights, and computer applications. Consultation on U.S.S.R.-related advertising, public relations, marketing, abstracting, editing, proofreading, creation of glossaries and phrase books, tutoring, and examination of translators' and interpreters' skills also offered.

Conner, R. Michael
8008 Gault Street
Austin, TX 78758
Phone: (512) 467-8870

Services: Russian-English*
translation. Special proficiency in
earth sciences, geology, geophysics,
meteorology, and oceanography.

Costello, Sally L.
6 Mill Lane
Rockport, MA 01966
Phone: (617) 546-7140

Creskoff, Ellen Hood
605 Westbury Apartments
271 S. 15th Street
Philadelphia, PA 19102
Phone: (215) 545-1977
Services: Russian-English* and
Bulgarian-English translation.
Special proficiency in medical
sciences, chemistry, biochemistry,
biological sciences, ecology,
environmental science, and
agriculture. Also offered are
abstracting and indexing services and
camera-ready copy.

Daniels, Ernestine R.
610B Gadd Road
Hixson, TN 37343
Phone: (615) 870-1473
Services: Russian-English
translation only. Specialty:
chemical and other scientific
literature. Formerly freelanced for
Plenum Publishing Co. in above
specialty.

Daniels, Guy
315 E. 86th Street, Apt. 11LE
New York, NY 10028
Phone: (212) 289-7207
Services: Russian-English
translation. Specializes in editing,
social sciences, and literature.

Dearner, Dolly A.
2405 NW 17th Street
Oklahoma City, OK 73107
Phone: (405) 528-5618
Services: Romanian-English*
translation. Special proficiency in
humanities, medical sciences, and
linguistics.

Diamant, Gabriel G.
6600 Boulevard East
W. New York, NJ 07093
Phone: (201) 861-2065
Services: English-Russian*,
English-Hungarian*, Russian-
English, Hungarian-English*.
Special proficiency in political
science and electronics. Interpreting
services are also offered. Graduate
of Moscow Power Engineering
Institute (ME). Well-rounded in
international trade negotiations.
Possesses thorough knowledge of the
Soviet and East European business
environment.

Dilson, Jesse
201 E. 30th Street
New York, NY 10016

Phone: (212) 685-3121
Services: Areas of specialty include science and technology.

Duncan, Albert H.
P.O. Box 669
Bodega Bay, CA 94923
Phone: (707) 875-3900
Services: Russian-English* and English-Russian* translation, specializing in political sciences, economic, military and naval sciences, aerospace industry, transportation and railroads, and maritime commerce and industry.

Fiske, William K.
454 W. 44th Street, Apt. 4RW
New York, NY 10036
Phone: (212) 265-0210
Services: Russian-English* and Czech-English* translation. Special proficiency in arts, humanities, business, and earth sciences.

Fletcher, George R.
c/o CompuLingua Translation Services
198 Broadway, Suite 1107
New York, NY 10038
Phone: (718) 788-7782, (212) 227-1994
FAX: (212) 693-1489
Services: Russian-English translation. Special proficiency in education, law, telecommunications, advertising, public relations, and agriculture. Also offers abstracting and editing services as well as court interpretation. Specializes in documents and educational evaluation from foreign countries.

Flick, Cathy
302 S.W. Fifth Street
Richmond, IN 47374
Phone: (317) 962-3427
Services: Russian-English translation. Specializes in science.

Fox, Leonard
278-A Meeting Street
Charleston, SC 29401
Phone: (803) 722-2531
Services: Georgian-English* translation. Special proficiency in humanities, linguistics, religion, philosophy, fiction, poetry, and theater. Also offers abstracting, editing, and proofreading services.

Frentz, L. Brand
Rt. 2, Box 18A
Mankato, MN 56001
Phone: (507) 947-3268, (507) 345-4505
Services: Russian-English* translation. Special proficiency in biography, history, humanities, law, political science, and military and naval sciences.

Gallagher, William B., M.D.
3891 N. Hillwood Cir.
Tucson, AZ 85715

Phone: (602) 298-3489
Services: Russian-English translation. Special proficiency in medical sciences, instrumentation, and techniques; health care; pharmacy. Also offers abstracting services.

Gallagher, Paul B.
2106 1/2 N. High Street #3
Columbus, OH 43201
Phone: (614) 294-3091
Services: Russian-English* translation. Special proficiency in linguistics, genetics, earth science, chemistry, metallurgy, glass, and ceramics. Also offers abstracting, editing, proofreading services, and consulting.

Gingold, Kurt (Dr.)
35 Windsor Ln.
Cos Cob, CT 06807
Phone: (203) 869-2742
Services: Russian-English* translation. Special proficiency in biochemistry, chemistry, and chemical engineering, medical sciences, patents, trademarks, copyrights, pharmacy, and pharmacology.

Gorzkowska, Regina
908 S. 47th Street
Philadelphia, PA 19143-3619
Phone: (215) 724-6477

Services: Russian-English and English-Russian translation services are provided.

Graf, Angelia
Department of Foreign Language
Virginia Polytechnic Institute
Blacksburg, VA 24061
Phone: (703) 961-5361
Services: Russian-English and English-Russian translation. Specializes in literature and social sciences.

Grier, Ella Feodorovna
450 Noble Boulevard
Carlisle, PA 17013
Phone: (717) 245-2804
Services: English-Russian*, Russian-English, and Bulgarian-English translation. Special proficiency in mechanical, electrical, and chemical engineering; petroleum, natural gas, and fossil fuels; building; construction; and computer applications. Also offers simultaneous interpretation, camera-ready copy, editing, proofreading, commercial documentation, promotional and training films in Russian, and consultation on advertising in the Soviet Union.

Grimes, William J.
P.O. Box 55
Hingham, MA 02043
Phone: (617) 749-1540
FAX: (617) 749-8738

Services: Russian-English* translation. Special proficiency in automotive industry, electrical and mechanical engineering, medical sciences, patents, trademarks and copyrights, transportation, and railroads. Also offers word processing and communications capability.

Gwirtsman, Joseph J.
21 Hemlock Terrace
Springfield, NJ 07081
Phone: (201) 379-3947
Services: English-Russian*, English-Polish*, Russian-English, and Polish-English translation. Special proficiency in petroleum, natural gas and fossil fuels, plastics and rubber, chemical engineering, biochemistry, and chemistry. Also offers abstracting, editing, and proofreading services.

Hall, Marie J.
Box 1745, Route 1
Bar Harbor, ME 04609
Phone: (207) 288-3104
FAX: (207) 288-9336
Services: Translates Russian-English and Polish-English. Special proficiency in agriculture, medical sciences, oceanography, political science, psychology, and psychiatry. Also offers abstracting, editing, and proofreading services as well as escort interpreting and camera-ready copy.

Hanff, Konstanty Z.
3 E. 15th Street
New York, NY 10003
Phone: (212) 255-0754
Services: English-Russian, Russian-English, English-Ukrainian, Ukrainian-English, Russian-Ukrainian, Serbo-Croatian-English*, and Ukrainian-Russian translation. Specializes in advertising, law, medicine, and science.

Hetzel, Eustace P.
7612 Cecelia Street
Downey, CA 90241
Phone: (213) 927-4585
Services: Translates Russian-English*. Special proficiency in aerospace industry, physical sciences, and mechanical engineering.

Jacobson, Helen Saltz
55 Thompson Hay Path
Setauket, NY 11733
Phone: (516) 751-0371
Services: Russian-English translation. Specializes in medicine and literature.

Jacolev, Leon
30 The Fairway
Upper Montclair, NJ 07043
Phone: (201) 748-5673
Services: Translates English-Russian* and Russian-English. Special proficiency in industry, technology, chemistry, chemical

engineering, patents, trademarks, copyrights, petroleum, natural gas, and fossil fuels, pharmacy, and pharmacology. Also offers editing services, consultation in foreign scientific documentation and terminology, lexicography, creation of specialized dictionaries or reference collections, and Russian-English interpretation.

Johanson, Astrid
c/o Bell Laboratories
600 Mountain Avenue
Murray Hill, NJ 07974
Phone: (201) 792-5826, (201) 582-6066
Services: Translates Russian-English and Estonian-English*. Special proficiency in telecommunications, physics (esp. solid-state physics), computer science and applications, systems analysis, and electronics. Also offers database search services.

Kawecki, Alicja T.
4AD Foxwood Drive
Morris Plains, NJ 07950
Phone: (201) 582-3817
Services: Russian-English, Polish-English, and Ukrainian-English* translation.

Keasbey, William P.
5031 Alta Vista Road
Bethesda, MD 20814

Phone: (301) 530-5031
Services: Translates Russian-English*. Special proficiency in economics, commerce, political science, industrial engineering, ecology, and environmental science.

Keesan, Cynthia
504 Hiscock #1
Ann Arbor, MI 48103
Phone: (313) 995-9463
Services: Translates Russian, Serbo-Croatian, Macedonian, Bulgarian, Czech, Slovak, Polish, Ukrainian, and Romanian into English. Can supply names of other translators from English into these languages (Hungarian, Finnish...). Training and experience in life sciences and medicine, chemistry, geology, applied sciences (esp. ecology, horticulture), math, linguistics, architecture/construction, patents, transcripts. Special low rates to nonprofit organizations and refugees. Fully computerized (modem, fax).

Kertesz, Francois
112 Wendover Cir.
Oak Ridge, TN 37830-8246
Phone: (615) 483-6225
Services: Translates Russian, Hungarian*, and Romanian* into English, as well as English-Hungarian*. Special proficiency in glass and ceramics, metallurgy, chemistry and chemical engineering,

nuclear science and engineering, and physics. Also offers abstracting and indexing services, database development, and camera-ready copy.

Koorbanoff, Alex
5525 Twin Knolls Road
Suite 323
Columbia, MD 21045
Phone: (301) 995-3022
FAX: (301) 995-0805
Services: English-Russian, Russian-English interpreting, translating, abstracting, editing, and quality control. Special proficiency in aerospace and scientific space issues, business negotiations, political science, naval and military sciences. Camera-ready copy is provided. Koorbanoff travels extensively supporting business negotiations. Tested and certified by various U.S. government agencies.

Lotyczewski, Agnieszka T.
11 Terrace Street
Norwich, NY 13815
Phone: (607) 334-9070
Services: Translates Russian-English*, Polish-English, and English-Polish*. Special proficiency in chemistry, biology, medical sciences, pharmacology, veterinary medicine, and the cosmetics industry.

Marcinik, Roger
P.O. Box 060411
Palm Bay, FL 32906
Phone: (305) 725-1610

Services: Russian-English translation.

Martin, Joan M.
922 Shirley Manor Road
Reisterstown, MD 21136
Phone: (301) 833-3248
Services: Translates Russian-English. Special proficiency in military and naval sciences, medical sciences, religion, theology and scripture, philosophy, and the aerospace industry. Also offers abstracting service.

Mayer, Claudius Francis
5513 39th Street, NW
Washington, DC 20015
Phone: (202) 966-3723
Services: Translates Czech*, Polish, Romanian*, and Serbo-Croatian* into English, as well as English-Hungarian*. Special proficiency in medical sciences, anthropology, archeology, military and naval sciences, agriculture, biology, and genetics. Also offers abstracting, editing, indexing, proofreading, bibliography, and research services.

McGlothlin, William C.
717A Old County Road
Belmont, CA 94002
Phone: (415) 591-2875
Services: Translates Russian*, Bulgarian, and Ukrainian* into English. Special proficiency in

biological, medical, physical, and agricultural sciences; and the aerospace industry. Also offers abstracting, editing, and proofreading services.

Morrow, Theodore E.
1663 Woodford Way
Blue Bell, PA 19422
Phone: (215) 277-0672
Services: Translates Romanian-English*, Russian-English, and Czech-English*; also works with Estonian, Latvian, Lithuanian, Azeri, Ukrainian, and Turkish. Special proficiency in chemical engineering, religion, theology and scripture, philosophy, medical sciences, patents, trademarks, copyrights, and history. Also offers editing and proofreading services, word processing, and computer programming.

Nelles, Peter
Nelles Translations
18 S. Michigan Avenue, Suite 1000
Chicago, IL 60603
Phone: (312) 236-2788
FAX: (312) 236-0717
Services: Translates Russian-English*. Special proficiency in electronics, textiles, patents, trademarks, and copyrights, metallurgy, as well as medical instrumentation and techniques.

Olaechea, Marilyn
6140 Dayton Road
Springfield, OH 45502
Phone: H: (513) 864-5709, O: (513) 257-2891
Services: Russian-English* translation. Specialization in medicine and medicinal sciences, immunology, radiology, microbiology, bacteriology, virology, anatomy, and physiology.

Olkhovsky, Yuri
12409 Braxfield Court, #4
Rockville, MD 20852
Phone: H: (301) 881-5326, W: (202) 994-6336
Contact: Yuri Olkhovsky
Services: Translation and interpretation in Russian-English, Ukrainian-English, English-Russian, and English-Ukrainian. Extensive experience since 1956 in government translation for official Soviet delegations visiting the U.S. Special proficiency in political, economic, and military subjects.

Osorio, Pedro
133 66th Street W.
New York, NJ 07093
Phone: (201) 868-4984
Services: Translates Romanian-English*. Special proficiency in economics, history, journalism, law, medical sciences, religion, and philosophy.

147

Papinako, Ilya
14100 W. 94th Terrace
Lenexa, KS 66215
Phone: (913) 492-6076
Services: English-Russian and Russian-English translations. Experienced in simultaneous interpreting. Special proficiency in coal preparation and handling, commerce, drilling, equipment, geology, mechanical engineering, mobil equipment, power plant design, and textile industry.

Potyomkina, Anna
50 The Lynnway, Apt. 826
Lynn, MA 01902
Phone: (617) 581-3011
Services: English-Russian* and Russian-English translation. Special proficiency in maritime commerce and industry, petroleum, natural gas and fossil fuels, chemistry, physics, health care, and dentistry. Also offers abstracting and indexing services.

Priest, Peter F. H.
P.O. Box 3180
Terre Haute, IN 47083
Services: English-Russian* and Russian-English* translation. Special proficiency in chemical engineering, patents, trademarks, copyrights, petroleum, natural gas and fossil fuels, pharmacology, veterinary medicine, computer science, and systems analysis. Also offers word processing in Russian and English, editing, terminology research, and typesetting in Russian.

Radzai, Ronald B.
6304 Monadnock Way
Oakland, CA 94605
Phone: (415) 562-3882
FAX: (415) 562-1187
Services: Translates Russian, Polish, Czech, Slovak, Ukrainian, Bulgarian, Serbo-Croatian, Hungarian, Romanian to English. Also works with Western and Northern European languages. All subject matter handled.

Renfield, Richard L.
2200 Leeland Drive
Falls Church, VA 22043
Phone: (703) 532-5271
Services: Russian-English translation.

Roder, Antonio
3875 Magnolia Drive
Palo Alto, CA 94306
Phone: (415) 493-5168
Services: Translates Romanian-English* and English-Romanian. Special proficiency in computer science and applications, systems analysis, electronics and electrotechnology, physics, and solid-state physics. Also offers abstracting, editing, and interpreting services.

148

Safonov, Dr. Sidonie H.
1643 Krameria Street
Denver, CO 80220
Phone: (303) 394-4360 (Home); (303) 236-6956 (Office)
Services: Russian-English*, Polish-English, and English-Russian* translation. Specialization in humanities, education, literature (theory and criticism), civil and hydraulic engineering, and political science.

Samu, Janos
46 Shaftsbury Avenue
Hopewell, NJ 08525
Phone: (609) 466-9105, (609) 924-6789
FAX: (609) 466-0864
Services: Translates English-Russian*, English-Hungarian*, Russian-English, Hungarian-English*, and Polish-English.
Special proficiency in advertising and public relations, glass and ceramics, computer applications, law, patents, trademarks, and copyrights. Also offers consecutive, court, and escort interpreting; abstracting, editing, and proofreading services; camera-ready copy; and film dubbing and subtitling.

Sargent, Peter
Rt. 1 Box 447
Hamilton, VA 22068
Phone: (703) 338-4875
Services: Russian-English and

Chinese-English translation.

Schuldt, M. Lesley
4645 NW Kahneeta Drive
Portland, OR 97229
Phone: (503) 645-3615
Services: Russian-English translation.

Schultz, Arlo A.
16450 NE 18th Street
Bellevue, WA 98008
Phone: (206) 747-1325
FAX: (206) 641-0408
Services: Translates Russian-English*. Special proficiency in economics, law, and education.

Schwartz, Marian B.
1207 Bickler Road
Austin, TX 78704
Phone: (512) 442-5100
Services: Translates Russian-English*. Special proficiency in literature, history, political science, economics, art, and biography. Also offers editing services.

Shkolnik, Alexander
962 S. El Camino Real #202
San Mateo, CA 94402
Phone: (415) 343-3805
FAX: (415) 342-8723
Services: Translates English-Russian* and Russian-English. Special proficiency in chemistry, mechanical engineering, metallurgy,

agriculture, food and nutrition, patents, trademarks, and copyrights. Also offers abstracting, typesetting, patent searches, and foreign patent filing services.

Smikun, Emanuel
805 Ditmas Avenue
Brooklyn, NY 11218
Phone: (718) 941-5703
FAX: (718) 941-5703
Services: English-Russian and Russian-English translations and conference/simultaneous interpreting.

Spiegler, Paul A.
7 Sierra Vista Lane
Valley Cottage, NY 10989
Phone: (914) 358-9443
Services: Russian-English translation.

Stackhouse, Kathy
300 S. Lang Avenue
Pittsburgh, PA 15206
Phone: (412) 391-0378
Services: Translates Russian-English* and English-Russian. Special proficiency in metallurgy, mining, petroleum, natural gas and fossil fuels, transportation and railroads, military and naval sciences, and aerospace industry. Also offers abstracting, editing, proofreading, w o r d p r o c e s s i n g, a n d telecommunications services; camera-ready copy; and paste-ups.

Stacy, Charles M.
2006 Reagan Boulevard
Carrollton, TX 75006
Phone: (214) 416-8039, (214) 418-3571
FAX: (214) 418-3833
Services: Translates Russian-English*. Special proficiency in petroleum, natural gas and fossil fuels, law, and commerce.

Stone, Lydia Razran, Ph.D.
1111 Westmoreland Road
Alexandria, VA 22308
Phone: (703) 768-5441, (202) 488-5854, 863-6269
Services: Translates Russian-English*. Specialist in Soviet life sciences for NASA. Special proficiency in medical and behavioral sciences, literature, humanities, ecology, environmental sciences, and education. Also offers editing and abstracting services, and camera-ready copy. PC, modem.

Stonehill, Paul
5700 Etiwanda
Tarzana, CA 91356
Phone: (818) 344-7442, (213) 627-6171
Services: Specialty areas include advertising, business, entertainment, finance, legal, medical, and science and technology.

Tapp, Linda
1861 Mintwood Place, NW
Washington, DC 20009

150

Phone: (202) 328-3280
Services: Translates Russian-English. Also escort and consecutive interpretation. State Department certification.

Teague, Ben
P.O. Box 129
Athens, GA 30603
Phone: (404) 543-0860
FAX: (404) 546-6539
Services: Russian-English* translation. Special proficiency in mechanical, nuclear, chemical, civil, and hydraulic engineering; physics; geology; and geophysics.

Tornquist, David A.
2 Wilbur Avenue
Newport, RI 02840
Phone: (401) 846-9013
FAX: (401) 847-2970
Services: Translates Russian-English*, Serbo-Croatian-English*, and English-Serbo-Croatian*. Special proficiency in computer science and applications, systems analysis, economics, finance, commerce, and medical sciences. Also offers consecutive and escort interpretation in Serbo-Croatian.

Townsend, Sylvia Linner
30 Ardmore Road
Kensington, CA 94707
Phone: (415) 524-5097
Services: Russian-English*, Czech-English*, and Hungarian-English*. Special proficiency in literature, behavioral sciences, history, and business administration.

Tschen, Jung
P.O. Box 753
Cary, NC 27512-0753
Phone: (919) 467-8346
Services: Translates English-Russian* and Russian-English. Special proficiency in military and naval sciences, and commerce. Also offers escort interpreting and proofreading services.

Valliere, Robert J.
10 Radcliff Road
Beverly, MA 01915
Phone: (617) 927-7784
Services: Translates Russian-English*. Special proficiency in petroleum, natural gas and fossil fuels, mechanical engineering, cybernetics and robotics, business and trade, transportation, military and naval sciences, and economics. Also offers editing and proofreading services, terminology research, glossary compilation, and camera-ready copy.

Virden, Emerson H., Jr.
1541 Clearview Avenue
Blue Bell, PA 19422
Phone: (215) 272-0571
Services: Russian-English*

translations. Special proficiency in metallurgy.

Walsh, P. Hartley
533 2nd Street, SE
Washington, DC 20003
Phone: (202) 707-7630
Services: Russian-English translation services.

Weppner, Eileen
1491 High Street
Boulder, CO 80302
Phone: (303) 494-8325
Services: Translates Russian-English*. Special proficiency in food, nutrition, astronomy, astrophysics, physics, oceanography, meteorology, science, and linguistics. Also offers English language proofreading and editing.

Willis, John M.
177 Doorack Lane
Kirkwood, MO 63122
Phone: (314) 822-4471
Services: Translates Russian-English. Special proficiency in geography, physical sciences, computer applications, mathematics, statistics, aerospace industry, geology, and geophysics.

Zane, Michael S.
3 Deer Run
Watchung, NJ 07060

Phone: (201) 754-6048
Services: Translation from English-Russian*, German-English, English-Polish, Russian-English*, Polish-English, and Lithuanian-English*. Special proficiency in law and automotive industry along with medical and physical sciences. Also offers both medical and technical writing and editing services, on economics, finance, commerce, and medical sciences. Also offers consecutive and escort interpretation in Serbo-Croati.

SECTION 11

INFORMATION SOURCES

Many have claimed that information on the Soviet Union is not readily available. The fact is, information on the Soviet Union is not a scarce commodity, but knowing where to find it is half the battle. This section provides leads on finding information and lists a wide selection of books, periodicals, articles and on-line databases. These information sources provide an extensive variety of data, ranging from legal matters to industry-specific subjects.

ELECTRONIC INFORMATION SERVICES

Moscow International Business Network
119 Peterborough Street, #4
Boston, MA 02215
Phone: (617) 262-4010
Contact: George Laughead
Services: The firm offers a worldwide computer-accessed electronic data service, providing editorial and commercial information on a variety of subjects relating to U.S.-Soviet trade. The service can be accessed through Tymnet, Telenet, Datapac (Canada), Transpac (France) and KDD (Japan).

NEXUS
Publisher: NEXUS Corp.
7700 Leesburg Pike
Falls Church, VA 22043
Phone: (703) 847-6644

Description: Nexus is an on-line database services that provides a wide range of information from periodicals and other publications for a fee to users.

Reuters Information Services
Publisher: Reuters Europe
85 Fleet Street
London
England
FAX: (1) 353-9909
Contact: Gregory Kats
Description: A new on-line information service containing information pertinent to U.S.-Soviet trade.

SOVSET' Computer Network
Publisher: Center for Strategic and International Studies-Soviet Studies
Washington, DC
Phone: (202) 775-3257

Contact: Dawn Mann
Description: The center operates an international computer network for the field of Soviet and East European studies. Basic services include electronic mail, computer conferencing, and a data library.

World Trade Center Washington DC
1101 King Street, Suite 700
Alexandria, VA 22314
Phone: (703) 684-6630
FAX: (703) 684-2918
Telex: 5106004086
Contact: Yvonne Morales
Description: Through membership, the center provides a computerized international buyer-seller information network, databases on investment opportunities, and seminars.

PERIODICALS

American Association of Exporters and Importers (AAEI)
11 West 42nd Street
New York, NY 10036
Phone: (212) 944-2230
Description: International business practices, U.S. export controls, transportation, foreign product standards, exchange rates, financing, legislation, government trade policy, countertrade, and barter.
Frequency: Publishes weekly and monthly publications, special bulletins, and reports.

ASET Industrial Monitor
ASET Consultants, Inc.
8350 Greensboro Drive, Suite 805
McLean, VA 22102
Phone: (703) 790-1922
FAX: (703) 883-1305
Frequency: Weekly or Monthly
Price: $125 per topic per month
Description: Custom-tailored monitoring/clipping service; ASET tracks and reports on subjects requested to help keep clients apprised of information that may affect their interests and business in the Soviet Union and Eastern Europe.

BLOC
350 Broadway, Suite 1205
New York, NY 10013
Phone: (212) 966-0655
FAX: (212) 966-0898
Publisher: Richard Fuchs
Editor-In-Chief: Stuart Anderson
Advertising Director: Henry Foxbrunner
Description: The magazine provides in-depth reports on East-West trade issues, including transportation, finance, insurance, and legal affairs; articles on economic trends in computers, medicine, and agriculture; regular columns on currency and finance, science and technology, and travel; reports from each country on political trends and social realities.
Description: Bulgaria,

154

Czechoslovakia, Hungary, Poland, Romania, the Soviet Union, Yugoslavia.
Frequency: Bi-monthly
Circulation: 26,605 in the U.S. paid and nonpaid. September/October 1989 issue audited by Verified Audit Circulation.
Distribution: Business corporations, export/import companies, government agencies, commercial banks, investment and private banks, other financial and trade institutions, professional and university organizations.
Subscription Price: $89
Advertising Rates: For 1 time black and white: full page/$6000; 2/3 page/$4200; 1/2 page/$3600; 1/3 page/$2760. For color - additional $2500. Inside front cover - 75% premium. Inside back cover - 25% premium. Back cover - 50% premium.
Premier Issue: October/November 1989.

Briefing Paper #1; Socialist-Capitalist Joint Ventures in the U.S.S.R.
Author: Alan B. Sherr
Year Published: 1988
Publisher: Center for Foreign Policy Development
Brown University
Providence, RI 02912
Inquiries call: (401) 863-3465

Bulletin on Current Research in Soviet and East European Law

Centre for Russian and East European Studies
University of Toronto
100 St. George Street, Rm. 1022
Toronto, Ontario, Canada, M5S 1A1
Editors: Yuri Luryi and Peter Solomon
Description: Book reviews, articles, laws, journals.
Frequency: Three times a year in February, June, and October.
Subscription Rate: $7.50

Bulletin of Commercial Information for Foreign Businessmen
U.S.S.R. Chamber of Commerce and Industry
2-y Lesnoy Per., 10
Moscow 103055
Phone: 251-33-51
Telex: 411126
Published in English by: International Trade Press
P.O. Box 14101
San Francisco, CA 94114
Phone: (415) 495-4765
Description: Decrees and resolutions by the U.S.S.R. Council of Ministers concerning developments in trade procedures and regulation, partnership offers, import offers, and export offers.
Frequency: Quarterly.
Subscription Price: $125.00
Premiere Issue: 1989

Business Eastern Europe
Business International S.A.
Schwarzenbergplatz 8/7

A-1030 Vienna, Austria
Phone: (0222) 72-41-61/65
Telex: 133 931
For subscriptions contact:
BI Customer Service Department
40 Duke Street
London W1A IDW
Phone: (1) 493-6711
FAX: (1) 499-9767
Managing Editor: George W. Hamilton
Description: A weekly report to managers of East European operations containing global business and advice. Includes current East European developments, lists of Western sales, cooperation, licensing, and market opportunities categorized by industry, and general articles on the East European markets.
Subscription Price: $800-1000

Business America
International Trade Administration
U.S. Department of Commerce, Room 3414
14th and Constitution, NW
Washington, DC 20230
Phone: (202) 377-3251
Editor: Douglas F. Carroll
Description: With the mission of helping American companies sell their products overseas, this magazine of the U.S. Department of Commerce contains trade leads, marketing advice, export tips, and information about the foreign trade activities of the U.S. Department of Commerce. Editorial focus is worldwide.
Frequency: Bi-weekly
Subscription Price: $49

Superintendent of Documents, U.S. Government Printing Office, Washington, DC 20402
Single Copy Price: $2.25
Premiere Issue: First published by the U.S. State Department under another name in October of 1980.

Business Contact
Publisher: Co-published by the Soviet advertising agency Vneshtorgreklama and the Austrian publishing house Globus.
Premier Issue: 1990 to replace Export Magazine

Communist Economies
Centre for Research into Communist Economies
c/o 2 Lord North Street
London SW1P 3LB, United Kingdom
Editors: Ljubo Sirc, Jacek Rostowski and Roger Clarke
Send Subscription Requests to:
Carfax Publishing Company
85 Ash Street
Hopkinton, MA 01748
Description: Concerned primarily, but not exclusively, with the economies of the U.S.S.R. and Eastern Europe.
ISSN: 0954-0261
Frequency: Quarterly
Subscription Price: $160, Individuals pay $80
Premiere Issue: March 1989

Countertrade and Offset Intelligence (COI)
Countertrade and Offset Intelligence Ltd.

156

9 Cavendish Square
London W1M 9DD, England
Phone: 01-631-1801
FAX: 01-631-4879
Telex: 295117 BGMLG
Editor: Jonathan Bell
Subscriptions: Andrea Gardner
Description: Each issue focuses exclusively on the subject of countertrade, offset, and non-conventional trade finance techniques worldwide.
Subscription Price: 235 Sterling (or equivalent in freely convertible currency)
Frequency: Monthly

Country Report: U.S.S.R.
The Economist Intelligence Unit
Business International
40 Duke Street
London W1A 1DW, U.K.
Phone: 01 493 6711
FAX: 499 9767
Telex: 266363 EIU G
Description: Political, economic, and business developments in the Soviet Union. Quarterly and annual statistics on the Soviet economy.
Frequency: Quarterly
Subscription Price: $175

Daily Report: Soviet Union
Author: Foreign Broadcast Information Service
Year Published: 1952-present
Publisher: FBIS
Washington, DC
Description: Provides English

language translations of Soviet broadcasts and serials. Hard copy issues are held for most recent two years. Older issues are held on microfilm of microfiche. Monthly indexes lag about five months behind.

Eastern European & Soviet Telecom Report (EESTR)
2940 28th Street, NW
Washington, DC 20008
Phone: (202) 234-2138
FAX: (202) 483-7922
Publisher: ITC, Inc.
Editor-in-Chief: S. Blake Swesrud
Description: EESTR is a Washington-based monthly newsletter focused on current developments affecting the telecommunications, computer, information technology and broadcasting industries in Eastern Europe and the Soviet Union.
Price: $479/year. Two month initial subscription $90.
Premiere Issue: May 1990

East European Politics and Societies (EEPS)
University of California Press
Periodicals Dept.
2120 Berkeley Way
Berkeley, CA 94720
Editor: Ivo Banac
Description: EEPS is a scholarly journal that examines important historical, cultural, political, social, and economic issues in Eastern Europe.
Subscription Price: $25 per year

(individual), $20 (student), $43 (institution).
Frequency: Tri-annually

East/West Technology Digest
Welt Publishing Company
1413 K Street, NW, Suite 800
Washington, DC 20005
Phone: (202) 371-0555
Telex: 281 409
ISSN: 0145-1421
Editors: Lawrence Holland and Jerry A. Orvedahl
Publisher: Leo G. B. Welt
Description: A monthly digest of new technology from the Soviet Union and Eastern Europe.
Frequency: Monthly
Subscription Price: $99

East European Markets
Financial Times Business Information
Tower House
Southampton Street
London WC2E 7MA
Phone: 071-240 9391
FAX: 071-240-7946
Telex: 296926
Editor: Margie Lindsay
Publisher: John McLachlan
Description: Newsletter format. Articles, categorized by country, detail trade agreements, joint ventures, company profiles, and basic economic news.
Frequency: every two weeks
Subscription Price: $654

East-West Business Analyst
Debos Oxford Publications, Ltd.
Kennett House, Suite 2
108-110 London Road
Oxford OX3 9 AW, UK
Publisher: Centre for the Study of East-West Commerce
Description: Provides analysis of economic and legal affairs on East-West commerce.
Frequency: Monthly

Eastern European Economics
M.E. Sharpe, Inc.
80 Business Park Drive
Armonk, NY 10504
Phone: (800) 541-6563 or (914) 273-1800
Editor: Josef Brada
Publisher: M.E. Sharpe
Description: A journal of translations covering a variety of themes, from price reform to central planning, from enterprise autonomy to income inequalities. Issues focus on integral themes or individual country studies. The goal is to present articles that represent departures from conventional economic thinking or that are emblematic of official policy.
Frequency: Quarterly
Subscription Price: $235.00
Premier Issue: 1962

Eastern Europe TIMES
1401 Wilson Boulevard, 5th Floor
Arlington, VA 22209

Business Phone: (703) 527-0039
Business FAX: (703) 527-8679
Editorial Phone: (703) 527-1207
Editorial FAX: (703) 527-0321
Publisher: Adams Publishing Company
Description: This daily newsletter covers business in Eastern Europe. Eastern European TIMES is published in Berlin and Washington, DC.
Frequency: Daily
Subscription Price: $827 per year
Other publications: Inside Eastern Europe, weekly, $347 per year; Eastern Europe Week, weekly, $150 per year; Eastern Europe Law Week, weekly, $667 per year.

Economic Newsletter
Russian Research Center
Harvard University
1737 Cambridge Street
Cambridge, MA 02138
Phone: (617) 495-4037
FAX: (617) 495-8319
Telex: 4948261
Program Coordinator: Judith Mehrmann
Description: Articles on the Soviet economy and developments.
Frequency: Monthly
Subscription Price: $25

Ecotass
Pergamon Press
Maxwell House
Fairview Park
Elsmford, NY 10523

Phone: (703) 487-4630

Expocourier
1a Sokolnicheskiy val
Moscow 107113
Phone: 268-64-93
Telex: 411185 EXPO SU
Editor-in-Chief: S. V. Mikhaylov
Description: The publication is a four-color magazine focusing on trade exhibitions in the Soviet Union as well as the Soviet Economy.
Frequency: 2-3 times/year
Advertising Rates: Full page/800 rubles; half page/500 rubles; quarter page/300 rubles; inside front and back cover/2200 rubles; back conver/2560 rubles. Additional 20% per color.
Subscription Rate: 14 rubles

Export Control News
Publisher: Martin Kalin
MK Technology*Deltac
1920 N Street, NW
Suite 600
Washington, DC 20036
Phone: (202) 463-1250
FAX: (202) 429-9812
Telex: 6503140383
Description: Updates export regulation changes, discuss effect of changes on U.S. exports, and trends in administration policy.
Frequency: Monthly
Subscription Price: $250, international: $337, Government rate: $225

FBIS (Foreign Broadcast Information Service):
U.S.S.R. Serial Reports
U.S. Department of Commerce
NTIS
5285 Port Royal Road
Springfield, VA 22161
Phone: (703) 487-4630
Price per Copy: $7 domestic; $14 foreign
Content: The series covers broadcast information on politics, economics, culture, and science in English translation.

Financial Times
FT Publications
14 East 60th Street
New York, NY 10022
Phone: (212) 752-4500

Foreign Trade
Frequency: Monthly
Subscription: $53
Contact: Available from Victor Kamkin Books, Rockville, MD.

Geonomics
Geonomics Institute
14 Hillcrest Avenue
P.O. Box 682
Middlebury, VT 05753
Phone: (802) 388-9619
FAX: (802) 388-9627
Editor: George Bellerose
Description: A newsletter of the Geonomics Institute for International Economic Advancement. Articles

center primarily on Soviet and Eastern European trade.
Frequency: Bi-monthly

Interflo
P.O. Box 42
Maplewood, NJ 07040
Phone: (201) 763-9493
ISSN 0748-4631
Editor/Publisher: Paul Surovell
Description: Index of news about bilateral and multilateral Soviet trade.
Frequency: Monthly
Subscription Price: $110

International Leadership
American Center for International Leadership
522 Franklin St
Columbus, IN 47201
Phone: (812) 376-3456
Editor: Tom Henry
Description: Newsletter format. Articles primarily concern ACIL's international programs with the Soviet Union, Hungary, and the West. ACIL sponsors binational and multinational seminars on business, trade, and economics, as well as on scientific, human rights, and cultural issues.
Frequency: Quarterly
Subscription Price: Free.

Joint Publications Research Service Reports
Year Published: 1975-present
Publisher: NTIS

Springfield, VA
Description: JPRS publishes monthly editions of collected Soviet material on a variety of subjects.

Journal of Commerce
110 Wall Street
New York, NY 10005
Phone: (212) 425-1616

Journal of the U.S.-U.S.S.R. Trade and Economic Council
U.S.-U.S.S.R. Trade and Economic Council, Inc.
805 Third Avenue
New York, NY 10022
Phone: (212) 644-4550
Description: Expansion and implementation of U.S.-Soviet trade.
Frequency: Bi-monthly

JPRS (Joint Publication Research Service):
U.S.S.R. Serial Reports
U.S. Department of Commerce
NTIS
5285 Port Royal Road
Springfield, VA 22161
Phone: (703) 487-4630.
Price per Copy: $7 domestic; $14 foreign

Licensintorg
31 Ul. Kakhova
Moscow 113461
Phone: 331-95-55
Editor: Nikolay I. Petrov

Description: Licensintorg is a four-color magazine focusing on licensing opportunities for English-speaking Western business readers.

Link Contact Dossier
Publisher: Co-published by Swiss-Soviet joint venture partners: U.S.S.R. Bank for Housing and Social Construction and the Swiss firm of Ton Koper Creative Division.
Description: Newsletter for Western firms investigating the Soviet market.
Subscription Price: $800

Moscow News
16/2 Ul. Gorkogo
Moscow 103829
Phone: 229-90-00 (information) and 209-12-49 (letters)
Editor-In-Chief: Yegor Yakovlev
Editor of English Edition: Vladimir Pichugin
Description: A newspaper of weekly Soviet news published for friendship and cultural relations with foreign countries and Novosti Press Agency. Published in Russian, Estonian, English, Arabic, French, German, Greek, Hungarian, Italian, and Spanish.
Frequency: Weekly
Subscription Price: $23 per year

Moscow Narodnyy Bank Press Bulletin
Economics Department
Moscow Narodnyy Bank

32 King William Street
London EC4P JS, England
Description: A weekly available free
to companies who apply in writing.

Multinational Monitor.
November/December 1987, U.S.S.R.
Open for Business
Editor: Ellen Hosmer and Jonathan
Dunn
Publisher: Essential Information,
Inc.
Washington, DC
Inquiries call: (202) 387-8030

New Times
Pushkin Square
Moscow 103782
Phone: 229-88-72, 209-07-67
FAX: 200-41-92, 200-10-38
Telex: 411164a NEWT SU
Editor-In-Chief: Vitaliy Ignatenko
Editor of English Edition: N.
Agaltsev
Description: Magazine format.
Articles on world affairs, written by
Soviets. Content focuses on Soviet
international news, with frequent
articles on business and trade.
Frequency: Weekly
Subscription Price: $66 per year

New Outlook
American Committee on U.S.-Soviet
Relations
109 Eleventh Street, SE
Washington, DC 20003
Phone: (202) 546-1700

Editor: Robert E. Berls, Jr.
Director, U.S.-U.S.S.R. Trade
Program: Margaret Chapman
Description: News and information
regarding U.S.-Soviet relations,
including coverage of political,
economic, trade, defense, and cultural
issues.
Frequency: Quarterly
Subscription Price: $12.00
Premier Issue: Winter 1989. The
successor to the American
Committee's former newsletter
Outlook.

News from the Ukraine
Frequency: Weekly
Subscription Price: $19
Available through Kamkin's
Bookstore (301) 881-1637.

Outlook
1782 Wyrinck Avenue
San Jose, CA 95124
Phone: (408) 723-5135
FAX: (408) 371-4474
Editor: Andrew Jakes
Description: Covers emerging
markets in Eastern Europe, the
effects of Europe 1992, and business
and joint venture information.
Frequency: Bi-monthly
Subscription Price: In U.S.: $144-
12 issues. *Canada and International:*
$200-12 issues
Premier Issue: April 1, 1990

PlanEcon Report
PlanEcon, Inc.
1111 4th Street, NW

Suite 801
Washington, DC 20005-5603
Phone: (202) 898-0471
FAX: (202) 898-0445
Editor: Dr. Jan Vanous
Description: Focuses on major macroeconomic and trade developments in the U.S.S.R. and Eastern Europe. *Frequency:* Weekly
Subscription Price: $1,300

Report on the U.S.S.R.
Radio Free Europe/Radio Liberty, Inc.
1775 Broadway
New York, NY 10019
Phone: (212) 397-5300
FAX: (212) 397-5374
For Subscriptions, contact: Irina Klionsky
Frequency: Weekly
Subscription Price: $85

Reprints from the Soviet Press
Compass Point Publications
P.O. Box 20673
New York, NY 10025
Preliminary translations received from Novosti Press Agency, Moscow.
ISSN 0034-4931
Description: Current articles, speeches, documents, and reports, unabridged, for those who wish to be informed beyond newspaper depth on Soviet affairs and Soviet points of view. Topics include economics, politics, foreign affairs, agriculture, industry, labor, science, law, and the unfolding process of perestroika.

Frequency: Bi-weekly, 24 issues per year
Subscription Price: $60.00 per year, single copies $2.75. Micro film available from University Microfilms International, 300 N. Zeeb Road, Ann Arbor, MI 48106.

RSEEA: Newsletter for Research on Soviet and East European Agriculture
Center for Business and Economic Research
School of Business, Economics, and Management
University of Southern Maine
96 Falmouth Street
Portland, ME 04103
Phone: (207) 780-4411
ISSN 8756-8942
Editor: Frank Durgin, Jr.
Description: Disseminates primary information among researchers in academia and government. Contains news on trade developments, articles, papers, conference listings, statistical materials, legislative information, book reviews, and special reports.
Subscription Price: $25, except for businesses, universities, and the government, which pay $35.

Soviet Business Law Report
1350 Connecticut Avenue, NW
Suite 1000
Washington, DC 20036
Phone: (202) 862-0990
FAX: (202) 862-0999
Publisher: Buraff Publications, A Division of The Bureau of National Affairs, Inc.

Description: Information and updates on Soviet business law. Designed to guide the lawyer through Soviet legal and regulatory complexities in order to provide accurate, confident counsel to American trading clients. Articles cover joint venture law, labor regulations, environmental regulation, company and commercial law, and changes in taxation. *Frequency:* Monthly
Subscription Price: $970 -- charter price until June 1, thereafter $1,270

Soviet and Eastern European Foreign Trade
M.E. Sharpe, Inc.
80 Business Park Drive
Armonk, NY 10504
Phone: (800) 541-6563 or (914) 273-1800
Editor: Josef Brada and Marvin Jackson.
Publisher: M.E. Sharpe.
Description: Geared as much to the business executive as to the academic specialist, the journal publishes materials from the region that are reflective both of current policy and of innovative thinking. The issues feature diverse topics as well as central themes.
Frequency: Quarterly
Subscription Price: $235.00
Premier Issue: 1965

Soviet Business and Trade With News From Eastern Europe
Welt Publishing Company

1413 K Street, NW, Suite 800
Washington, DC 20005
Phone: (202) 371-0555
Telex: 281 409 TAOA UR
ISSN 0731-7727
Publisher: Leo G. B. Welt; Diedre E. White, Executive Editor
Editors: Jerry A. Orvedahl, Lawrence Holland
Description: Four color newsletter with summaries of trade negotiations and other trade news from the Soviet Union and Eastern Europe.
Frequency: Bi-weekly
Subscription Price: $249

Soviet Life
1706 18th Street, NW
Washington DC 20009
Phone: (202) 328-3237
Editor: Sergei S. Ivanko
Managing Editor: Victor L. Karasin
Description: A comprehensive magazine about life in the Soviet Union, including business, trade, and economic policy.
Subscription Rate: $18/year

Soviet-American Trade
P.O. Box 18394
Washington, DC 20036
Phone: (301) 907-8125
Editor: Robert Cullen
Format: Newsletter
Description: Commercial news and other economic, financial, political, and legal issues affecting East-West Trade.
Frequency: Monthly
Subscription Price: $285 per year U.S.; $300 foreign

Surviving Together: A Journal on Soviet-American Relations
ISAR (Institute for Soviet-American Relations)
1601 Connecticut Avenue, NW
Washington, DC 20009
Phone: (202) 387-3034
Editors: Harriett Crosby, Nancy A. Graham, Eliza Klose, Anne Hunt
ISSN: 0859-6286
Description: Covers U.S.-Soviet cultural, political, scientific, academic, and business relations and initiatives undertaken in the private sector by individuals and organizations. Includes press and editorial abstracts on current events in the U.S.S.R., as well as news about exchanges, public education programs, travel, legislation, and reviews of current books and materials.
Frequency: Tri-annually
Subscription Price: Students/$15; Individuals/$25; Libraries and Institutions/$40.
Single Copy Price: $10

Tax Planning International Review
BNA International, Inc.
17 Dartmouth Street
London SW1H 9BL
Phone: International toll-free service 800 number 44-(1)997-4909
Editors: Sondra Beecroft, Linda O'Mahoney, London; Leonard L. Silverstein, Washington
Description: Each issue provides information on new tax laws in various countries around the world and how these laws can affect businesses operating there. There is also expanded coverage of U.S. tax legislation affecting foreign trade and business.
Subscription Price: $504 per year; back issues available on request.
Frequency: Tax Planning International is a two-part information service, Tax Planning International Review is a monthly journal of international developments and opportunities, and Tax Management International Forum is a quarterly analysis of international tax law problems.

The American Export Marketer
Welt Publishing Company
1413 K Street, NW
Suite 800
Washington, DC 20005
Phone: (202) 371-0555
Subscription: $199.

The Pacific Business Herald
Delin Joint Stock Company
Vladivostok
Description: Information on export goods manufactured in the U.S.S.R., Asia and the Pacific.
Premiere Issue: Forthcoming

The Current Digest of the Soviet Press
3857 North High Street
Columbus, OH 43214
Phone: (614) 292-4234
Executive Editor: Robert S. Ehlers

Description: A selection of the contents of the Soviet press translated into English. Translations, intended for use in teaching and research, are presented as documentary material, without elaboration or comment.
Frequency: Weekly, 52 issues per year, with four quarterly indexes.
Subscription Price: $705 per year with four indexes included at no extra charge, special high school rate of $90, single copies available at $8.50 each, microfilm and microfiche are $200 per volume (year).
Premier Issue: 1949 by The American Council of Learned Societies and the Social Science Research Council.

The Harriman Institute Forum
The W. Averell Harriman Institute for Advanced Study of the Soviet Union
Columbia University
420 West 118 Street, 12th floor
New York, NY 10027
ISSN: 0896-114X
Editor: Leslie Auerbach
Description: Feature article each month on a contemporary issue in the Soviet Union.
Frequency: Monthly
Subscription Price: U.S./Canada: $30/yr, $50/2 yrs; outside U.S./Canada: $40/yr, $75/2 yrs; back issues: $3 each

The International Information Report
Washington Researchers Publishing, Ltd.
2612 P Street, NW
Washington DC 20007
Phone: (202) 333-3533
Price: $120/year
Description: Economic news, information, and contacts from around the world.
Frequency: Monthly

The Soviet Travel Newsletter
International Intertrade Index
Box 636 Federal Square
Newark, NJ 07101
Publisher: International Intertrade in cooperation with Intourist
Editor: John E. Felber
Description: Four-page listing of general news focused on travel issues. Includes helpful tips for Western businessmen traveling to the Soviet Union.
Frequency: Bi-weekly
Price per Copy: $1 with self-addressed stamped envelope; annual subscription $62.00
Premiere Issue: 1989. Replaced Intourist News.

U.S.S.R. Agriculture and Trade Report
Publisher: U.S. Department of Agriculture, Economic Research Service
To order call: (800) 999-6779

U.S.S.R. Technology Update
7700 Leesburg Pike, Suite 250
Falls Church, VA 22043
Phone: (703) 556-0278
FAX: (703) 556-0494
ISSN: 0892-497X
Description: Articles and briefs on Soviet and East European science, technology, and trade. Comprehensive and current listing of Soviet patents in the U.S. Annual index.
Frequency: Bi-weekly
Subscription Price: $400; special rates for academic institutions and students

U.S.S.R. Currents
P.O. Box 65861
Washington, DC 20035-5861
Editor: Steven Stomski
Description: Articles and brief summations of events and news appearing in the Western news media.
Frequency: Bi-weekly
Subscription Price: $225.00, except for nonprofit and academic institutions, which pay $175.00, and students, who pay $150.

Vestnik MID SSSR
Publisher: Co-published by the U.S.S.R. Ministry of Foreign Affairs and the Austrian firm ABV.
Description: Periodical on Soviet foreign affairs, including trade and economic relations. Published in English for distribution in the West.
Premiere Issue: Forthcoming

World Trade
4940 Campus Drive
Newport Beach, CA 92660
Phone: (714) 641-1404
FAX: (714) 957-0922
Editor and Publisher: Drew Lawler
Managing Editor: William Lobdell
Description: A comprehensive, glossy four-color magazine on the various aspects of worldwide trade, including banking and finance, imports and exports, insurance, site selection, transportation, and company profiles.
Frequency: Monthly
Subscription Rate: $24 within the U.S. and $34 outside the U.S.

BOOKS

Note: Most publications from the Soviet Union may be ordered from:

Victor Kamkin Bookstore, Inc.
Boiling Brook Parkway
Rockville, MD 20852
Phone: (301) 881-5973
Call or send for catalog.

Quarterly Report to the Congress and the Trade Policy Committee on Trade Between the United States and Nonmarket Economy Countries.
Publisher: U.S. Trade Commission
Office of the Secretary
500 E Street, SW
Washington, DC 20436
Phone: (202) 252-1263

167

A Yellow Light on U.S.-Soviet Joint Ventures
Author: Juliana Geran Pilon
Year Published: 1988
Publisher: The Heritage Foundation
Washington, DC
To order call: (202) 546-4400
Number of Pages: 11
Description: Assessment of U.S. business activity in Soviet territory.

A New Look At Doing Business in the Soviet Union, Commercial Law and Practice Course handbook Series, No. 506
Author: Eugene Theroux, Chairman
Publisher: The Practising Law Institute
New York
Price: $392

Abstracts Soviet and East European Series
Publisher: Pergammon Press
Maxwell House
Fairview Park
Elmsford, NY 10523
Director of Publication: Michael Kaser
Editor: Raymond Hutchings
Description: Each issue contains printed summaries of articles and news from the Soviet and East European press, as well as abstracts of these on microfiche. Includes coverage of foreign trade and payments, economic planning, industry and finance.
Subscription Price: $410 for first subscription; additional subscriptions are available to individuals at $77.
Frequency: Tri-annual

Agricultural Statistics of Eastern Europe and the Soviet Union, 1965-1985
Author: Nancy J. Cochrane
Year Published: 1989
Publisher: U.S. Department of Agriculture, MD
To order call: (800) 999-6779 and order #SB-778
Price: $8
Number of Pages: 129
References or Bibliography: The data on this report are also available on diskette.
Description: Contains 110 tables with data on land use, farm structure, population, farm machinery, corn production, livestock, inventories and production, and per capita consumption of selected foods. Countries covered are the Soviet Union, Bulgaria, Czechoslovakia, East Germany, Hungary, Poland, Romania, and Yugoslavia.

American Business and U.S. Export Control Policy, 1979-1988
Author: Steven Elliot-Gower
Publisher: University of Georgia Center for East-West Trade Policy

ASET Briefing Book: Selling to the Soviet Health Care Industry
Author: ASET Consultants, Inc.

Year Published: 1990
Publisher: ASET Consultants, Inc.
8350 Greensboro Drive, Suite 805
McLean, VA 22102
Phone: (703) 790-1922
Price: $145
Number of Pages: 110
Description: The briefing book provides industry-specific information about selling medical equipment to the Soviet Union, the Soviet medical consumer environment, equipment certification procedures, negotiating tips, details about the Soviet health care industry, a listing of international activities between the Soviet Union and foreign countries in the medical field, and more.

Can Russia Change? The U.S.S.R. Confronts Global Interdependence
Author: Walter C. Clemens, Jr.
Year Published: 1989
Publisher: Unwin Hyman Publishers
Phone: (800)-547-8889
Description: The political and historical context of the new Soviet policy on foreign economic relations.

COMECON, Trade and the West
Author: Wallace and Clarke
Year Published: 1986
Publisher: St. Martin's Press
Scholarly and Reference Division
New York, NY
Phone: (800) 221-7945
Price: $32.50

Commersant
in the U.S.:
c/o Refco, Inc.
111 West Jackson Boulevard, Suite 1700
Chicago, IL 60604
Phone: (312) 930-6500
FAX: (312) 930-6534
Telex: 253322 REFCO CGO
In Moscow:
Khoroshevskoye Shosse, 41
Moscow, 123308
FAX: 335-28-25
Telex: 411712 POSTF SU
Editor: Vladimir Yakovlev
Description: Commersant is an independently owned weekly newspaper published every Monday in Moscow and in the United States. The 16-page paper is geared towards financial news in the Soviet Union. It also includes timely information regarding exhibits and cultural attractions and includes a weather map. All reporting, writing and graphics is performed solely by the Soviets. Translations are performed by two American editors on staff in the Commersant office in Moscow.
Subscription Price: $265 in the U.S. and $380 in all other international locations.
Advertising Rates: full page/$4,000; 1/2 page/$2,400; 1/4 page/$1,440; 1/8 page/$720; and 1/16 page/$360.

Communist Entrepreneurs: Unknown Innovators in the Global Economy
Author: John W. Kiser III

Year Published: 1989
Publisher: Franklin Watts
Price: $19.95
Number of Pages: 225
Description: This book profiles individuals in the Soviet Union and Eastern Europe who have been technological entrepreneurs for a variety of innovative new products and processes.

Comparative Economic Systems
Author: Richard L. Carson
Year Published: 1989
Publisher: M.E. Sharpe, Inc.
New York, NY
Price: Hardcover $60
Number of Pages: 752
Description: This book explores the major topics in comparative economic systems. The text is organized into three parts: the first is a discussion of property rights and the role of the state in the context of historical evolution. Part two examines the varieties of socialist organization. Part three presents the capitalist alternatives, such as the Japanese economy.

Considering a Joint Venture with the Russians?
Author: Jeffery A. Burt
Year Published: 1989
Publisher: The International Executive,
November-December 1989
Description: The article reviews salient points of Soviet legal codes concerning joint venture law.

Contract Law in the U.S.S.R. and the United States
Author: Allan Farnsworth and Viktor P. Mozolin
Year Published: 1987
Publisher: University Press of America, MD
Price: Hardcover $39.75
Number of Pages: 350
Description: Offers in depth accounts of American and Soviet contractual law, by an American and Soviet author, respectively. Similarities and differences between the systems are discussed in a jointly-written afterword.

Countertrade: Practices, Strategies, and Tactics
Author: C. G. Alexandrides and Barbara L. Bowers
Publisher: Wiley Press
Price: $24.95
Number of Pages: 250

Crisis and Reform in Socialist Economies
Author: Editors: Peter Gey, Jiri Kosta, and Wolfgang Quaisser
Year Published: 1987
Publisher: Westview Press
Boulder, CO
Price: $39.50
Number of Pages: 196

Data Goods and Data Services in the Socialist Countries of Eastern Europe
Publisher: United Nations Publications

Sales Room DC2-0853, Dept. 355
New York, NY
Phone: (212) 963-8302
Price: $13.50
Number of Pages: 103
Description: This study reviews the role of the CMEA member countries of Eastern Europe, in data-services and data-goods, the impact of transborder data-flows on the development process, and policy options.

Debt Problems of Eastern Europe
Author: Iliana Zloch-Christy
Year Published: 1988
Publisher: Cambridge University Press
New York
Price: $39.50
Number of Pages: 240
References or Bibliography: Includes tables and diagrams.

Delovaya Moskva [Business Moscow]
Author: Vneshtorgreklama
Year Published: 1989
Publisher: Vneshtorgreklama Moscow; the book can be ordered from Victor Kamkin, Rockville, MD.
Price: $50
Number of Pages: 340
Description: This book contains information on the Soviet Union; explains the role of joint ventures in the reorganization of the Soviet economy; provides a directory of ministries, departments, and foreign trade organizations; provides a list of

foreign commercial representatives; provides customs guidelines for foreigners entering and leaving the Soviet Union; and lists a variety of services offered to foreigners.

Directory of Foreign Trade Organizations in Eastern Europe: Bulgaria, Czechoslovakia, East Germany, Hungary, Poland, Romania, and the Soviet Union
Author: Vance T. Petrunoff
Year Published: 1989
Publisher: International Trade Press
San Francisco, CA
Number of Pages: 293

Directory of Soviet and East European Companies in the West
Author: Robert B. Morgan
Year Published: 1979
Publisher: East-West Project
Carleton University, Ottawa
Description: A useful dictionary for company names, addresses, ownership and commercial activities information. Table of contents is well organized and easy to use for locating East European company per Western country. Carleton University (Ottawa, Canada) began publishing this directory annually in 1983. These recent issues are held in the New York Public Library.

Doing Business in the Soviet Union
Author: Waterhouse
Year Published: 1990
Publisher: Waterhouse

171

Southwark Towers
32 London Bridge Street
London, SE1 95Y
Phone: (1) 407-8989
Number of Pages: 71
Description: The book includes information on the investment climate, business practices, auditing and accounting practices, and taxation in the Soviet Union.

Doing Business with the Soviet Union
Author: The American Management Association
Year Published: 1988
Publisher: A.M.A. Membership Publication Division
New York

East-South Relations in the World Economy
Editor: Marie Lavigne
Year Published: 1988
Publisher: Westview Press
Boulder, CO
Price: $44.95
Number of Pages: 288
References or Bibliography: Includes tables, figures, appendix, and bibliography.

East-South Trade
Editor: Marvin Jackson
Year Published: 1985
Publisher: M.E. Sharpe, Inc.
New York
Price: Paper $29.95

Number of Pages: 280
References or Bibliography:
Description: Economics and political economics.

East-West Joint Venture Contracts
Publisher: United Nations Publications
Sales Room DC2-0853, Dept. 355
New York
Phone: (212) 963-0832
Price: $50
Number of Pages: 224
Description: The purpose of this guide is to facilitate the drafting of East-West joint venture contracts, by drawing
attention to the main legal issues involved in this kind of transaction, and suggesting ways of resolving these issues, within the framework of the applicable law. The book reflects practical experience from current joint ventures and concentrates on the Soviet Union, Romania, Poland, Hungary, Czechoslovakia and Bulgaria. Model joint venture contracts and charters are also included in the book.

East-West Agricultural Trade
Author: James R. Jones
Year Published: 1986
Publisher: Westview Press
Boulder, CO
Price: $38
Number of Pages: 256

East-West Joint Ventures: Economic, Business, Financial, and Legal Aspects
Publisher: United Nations Publications
U.N. Pub., Sales Section Rm. DC2-0853 Dept. 800D
New York, NY
Phone: (212) 963-8302
Price: $45
Number of Pages: 189
Description: A comparative view of joint ventures in socialist countries.

East-West Trade and the Atlantic Alliance
Author: Editors: David A. Baldwin and Helen V. Milne
Year Published: 1990
Publisher: St. Martin's Press
New York
Phone: (800) 221-7945

Eastern Bloc Polymer Access Report
Kiser Research, Inc.
P.O. Box 33608
Washington, DC 20033
Phone: (800) 333-0877

Economic Relations with the Soviet Union: American and West German Perspectives
Author/Editor: Angela E. Stent
Year Published: 1985
Publisher: Westview Press
Boulder, CO
Price: $32
Number of Pages: 200

Economic Reforms in Eastern Europe and the Soviet Union, The Vienna Institute for Comparative Economic Studies Yearbook I
Editor: Hubert Gabrisch
Year Published: 1988
Publisher: Westview Press
Boulder, CO
Price: $29.50
Number of Pages: 214
References or Bibliography: Includes tables, notes, and appendices.
Description: The authors analyze the chances for success and the limits of the last wave of economic reforms in Poland, Czechoslovakia, Bulgaria, and the Soviet Union. Special aspects of reform in banking, trade, and joint ventures in the CMEA area are also discussed.

Economics and Politics in the U.S.S.R.: Problems of Interdependence
Author/Editors: Hans-Hermann Hohmann, Alec Nove, and Heinrich Vogel
Year Published: 1986
Publisher: Westview Press
Boulder, CO
Price: $37
Number of Pages: 306

Eroding Empire: Western Relations with Eastern Europe
Author: Lincoln Gordon
Year Published: 1987
Publisher: Brookings Institution

173

Washington, DC
Description: The volume contains a collection of essays on East-West trade and economic relations. It has valuable economic tables on East-West trade covering the years 1960-1985.

Exporter's Guide to Federal Resources for Small Business
Author: 1988 Interagency Task Force on Trade
Year Published: 1988
Number of Pages: 113
Description: The book is a compendium of federal international trade programs.

Finansy, dengi i kredit SSSR: bibliograficheskiy ukazatel
Author: Nauchnaya biblioteka Ministerstva finansov SSSR
Year Published: 1986
Publisher: Finansy i statistika
Description: A comprehensive bibliography on books, brochures, and articles on all aspects of the Soviet economy, published from 1976-1985.

Foreign Trade with the U.S.S.R.: A Manager's Guide to Recent Reforms
Author: Boris Bubnov
Year Published: 1987
Publisher: Pergamon Press
New York and Oxford

Foreign Trade in Eastern Europe and the Soviet Union, The Vienna Institute for Comparative Economic Studies Yearbook II
Editor: Michael Friedlander
Year Published: 1989
Publisher: Westview Press
Boulder, CO
Price: $22.50
Number of Pages: 192
Description: The yearbook discusses current trade issues related to the CMEA countries. Beginning with a survey of reforms in trade and trade policies, the contributors examine what the Soviet Union is doing to attract foreign capital and how individual East European countries are adjusting their trade policies.

Gorbachev and Glasnost': Viewpoints from the Soviet Press
Author: Editor: Isaac J. Tarasulo
Year Published: 1989
Publisher: Scholarly Resources, Inc., DE
Price: Paper $12.95
Number of Pages: 388
References or Bibliography: Includes index, glossary, and bibliographies.
Description: The book is a collection of recent articles translated from the Soviet press providing a unique window on Gorbachev's Soviet Union and the passionate struggle being waged between reform advocates and their conservative opponents for control of the future of their country.

174

Gorbachev's Struggle for Economic Reform: The Soviet Reform Process
Author: Anders Aslund
Year Published: 1989
Publisher: Cornell University Press
Ithaca, NY
Price: Hardcover $38.50, Paper $12.95
Number of Pages: 269
Description: The book represents an insider's view on the progress of Soviet economic reform. Aslund explains how the reform developed and what determined its design and the timing of its implementation.

Growth and Inflation in the Soviet Economy
Author: Fyodor I. Kushnirsky
Year Published: 1989
Publisher: Westview Press
Boulder, CO
Price: $38.95
Number of Pages: 319
Description: This book combines a theoretical analysis of the methodology used by Soviet planners to gauge economic progress with case studies from the machine-building and manufacturing sector to answer key questions about the Soviet economy. The author concludes with an assessment of the impact of the internal criticism of official statistics spurred on by glasnost'.

Guide to Joint Ventures in the U.S.S.R.: What the Businessman Should Know

Author: The International Chamber of Commerce, No. 456
Year Published: 1988
Publisher: ICC Publishing Corp.
New York
Number of Pages: 300
Description: A collection of information about Soviet legislation relating to joint ventures in the Soviet Union as well as laws and regulations generally affecting the activities of an enterprise in the Soviet Union, including surveys and comments on such legislation.

Handbook of Economic Statistics
Author: United States Central Intelligence Agency
Year Published: 1975-present
Publisher: CIA
Washington, DC
Description: The handbook includes statistics for all communist countries. Includes a section on Soviet economic performance data on commodities.

Hosting Soviet Visitors: A Handbook
Author: This handbook is co-sponsored by The Institute for Soviet-American Relations and the Delphi International Group
Year Published: 1990
Publisher: Delphi Press
Washington, DC
To order call: (202) 466-7951
Price: $4.95 each plus $1 postage
Description: The handbook includes information on the history of U.S.-

Soviet exchange, the variety of existing exchange programs, how to start your own exchange, host preparation, how to design professional cultural programs for Soviet guests, what to expect from Soviet visitors, and the cultural values of the Soviet people.

How to do Business with the Russians: A Handbook and Guide for Western World Business People
Author: Misha G. Knight
Year Published: 1987
Publisher: Quorum Books
New York
Description: This book describes the steps involved in initiating and doing business with the Soviets, supported by case-study examples. Some topics are illustrated with helpful figures and tables. Essential reading for anyone interested in forming a U.S.-Soviet joint venture.

Information Moscow
Author: U.S. Information Moscow
Year Published: 1987
Publisher: U.S. Information Moscow
San Francisco, CA
Description: A directory/handbook for U.S.-Soviet trade. Includes U.S. and Soviet listings.

Information Moscow
Author: Jupiter Associates, Ltd.
Year Published: 1989-90
Publisher: Jupiter Associates, Ltd.

21 The Waldrons
Croydon, London, CRO 4HB
Number of Pages: 395
Description: The directory provides detailed information about Soviet organizations, services, diplomatic corps, foreign correspondents, and more.

Inside Perestroika: The Future of the Soviet Economy
Author: Abel Aganbegyan
Year Published: 1989
Publisher: Harper and Row
Price: $19.95
Number of Pages: 256
Description: Written by President Gorbachev's architect for restructuring the Soviet economy, this book examines the current restructuring and makes future predictions on the Soviet economy.

International Technology Flows and the Technology Gap
Author: Jan Monkiewicz
Year Published: 1989
Publisher: Westview Press
Boulder, CO
Price: $33.50
Number of Pages: 220
Description: The thrust of this book is to examine under what conditions and to what extent international technology transfer has succeeded, with a particular focus on the socialist countries of Eastern Europe and their joint efforts through the CMEA.

International Joint Ventures
Author: James Dobkin, Jeffrey Burt,
Kenneth J. Krupsky, and Mark J.
Spooner
Publisher: Federal Publications, Inc.
For mailing call: (202) 337-7000
Price: $80 plus $3.50 shipping
Number of Pages: 1989
Description: The book contains
information on the structuring and
financing of existing joint ventures.

**International Business in
Gorbachev's Soviet Union**
Author: Margie Lindsay
Year Published: 1989
Publisher: St. Martin's, Press
Scholarly and Reference Division
New York
Phone: (800) 221-7945
Price: $49.95
Number of Pages: 218
Description: An analysis of the
major elements of the restructuring
of the Soviet Union under
Gorbachev, including details of joint
venture law, changes in the Soviet
management systems, and other
important reforms affecting the
international business community.
Also included is a balanced view of
the new market opportunities
opening up to those interested in the
Soviet market.

**International Business in
Gorbachev's Soviet Union**
Author: Margie Lindsay
Year Published: 1989

Publisher: St. Martin's Press
Scholarly and Reference Division
New York
Phone: (800) 221-7945

**Introductory Guide to Joint Ventures
in the Soviet Union**
Author: U.S. Department of
Commerce
Year Published: 1990
Publisher: U.S. Department of
Commerce
International Trade Administration
U.S.S.R. Division, Rm. 3413
Washington, DC
Number of Pages: 23
References or Bibliography: A
bibliography of selected readings is
included.
Description: This publication
provides a general overview of the
prospects for joint venturing in the
Soviet Union. Chapter headings
include: "Get to Know the Market,"
"Success Requires Clearly Defined
Goals," "Soviet Goals for Joint
Ventures in the West," "Finding a
Joint Venture Partner," "Establishing
a Joint Venture Partner," and
"Operation of a Joint Venture."

**Investment and Reindustrialization in
the Soviet Economy**
Author: Boris Z. Rumer
Year Published: 1985
Publisher: Westview Press
Boulder, CO
Price: $28.50
Number of Pages: 145

Joint Ventures in the Soviet Union
Publisher: Transnational Juris Publications
New York
To order call: (914) 693-0089
Price: $125
Description: An annotated compendium detailing the complex world of Soviet joint venture legislation.

Joint Venture Operations in the U.S.S.R.
Author: Peat Marwick Main and Co.
Publisher: Peat Marwick Main and Co.
New York
Phone: (212) 872-6758
Contact: Nina Dimas
Description: An informational study.

Joint Ventures as a Form of International Economic Cooperation
Author: United Nations Centre on Transnational Corporations
Year Published: 1988
Publisher: United Nations
New York
Description: This work is a detailed examination of Soviet-international joint venture projects. The report includes models for preparing joint venture studies, case-study examples, and useful checklists.

Joint Ventures in the Soviet Union: Law and Practice
Author: Eugene Theroux and Arthur

L. George
Year Published: 1988, 1989
Publisher: Baker and McKenzie
Washington, DC
Inquiries call: (202) 452-7000

Labour and Leisure in the Soviet Union
Author: Moskoff
Year Published: 1984
Publisher: St. Martin's Press Scholarly and Reference Division
New York
Phone: (800) 221-7945
Price: $27.50
Description: The conflict between public and private decision-making in a planned economy.

Legal and Practical Aspects of Doing Business with the Soviet Union
Author: Eugene Theroux
Year Published: 1987
Publisher: Pergamon Press
New York, Oxford

Legal Aspects of Doing Business in Eastern Europe and the Soviet Union
Author: Dennis Campbell
Year Published: 1986
Publisher: Kluwer Law and Taxation Publishers
Deventer, The Netherlands

Legal Regulations on Joint Ventures in the U.S.S.R., 2 volumes
Author: Sarah Carey

Publisher: U.S.S.R. Chamber of Commerce and Heron, Burchette, Ruckert and Rothwell
Phone: (202) 492-3000
Contact: Denee Clark, Steptoe and Johnson

Matekon
M.E. Sharpe, Inc.
80 Business Park Drive
Armonk, NY 10504
Phone: (800) 541-6563 or (914) 273-1800
Editor: John Litwack
Publisher: M.E. Sharpe.
Description: Translations of Russian and East European mathematical economics. The journal makes available in English the unique economic tradition pioneered by V.V. Novozhilov and Nobel laureate L. V. Kantorovich. Topics covered include problems of plan modeling, forecasting, analyses of consumption behavior, informatics, and general equilibrium theory.
Frequency: Quarterly
Subscription Price: $256.00

MEMO: New Soviet Voices on Foreign and Economic Policy
Author/Editor: Steve Hirsch
Year Published: 1989
Publisher: BNA Books
Washington, DC
Price: Hardcover $55
Number of Pages: 656
Description: The book is a collection of 36 significant articles from recent issues of MEMO, the influential monthly journal of the U.S.S.R. Academy of Sciences' Institute of World Economy and International Relations. Topics of pieces include the economy and foreign policy of the Soviet Union and East-West economic cooperation.

Michal Kalecki on a Socialist Economy
Author: Jerzy Osiatynski
Year Published: 1988
Publisher: St. Martin's Press Scholarly and Reference Division
New York
Phone: (800) 221-7945
Price: $47.50
Number of Pages: 201
Description: This book examines Kalecki's ideas on economic functioning, theories of long-run planning and growth under socialism, and his views on the cost-benefit analysis of investment as set against the earlier theory and practice of the Soviet Union and other CMEA countries. His ideas on social aspects of economic development are discussed.

Opening Up the Soviet Economy
Author: Jerry F. Hough
Year Published: 1988
Publisher: Brookings Institution
Washington DC
Description: This book is a study of the outlook and implications of Soviet economic reform and U.S.-

U.S.S.R. joint venture possibilities in the Gorbachev era.

Organizations Involved in Soviet-American Relations
Author: Institute for Soviet-American Relations
Year Published: 1986
Publisher: ISAR Publication
Washington, DC
Description: ISAR publishes an annual directory of American and Soviet organizations which are active in U.S.-Soviet affairs, particularly non-profit organizations.

Perestroika and the Economy
Editors: Anthony Jones and William Moskoff
Year Published: 1989
Publisher: M.E. Sharpe, Inc.
New York
Price: Hardcover $45
Number of Pages: 304
Description: Many shades of opinion are evident in this anthology of recent articles on such topics as central planning, the market mechanism, the property system, prices, incentives, autonomy and initiative, and issues of equity. Where some authors advocate radical change, others call for one-time adjustments, while perhaps the most daring call not so much for new policies as for an opening up of the system. Among the authors included here are Abalkin, Kurashvili, Latsis, 'Popkova', Torkanovskiy, and Shmelyev.

Personal Consumption in the U.S.S.R. and U.S.
Author: Igor Birman
Year Published: 1989
Publisher: St. Martin's Press
Scholarly and Reference Division
New York
Phone: (800) 221-7945
Price: $49.95
Number of Pages: 280
Description: This volume presents evidence indicating that the Soviets are at least five times worse off then their American counterparts in terms of living standards.

Perspectives on U.S.-Soviet Joint Ventures
Author: Erika D. Nobel and H. Randall Morgan
Year Published: July, 1989
Publisher: The CPA Journal; article available from ASET
Phone: (703) 790-1922
Price: Free
Number of Pages: 4
Description: The authors describe efforts underway to develop joint ventures in a wide range of industries. The legal aspects of joint ventures, as well as some of the typical problems confronted by Western partners are also discussed.

Planned Economies: Confronting the Challenges of the 1980s
Author/Editors: John P. Hardt and Carl H. McMillan
Year Published: 1987

Publisher: Cambridge University Press
New York
Price: $39.50
Number of Pages: 200
References or Bibliography: Includes tables and line diagrams.

Practical Aspects of Trading with the U.S.S.R.
Authors: Robert Starr and Sally March
Year Published: 1989
Publisher: Worldwide Information
New York
Description: The book contains business studies on Soviet commercial policies.

Predicasts Funk and Scott Index Europe Annual
Author: Predicasts, Inc.
Year Published: 1989
Publisher: Predicasts, Inc.
Cleveland, OH
Description: The annual includes East Europe and the Soviet Union. It covers company, product, and industry information compiled from over 750 publications.

Pressures for Reform in the East European Economies
Author: Joint Economic Committee of the U.S. Congress
Publisher: Joint Economic Committee Publications
Washington DC

To order call: (202) 224-5321
Number of Pages: vol. 1 - 284 pages, vol. 2 - 633 pages
Description: This is a study by the Joint Economic Committee of the U.S. Congress focusing on political, economic, and demographic trends in the countries of Eastern Europe.

Problems of Economics
M.E. Sharpe, Inc.
80 Business Park Drive
Armonk, NY 10504
Phone: (800) 541-6563 or (914) 273-1800
Editor: Murray Yanowitch and James W. Gillula.
Publisher: M.E. Sharpe.
Description: This journal scans the Soviet economic literature from Voprosy ekonomiki to EKO and permits its readers to follow principle theoretical and policy issues that constitute the core of Soviet economic discourse.
Frequency: Monthly
Subscription Price: $394.00

Public Figures in the Soviet Union, A Current Biographical Index 1984-Present
Year Published: 1990
Publisher: Chadwick-Healey Inc.
Alexandria, VA
Price: Base File thru 1987 $600, Bi-annual Updates thru present $175
References or Bibliography: Index is Bibliographic
Description: A comprehensive

current biographic index to public figures in the U.S.S.R., giving users references to articles, news items, and transcripts of speeches from a wide range of sources. Entries are in Russian language and published on computer output microfiche in a storage binder, with printed instructions.

Quarterly Report to the Congress and the Trade Policy Committee on Trade Between the United States and Nonmarket Economy Countries.
Office of the Secretary
U.S. Trade Commission
701 E Street, NW
Washington, DC 20436
Phone: (202) 523-5178

Reflections on Perestroika and the Foreign Economic Ties of the U.S.S.R.
Author: Bela Balassa
Year Published: 1989
Publisher: The World Bank
Washington, DC
Description: The volume contains policy, planning, and research working papers.

Reforming the Soviet Economy: Equality vs. Efficiency
Author: Ed A. Hewett
Year Published: 1988
Publisher: The Brookings Institution
Washington, DC
Number of Pages: 404

Description: The book analyzes the strengths and weaknesses of Soviet economic performance during the last quarter century.

Reorganization and Reform in the Soviet Economy
Editors: Susan J. Linz and William Moskoff
Year Published: 1988
Publisher: M.E. Sharpe, Inc.
New York
Price: Hardcover $37.50
Number of Pages: 160
Description: This volume of essays on the Gorbachev economic reforms provides an up-to-date and focused account of the process of perestroika in the Soviet economy.

Russian-English Foreign Trade Dictionary
Author: I. V. Voskresenskaya
Year Published: 1986
Publisher: Russkiy yazyk
Moscow
Description: The dictionary provides a useful collection of Russian-English business and foreign trade terms arranged by subject theme.

Socialist World Business Directory
Author: M. Z. Michalczonek
Year Published: 1986
Publisher: M.Z. Michalczonek
Sopot, Poland
Description: This address guide of business and trade arranged by

country is unique in that it comprises only the socialist world. The information is helpful regarding all communist nations. The Soviet Union is covered in greater detail in other guides and directories mentioned in this section.

Soviet Regional Economic Policy: The East-West Debate over Pacific Siberian Development
Author: Jonathan R. Schiffer
Year Published: 1989
Publisher: St. Martin's Press
Scholarly and Reference Division
New York
Phone: (800) 221-7945
Price: $49.95
Number of Pages: 384
Description: This book analyzes the complex interaction between economic and spatial planning by focusing on the regional dimension of the Soviet resource allocations decision-making process.

Soviet Foreign Trade: The Decision Making Process
Author: H. Stephen Gardner
Publisher: Kluwer Hijhoff Publishing
Boston, MA
Description: The book examines the changing institutional structure and economic attitudes that are employed in Soviet foreign trade decision making.

Soviet Foreign Trade: Today and Tomorrow
Author: Translated from Russian by Jane Sayers
Year Published: 1985
Publisher: Progress Publishers
Moscow
Number of Pages: 277
References or Bibliography: Includes bibliographical references.

Soviet Natural Resources in the World Economy
Year Published: 1983
Publisher: Jensen/Shabad/Wright
Price: Hardcover $100

Soviet Product Quality
Author: Malcolm R. Hill and Richard McKay
Year Published: 1988
Publisher: St. Martin's Press
Scholarly and Reference Division
New York
Phone: (800) 221-7945
Price: $45
Number of Pages: 221
Description: This volume presents a study of the quality of Soviet manufactured products based on a comparative examination of documented empirical data elicited from Soviet sources. The authors employ Soviet state standards, product specifications and expert assessment to analyze Soviet product quality as compared to that of Western manufacturers.

Soviet and East European Transport Problems
Editor: Ambler, et. al.
Publisher: St. Martin's Press
Scholarly and Reference Division
New York
Phone: (800) 221-7945
Price: $32.50

Soviet Joint Venture Legislation and Regulations, and Recent Related Legal Development
Author: Jeffery A. Burt
Publisher: Arnold and Porter
Washington, DC
Inquiries call: (202) 872-6962

State Register of Participants in the Foreign Economic Relations of the Soviet Union
Publisher: Mezhdunarodnaya Kniga
Ul. Dimitrova
Moscow 113095
FAX: 230-21-17
Price: $40 per volume

Statistical Abstract of East-West Trade and Finance
Author: Ronald G. Oechsler
Year Published: 1986
Publisher: Office of Trade and Investment Analysis
Washington, DC
Description: This report covers the years 1970-1985.

A Successful Joint Venture in the U.S.S.R.: Practical Handbook
Author: Matti Honkanen
Year Published: 1990
Publisher: International Law Centre, Helsinki, Finland
Price: $150
To Order: (800) 735-5301
Description: The book contains practical information and comprehensive models for establishing joint ventures in the Soviet Union.

Sun World
Phone: (202) 783-7173
Description: A television service available in Moscow, Sun World Moscow provides television and news service from the Washington, DC-based firm, Sun World Satellite News.

Survey of Views on the Impact of Granting Most Favored nation Status to the Soviet Union
Author: International Trade Commission
Year Published: 1989
Publisher: International Trade Commission
Phone: (202) 252-1809
Price: Free
Description: The report contains information collected from public hearings concerning trade with the Soviet Union.

Taxation in Centrally Planned Economies
Author: Wanless
Year Published: 1985
Publisher: St. Martin's Press
Scholarly and Reference Division
New York
Phone: (800) 221-7945
Price: $27.50

Technology Export from the Socialist Countries
Author: Jan Monkiewicz and Jan Maciejewicz
Year Published: 1986
Publisher: Westview Press
Boulder, CO
Price: $30
Number of Pages: 170

The American-Soviet Medical Market Journal
374 Congress Street, Suite 408
Boston, MA 02210
Phone: (617) 451-6633
FAX: (617) 451-6182
Associate Publisher: Richard P. Mills

The Europa Year Book
Author: Europa Publications Limited
Year Published: 1988
Publisher: Europa Publications
London
Description: This yearbook is an annual two-volume reference work covering international trade, economics, and politics. The yearbook includes statistical section for each country, and directories of important individuals.

The Reorganization of Soviet Foreign Trade
Author: M. M. Boguslavskiy and P. S. Smirnov
Year Published: 1989
Publisher: M.E. Sharpe, Inc.
New York
Price: Hardcover $75
Number of Pages: 224
Description: Description of the legal foundations underlying the recent changes in Soviet foreign trade operations. The book contains a chapter outlining the legal bases for the formation of joint ventures between Soviet and Western firms. Also included are ten appendices presenting in translation the most important recent Soviet legislation pertaining to foreign trade.

The Soviet Economic System: A Legal Analysis
Author: Olimpiad S. Ioffe and Peter B. Maggs
Year Published: 1987
Publisher: Westview Press
Boulder, CO
Price: $53.50
Number of Pages: 326
References or Bibliography: Includes notes and an index.

The U.S.S.R. in the 1990s: Struggling out of Stagnation
Author: Michael Ellman
Year Published: 1989
Publisher: The Economist Intelligence Unit
London

185

Price: $230 (including airmail postage)

Description: The report examines contemporary Soviet reforms and gives a detailed analysis of the serious problems found in various industrial sectors, agriculture, energy, and science. Looking at the future, in five separate scenarios, it examines the most likely paths along which economic reform will tread in the 1990s. It points out the possible implications of perestroika for Western companies, identifying some dos and don'ts of establishing joint ventures.

The Soviet Union and Eastern Europe: Recent Developments in Trade, Investment and Finance
Author: The American Bar Association
Year Published: 1988
Publisher: American Bar Association
New York

The Soviet Joint Enterprise Decree: Law and Structure
Author/Editors: David F. Kelley and Joshua B. Saul
Year Published: 1990
Publisher: Harvard Russian Research Center, MA
Price: $200
Description: Includes all relevant legislation pertaining to joint ventures, an Executive Overview of the laws, a listing of the first 188 joint ventures signed, and boilerplates

of an actual charter and agreement used in 1989.

The Economist Business Traveller's Guides: U.S.S.R.
Editor: Stephen Brough
Year Published: 1989
Publisher: $19.95
Price: 192
Number of Pages: Prentice-Hall New York
References or Bibliography: The book provides a wide range of practical information, ranging from business etiquette to communications for the Soviet Union.

The Second Economy in Marxist States
Author: Maria Los
Year Published: 1989
Publisher: St. Martin's Press Scholarly and Reference Division New York
Phone: (800) 221-7945
Price: $45
Number of Pages: 256
Description: A vivid, mosaic-like panorama of the hidden economies of ten Marxist states is presented in this collection. The view presented shows an unfolding interplay between the official and shadow economy which limits the dynamics and the process of change, particularly when considering the current reform movements in these states.

186

The Political and Legal Framework of Trade Relations Between the European Community and Eastern Europe
Editor: Marc Maresceau
Year Published: 1989
Publisher: Kluwer Academic Publishers, Hingham, MA
Phone: (617) 871-6600
Price: $72.50
Number of Pages: 750
Description: The book provides insight into the problems and prospects regarding the political and commercial climate both at the international and national level. Fully examined in this book are the positions of Western European countries in their relations with Eastern Europe; Eastern European enterprises in the EEC; export controls; financial cooperation and countertrade; and more.

The Shadow Economy
Author: Horst Brezinski
Year Published: 1990
Publisher: Westview Press
Boulder, CO
Price: $23
Number of Pages: 250
Description: The book assesses the shadow economy's operation in free market, socialist, and developing countries. The author develops a general theory of this phenomenon in different types of economies, at various stages of development, and in diverse geographical areas.

The Soviet Bloc in the IMF and the IBRD
Author: Valerie J. Assetto
Year Published: 1987
Publisher: Westview Press
Boulder, CO
Price: $30
Number of Pages: 208
References or Bibliography:
Includes tables, notes, bibliography and index.

The Soviet Economy: Continuity and Change
Editor: Morris Bornstein
Year Published: 1981
Publisher: Westview Press
Boulder, CO
Price: $23.95
Number of Pages: 381
Description: Information and analysis on the Soviet economic policy process.

The Soviet Challenge in the Gorbachev Era: Western Perceptions and Policy Recommendations
Author: The Aspen Strategy Group and the European Strategy Group
Year Published: 1989
Publisher: University Press of America, MD
Price: Hardcover $27.25, Paper $14.50
Number of Pages: 170
Description: This report examines and compares Soviet domestic economic and policy reforms, international trade and financial

reforms, reforms affecting Eastern Europe, reforms in military strategy and capabilities, and in foreign policy and arms control. It then makes recommendations about the methods and extent to which the West can influence these processes.

The Opening of the Soviet Market
Author: Business Week
Year Published: 1989
Publisher: Peters and Peters
New York
Number of Pages: 114
Description: Transcripts of the Business Week conference "The Opening of the Soviet Market: Implications of Perestroika for Global Business" held in New York, December 1989.

The Modern Uzbeks
Author: Edward Allworth
Year Published: 1990
Publisher: Hoover Institution Press, Stanford University
To order call: (415) 723-3373
Price: Hardcover $39.95, Paper $24.95
Number of Pages: 500
Description: The book examines some of the nationality dilemmas in the Soviet Union.

The Crisis in Soviet Agriculture
Author: Hedlund
Year Published: 1984
Publisher: St. Martin's Press

Scholarly and Reference Division
New York, NY
Phone: (800) 221-7945
Price: $27.50

The Coming Soviet Crash: Gorbachev's Desperate Pursuit of Credit in Western Financial Markets
Author: Judy Shelton
Publisher: The Hoover Institution Press, Stanford University

The List of Registered Joint Ventures in the U.S.S.R.
Author: Harvard Russian Research Center
Price: $100
Publisher: Harvard Russian Research Center
Cambridge MA
Phone: (617) 495-4037
Contact: Cathy Reed
Description: The entries in this publication include: registration number and date, Russian name of the JV, location of JV, foreign partner(s), Soviet partner(s), share ownership, planned business activity, and capital contributions of partners. The listing covers the first 543 joint ventures.

The Making of the Georgian Nation
Author: Ronald Grigor Suny
Year Published: 1988
Publisher: Indiana University Press, IN
Price: Hardcover $45, Paper $17.50

Number of Pages: 416
References or Bibliography: Includes maps, glossary, notes, bibliography, and index.
Description: A good book to consult for the background relationship of Russian dominance in the region.

The Soviet Impact on Commodity Markets
Author: Hutchings
Publisher: St. Martin's Press Scholarly and Reference Division
New York
Phone: (800) 221-7945
Price: $39.95

The Soviet Industrial Enterprise: Theory and Practice
Author: Freris
Publisher: St. Martin's Press Scholarly and Reference Division
New York
Phone: (800) 221-7945
Price: $39.95

The East European Motor Industry: Prospects and Developments
Author: ECHO
Year Published: 1989
Publisher: The Economist Intelligence Unit
London
Price: $485 (including airmail postage)
Description: This report examines trends in vehicle production, exports and imports in the Soviet Union, Czechoslovakia, Poland, Hungary, Romania, Bulgaria, and Yugoslavia. There is an analysis of prospects for the East European motor industry, including the potential impact of perestroika. The report is designed to assist manufacturers, suppliers, distributors, and analysts in evaluating the opportunities and challenges presented by this sector of the global motor industry.

The Future of the Soviet Economic Planning System
Author: David A. Dyker
Year Published: 1985
Publisher: M.E. Sharpe, Inc.
New York
Price: Hardcover $37.50, Paper $17.95
Number of Pages: 186

The Economic Challenge of Perestroika
Author: Abel Aganbegyan
Year Published: 1988
Publisher: Indiana University Press, IN
Price: Hardcover $18.95
Number of Pages: 278
References or Bibliography: Includes a forward, a map, 2 figures, tables, appendices, and an index.
Description: The author provides a candid examination of the Soviet economy and domestic economic debates.

The Belorussian Railroad Experiment, Staff Paper 48
Author: Center for International

Research (CIR)
Year Published: 1989
Publisher: U.S.   Bureau   of   the
Census
Phone: (301) 763-4086
Price: $10

The Development of Siberia
Author: Alan   Wood   and   R.   A.
French
Year Published: 1989
Publisher: St.   Martin's   Press
Scholarly and Reference Division
New York
Phone: (800) 221-7945
Price: $49.95
Number of Pages: 256
Description: The authors examine
how, despite severe climactic and
environmental difficulties, this vast
and little-known region has recently
played an increasingly important role
in the economies of the Soviet Union
and the rest of the world.

The Economies of Eastern Europe in a Time of Change
Author: Adam Zwass
Year Published: 1983
Publisher: M.E. Sharpe, Inc.
New York
Price: Hardcover $45
Number of Pages: 184

The Soviet Business Review
Dhalfelt International
120 Potter Road
Scarsdale, NY 10583

Phone: (914) 472-2084
Publisher: Ulf Nofelt
Description: Provides   inside
information on new projects, joint
ventures, financing, and economic
information. Also provides business
contacts   for   Soviet   companies
interested in establishing contacts in
the West.
Frequency: Monthly
Subscription Price: $275

The Turning Point: Revitalizing the Soviet Economy
Author: Nikolay   Shmelyev   and
Vladimir Popov
Publisher: Doubleday
New York
Phone: (800)-223-6834, ext. 9479 or
(202) 492-9479
Price: $22.95
Number of Pages: 330
Description: A book, written by two
leading   radical   reform   advocates,
explaining the failures of central
planning and recommending market-
oriented prescriptions.

The Soviet Union - Business, Travel and Security Seminar
Author: Overseas   Security
Management Incorporated
Year Published: 1985
Publisher: Overseas   Security
Management
Tysons Corner, VA
References   or   Bibliography:
Contains a directory of the addresses,
telephone, and telex numbers of

government and private business representatives in Moscow.
Description: This study provides information on business, travel, and security in the Soviet Union. Especially insightful ideas are offered in the chapters, "Negotiating with the Soviets," and "Security Advice".

Trade without Money: Barter and Countertrade
Author: Leo G. B. Welt
Publisher: Prentice-Hall Law and Business
Description: The book describes the specifics of barter and countertrade, including forms of countertrade, contract transactions, financing countertrade, creating a countertrade capability, and case studies.

Trade and Technology in Soviet-Western Relations
Author: Phillip Hanson
Publisher: Columbia University Press
New York
Price: $271
Description: The book focuses on commercial transactions involving machinery, expertise, licenses, and technology flows.

Trading with the U.S.S.R.
Author: International Marketing Information Series, Overseas Business Reports
Year Published: 1977

Publisher: U.S. Department of Commerce
Washington, DC
Price: Single report $0.80
Number of Pages: 56
References or Bibliography: Includes extensive bibliography.
Description: This publication is designed to introduce U.S. firms to the procedures for trading with the Soviet Union and to the trade practices and organizations with which they should be familiar before entering the Soviet market.

Transcripts of "Roundtable On Joint Venturing in the U.S.S.R.", 7 volumes
Author: Sarah Carey
Publisher: Heron Burchette, Ruckert, and Rothwell
Phone: (202) 492-3000
Inquiries contact: Denee Clark, Steptoe and Johnson

Ukrainian Business Outlook
Outlook International Inc.
213 Valley Street, Suite 254
South Orange, NJ 07079
Phone: (201) 672-6105
FAX: (201) 672-6105
Editor: Roman G. Kupchinsky
Description: A 12-page newsletter providing news and analysis of business in the Ukraine.
Frequency: 10 times a year.
Subscription Rates: $400 for institutions and $250 for individuals.

U.S.-Soviet Trade Alert
Global Trading Associates, Inc.
1155 Connecticut Avenue, NW
Suite 500
Washington, DC 20036
Phone: (202) 467-8589
FAX: (202) 452-8654
Telex: 4933729 WASH UI
Contact: William S. Loiry, Chairman
& CEO
Description: The U.S.-Soviet trade
industry's main fax newsletter,
containing the latest strategic
information on events, strategies,
announcements, and news.
Subscription: $89

U.S.-Soviet Trade Policy
Author: Carol Rae Hansen
Year Published: 1988
Publisher: Foreign Policy Institute,
Johns Hopkins University, School of
Advanced International Studies
Washington, DC
To order call: (202) 663-5773
Price: Paper $9
Number of Pages: 53
Description: Hansen shows how the
United States can balance competing
commercial and security objectives,
channel Mikhail Gorbachev's reform
campaign in positive directions, and
strike deals that benefit both sides.
The discussion brings together high
level government officials from all
departments and senior scholars from
SAIS.

**U.S.-Soviet Trade and Economic
Council: Determined to Sell Moscow**

the Rope that Could Hang America
Author: Ira Carnahan
Year Published: 1988
Publisher: The Heritage Foundation
Washington, DC
Phone: (202) 546-4400
Description: A pessimistic
assessment of U.S. business in the
Soviet Union.

**U.S.S.R. New Business Opportunities;
A Guide for Businessmen and
Managers**
Publisher: V/O Vneshtorgizdat
Moscow
Phone: 250-51-62

U.S.S.R. Facts and Figures Annual
Author: John L. Scherer
Year Published: 1977-present
Publisher: Academic International
Press
Gulf Breeze, FL
Description: This annual, published
since 1977, contains statistical data
and information on important events
in the Soviet Union.

**U.S.S.R. Participation in the General
Agreement on Tariffs and Trade
(GATT), Proceedings of an
International Conference**
Editor: Margaret Chapman
Year Published: 1989
Publisher: American Committee on
U.S.-Soviet Relations
Washington, DC
Inquiries call: (202) 546-1700

Description: The publication includes remarks and discussion from a conference held in Washington, DC in September 1988. The conference brought together senior trade figures from the government, the business community, academia, and the media for concerted exploration of the economic and political issues that affect the expansion of nonstrategic trade with the Soviet Union.

U.S.S.R.: New Management Mechanism in Foreign Economic Relations
Publisher: United Nations Publications
Sales Room DC2-0853, Dept. 355
New York
To order call: (212) 963-8302
Price: $12
Number of Pages: 22
Description: This study reviews perestroika and includes two annexes on setting up foreign trade firms and transferring import/export operations.

Uranium Enrichment: U.S. Imports of Soviet Enriched Uranium, GAO/RCED-90-70BR
Author: U.S. General Accounting Office
Year Published: 1990
Publisher: U.S. General Accounting Office
Phone: (202) 228-6427
Price: Free
Description: The volume discusses Soviet practices in the trade of enriched uranium and provides details on amounts purchased from Soviet and third-party sources.

U.S. Commercial Opportunities in the Soviet Union
Author: Chris C. Carvounis
Year Published: 1989
Publisher: Quorum Books, New York
Bibliography: Contains extensive bibliography.
Description: This book details considerations for planning U.S.-Soviet joint ventures.

Voices of Glasnost, Interviews with Gorbachev's Reformers
Author: Stephen F. Cohen and Katrina Vanden Heuvel
Publisher: W. W. Norton
To order call: (800) 223-2584 or (800) 223-4830
Price: $19.95
Number of Pages: 339
Description: A book compiled from discussions with leading reform advocates in the Soviet Union, including Politburo member Alexander Yakovlev, political commentator Fyodor Burlatsky, and economist Nikolay Shmelyev.

We Are Building a Long-Term Policy
Author: Mikhail Gorbachev
Year Published: 1988
Publisher: Novosti Press Agency Publishing House
Moscow

World Patents Index Database
Publisher: Derwent Incorporated
McLean, VA
Phone: (703) 790-0400
FAX: (703) 790-1426
Description: Weekly review of over 14,000 patent documents enables Derwent's large team of specialist editors and abstractors to produce new and highly informative titles and abstracts. Special subject classification codes are also added. All of the analyzed information is available on-line in the database and in a wide range of printed and microfilm services.

World Trade and Payments Cycles: The Advance and Retreat of the Post-War Order
Author: Richard Cohen
Year Published: 1989
Publisher: Praeger
New York

SECTION 12

RESEARCH CENTERS

A number of universities throughout the United States have research centers and resources that may be useful for business executives who are searching for information that is crucial for their business activities in the Soviet Union and Eastern Europe. Some of the universities maintain specialized libraries with English language and original Russian language sources.

Business executives should consider these research centers as yet another source of information, as well as a possible source for new staff, as a greater number of students graduate with an emphasis on Soviet economics, political, cultural training, and have completed preparatory work that is useful for companies trading with the Soviets. This section lists many of the research centers that are active in U.S.-Soviet trade and relations.

Center for Russian and East European Studies
University of Michigan
Lane Hall
Ann Arbor, MI 48109
Phone: (313) 764-0351
Contact: Don K. Rowney
Services: The Center offers joint degrees between Russian and East European Studies and Business Administration, Journalism, Law, and Public Policy. The Center also has special programs in Armenian, Polish, and Ukrainian studies. The Center is currently developing a program dealing with U.S.-Soviet trade and also conducts seminars on selected issues related to doing business in the Soviet Union.

Center for International Business and Trade
Georgetown University
1242 35th Street, Suite 501
Washington, DC 20057
Phone: (202) 687-6993
FAX: (202) 687-4031
Services: The Center publishes a newsletter with Atlantic Information Services, "Business Opportunities in Eastern Europe."

Center for Foreign Policy Development
Brown University
Box 1948
Providence, RI 02912
Phone: (401) 863-3465

FAX: (401) 274-8440
Telex: 3792135 CFPD
Contact: Dr. Alan Sherr, Associate
Director
Services: The Center has a Project
on Soviet Foreign Economic Policy
and International Security, which is
active in U.S.-Soviet trade. CFPD
publishes a series of conference
papers on "Superpower Commerce,"
as well as a joint venture briefing
paper series. The Center maintains
a database on Soviet-Western joint
ventures and trade agreements.

Center for East-West Trade Policy
University of Georgia
204 Baldwin Hall
Athens, GA 30602
Phone: (404) 542-2985
Contact: Dr. Gary Bertsch and Dr.
Martin J. Hillenbrand
Services: The Center is a policy-
oriented research institution studying
various aspects of East-West
economic relations. The Center
organizes seminars, conferences, and
workshops on various trade issues. In
addition, the Center conducts
research for other organizations.

**Center on East-West Trade,
Investment and Communication**
Duke University
2114 Campus Drive
Durham, NC 27706
Phone: (919) 684-5551
Contact: Dr. Jerry Hough

Services: The Center examines
issues related to business with the
Soviet Union and all East European
countries. The Center has post-
doctoral and other scholarly
programs.

**Center for the Study of Joint
Ventures**
SUNY Plattsburgh
Redcay Hall
Plattsburgh, NY 12901
Phone: (518) 564-4190
Contact: Dr. M. Zubaidur Rahman,
Director
Services: The Center conducts
research on Soviet trade and
investment issues with particular
focus on accounting, management,
and regulations concerning joint
ventures. In addition, the Center has
formal agreements with the following
organizations in the Soviet Union for
undertaking joint research and for
conducting conferences in the
U.S.S.R. and the U.S. on joint
ventures: Center for the Study of
Joint Ventures; faculty of Economics,
Moscow State University; Plekhanov
Institute of National Economy in
Moscow; and the All-Union Center
for Study and Development of Joint
Ventures of the All-Union
Federation of Trade Unions for Joint
Ventures in the U.S.S.R.

**Esalen Institute on Soviet-American
Relations**
3105 Washington Street

San Francisco, CA 94115
Phone: (415) 563-4731
FAX: (415) 931-0915
Telex: 4931349 ESAL SU
Contact: Dulce Murphy, Director
Services: The Institute sponsors an exchange program which develops projects in the fields of economics, politics, science, health, sports, psychology, philosophy, and literature. The program strives to create interactions between leading Soviets and Americans. The Institute also organizes a number of internship and training programs in the U.S. and Soviet Union.

Hoover Institution on War, Revolution and Peace
Stanford University
Stanford, CA 94305-2323
Phone: (415) 723-2300

Institute for Sino-Soviet Studies
The George Washington University
6th Floor
2130 H Street, NW
Washington, DC 20052
Phone: (202) 994-6340
Contact: James R. Millar, Director
Services: The Institute develops and promotes graduate education and comprehensive research programs in Russian-Soviet, East European, and East Asian studies. The Institute operates the Sino-Soviet Information Center, a specialized library with extensive collections on the Soviet

Union, Eastern Europe, and East Asia. Generally, researchers may make on-site use of the holdings without special permission. SSIC receives a number of very useful periodicals, both Chinese and Soviet. The phone number is (202) 994-7105.

Joseph H. Lauder Institute of Management and International Studies
The Wharton School of the University of Pennsylvania
102 Vance Hall
Philadelphia, PA 19104-6361
Phone: (215) 898-6182
Services: Joint degree programs with the University of Pennsylvania and the Johns Hopkins School of Advanced International Studies (SAIS) offer management education combined with grounding in language and business culture of the Soviet Union.

Library of Congress
10 1st Street, SE
Washington, DC 20540
Phone: (202) 287-5000
European Reading Room
Reading Room: Al Graham, Grant Harris
Services: Despite the wealth of specialized resources available elsewhere on Soviet business and trade, the Library of Congress remains a leading source of information on the Soviet Union.

197

Slavic holdings approach one million items and the Library receives approximately 20,000 titles per year from the Soviet Union. A good starting point for researchers is the European Reading Room, which can provide brochures on the various facilities, services, holdings, and publications of the Library, which relate to the Soviet Union.

National Council for Soviet and East European Research
1755 Massachusetts Ave.
Suite 304
Washington, DC 20036
Phone: (202) 387-0168
Contact: Robert H. Randolph
Services: The Council receives federal money which it then awards to individuals for post-doctoral research.

Russian and East European Center
University of Illinois at Champaign-Urbana
1208 West California Avenue
Urbana, IL 61801
Phone: (217) 333-1244

Russian Research Center (RRC)
Harvard University
1737 Cambridge Street
Cambridge, MA 02138
Phone: (617) 495-4037
Contact: Marshall Goldman, Associate Director

Services: The Russian Research Center holds conferences several times a year on joint ventures and other business topics. The RRC also publishes a handbook of companies involved in joint ventures and a monthly newsletter for $25 a year subscription.

Russian and East European Studies Program
University of Washington/Seattle
DR-05
Seattle, WA 98195
Phone: (206) 436-0250

School of Advanced International Studies
The Johns Hopkins University
1740 Massachusetts Ave., NW
Washington, DC 20036
Phone: (202) 663-5700

Ukrainian Research Institute
Harvard University
1583 Massachusetts Ave.
Cambridge, MA 02138
Phone: (617) 495-4053
FAX: (617) 495-8097
Services: Harvard's Ukrainian Research Institute has reciprocal relations with counterpart organizations in the Ukraine. Although the Center does not focus on business issues, the staff and the unique holdings of the center may be of use to entrepreneurs investigating

business opportunities in the
Ukraine.

**W. Averell Harriman Institute for
Advanced Study of the Soviet Union**
Columbia University
420 W. 118th Street
12th Floor, IAB
New York, NY 10027
Phone: (212) 854-4623
Contact: Douglas A. Evans, Program
Coordinator

SECTION 13

NONPROFIT ORGANIZATIONS

Companies and government agencies are not the only ones focusing on U.S.-Soviet trade. A variety of public service organizations also have it on their agenda, each with a particular angle.[1]

The Foundation For Citizen Diplomacy creates new U.S.-Soviet sister city programs, including trade components, as well as new U.S.-Soviet sister state programs, also including trade components. The Slepak Foundation advocates that human rights should be a priority in U.S.-Soviet trade and has developed the "Slepak Principles," seven principles that American companies are asked to adhere to when trading with the Soviet Union. The Geonomics Institute organizes conferences and workshops on U.S.-Soviet trade. The Massachusetts Soviet Trade Council holds regular breakfasts with speakers as a way of promoting the improvement of business conditions with the Soviet Union.

American Committee on U.S.-Soviet Relations
109 Eleventh Street, SE
Washington, DC 20003
Phone: (202) 546-1700
Contact: Margaret Chapman, Director U.S.-U.S.S.R. Trade Program
Services: The Committee is a nonpartisan, nonprofit, educational organization established in 1974 to strengthen public understanding of U.S.-Soviet relations by providing accurate information and informed, expert analyses. The Committee's programs deal with a broad range of issues between the two countries, including trade and economics, arms control and the military, the environment, and cultural and scientific exchanges. The Committee's "Forum on U.S.-Soviet Trade" brings together senior figures from the private sector, the government, academia, and the news media for exploration of the economic and political issues that affect the expansion of trade with the Soviet Union. The findings from these sessions--luncheon meetings, seminars, conferences, and briefings--provide an informed basis for policy proposals in the national interest.

---

[1]Some of the information for this section was contributed by ISAR, (The Institute for Soviet-American Relations), Washington, DC.

American Enterprise Institute for Public Policy Research
1150 17th Street, NW
Washington, DC 20036
Phone: (202) 862-5800
FAX: (202) 862-7178
Contact: Paul Vizza
Services: The Institute is a research and educational organization which performs analysis of national and international issues. It commissions studies in areas including foreign policy and international economics.

American Council of Learned Societies
800 Third Avenue
New York, NY 10022
Phone: (212) 888-1759
Services: The Council administrates post-doctoral grants in East European studies.

American Center for International Leadership (ACIL)
401 East Pratt Street, Suite 2415
World Trade Center
Baltimore, MD 21202
Phone: (301) 539-2245
Contact: Donna Veatch, Vice President for Programs
Services: The principle aim of the Center is the development of international understanding among individuals who have or will assume positions of responsibility at the local, national, and global levels. ACIL seeks to realize this aim by organizing leadership conferences in which emerging and established American leaders can meet with and conduct professional discussions with counterparts in other countries. Sponsor of the U.S.-U.S.S.R. Emerging Leaders Summit Program and the U.S.-U.S.S.R. Leadership Conference Program (continuation of the Chautauqua citizens diplomacy process).

American Association of Exporters and Importers (AAEI)
11 W. 42nd Street
New York, NY 10036
Phone: (212) 944-2230
FAX: (212) 382-2606
Contact: Eugene Milosh, President (formerly Vice-President of Operations, U.S.-U.S.S.R. Trade & Economic Council)
Services: The Association, founded in 1921, provides 1200 member firms with information on trade regulations, legislation and international developments affecting business through weekly and quarterly publications. AAEI also testifies before Congress and other levels of government to address trade restrictions and problems. Membership consists of multinational, medium- and small-size firms active in trading with PRC, Eastern Europe, and the U.S.S.R., especially consumer products and smaller enterprises such as textiles and apparel, footwear, toys, food products, chemicals and electronics.

202

Association of Joint Ventures, International Unions, and Organizations
2-y Novopodmoskovnyy Per., 4
125130 Moscow
Phone: 943-00-85, 159-01-47
Contact: Lev I. Weinberg, Chairman

Brookings Institution
1775 Massachusetts Avenue, NW
Washington, DC 20036
Phone: (202) 797-6000
FAX: (202) 797-6004
Contact: Ed Hewett, Senior Fellow
Services: The Institution is a nonpartisan organization involved in education, research, and publishing in areas including foreign policy, government, and economics.

Center for International Policy
Room 500
1755 Massachusetts Avenue, NW
Washington, DC 20036
Phone: (202) 232-3317
Services: The Center studies the impact of U.S. policy on human rights and social-economic conditions, primarily in the Third World.

Chamber of Commerce and Industry of the United States of America
U.S. Chamber of Commerce
1615 H Street, NW
Washington DC 20062
Phone: (202) 463-5482

Services: The U.S. Chamber of Commerce is a service organization which represents all U.S. industry and promotes U.S. exports.

Citizen Exchange Council
12 W. 31st Street
New York, NY 10001-4415
Phone: (212) 643-1985
FAX: (212) 643-1996
Telex: 4900001648 CEC UI
Contact: Michael C. Brainerd, Ph.D., President
Services: Founded in 1962, the Citizen Exchange Council (CEC) is a not-for-profit, nonpartisan cultural exchange organization devoted to fostering communication and cooperation between American and Soviet citizens. Understanding that Soviet cultural and historical contexts are crucial for maximizing business opportunities in the new Soviet Union, CEC can provide orientation seminars and educational travel programs for employees of American companies interested in gaining a deeper understanding of the current social, political, and economic environment in the Soviet Union. Consulting and facilitating services are available to American and Soviet businesses interested in publicizing their joint ventures by sponsoring cultural exchange projects. CEC's travel programs and conferences feature intense person-to-person interaction and professional dialogue

203

for a wide range of participants, including state legislators, religious and community leaders, journalists, filmmakers, artists, and students.

Council on International Educational Exchange (CIEE)
205 E. 42nd Street
New York, NY 10017
Phone: (212) 661-1414
FAX: (212) 972-3231
Telex: 423227/6730395
Contact: Adele Donchenko, Chairperson
Services: The Council assumes important educational responsibilities and develops, facilitates, and administers programs of international educational exchange throughout the world on behalf of its constituencies.

The Foundation for Citizen Diplomacy, Inc.
1155 Connecticut Avenue, NW
Suite 500
Washington DC 20036
Phone: (202) 467-8587
FAX: (202) 452-8654
Telex: 4933729 WASH UI
Contact: William S. Loiry, President
Services: The Foundation creates new U.S.-Soviet sister city programs, including trade components, as well as new U.S.-Soviet sister state programs, including trade components.

Geonomics Institute
14 Hillcrest Avenue
Middlebury, VT 05753
Phone: (802) 388-9619
FAX: (802) 388-9627
Contact: Michael P. Claudon, President
Services: The private, nonprofit Institute specializes in developing solutions to practical business and economic problems in the Soviet Union and Eastern Europe. Through business seminars and workshops, Geonomics brings together small multilateral groups of business people, researchers, and policy makers to develop policy and program recommendations. Recent projects include: a joint U.S.-Soviet draft of a foreign investment law for the Russian Republic; recommendations to develop commercial banking and capital markets in the Soviet Union; an analysis of the opportunities for Western business in German reunification and privatization in Hungary, Poland, and Czechoslovakia; an agricultural training program for the Soviet Union using family-sized farms as the development model.

Institute for Security and Cooperation in Outer Space
1336 A Corcoran Street, NW
Washington, DC 20009
Phone: (202) 462-8887

FAX: (202) 462-3576
Contact: Connie Van Pratt
Services: The Institute is a nonpartisan organization promoting international cooperation in outer space research and development.

Institute for Soviet-American Relations (ISAR)
1601 Connecticut Avenue, NW
Washington, DC 20009
Phone: (202) 387-3034
Contact: Eliza Klose
Services: ISAR's goal is to improve U.S.-Soviet relations through improved communications. The Institute publishes the journal Soviet-American Relations and the Handbook on Organizations Involved in Soviet-American Relations; the 1990 issue is now available.

InterCultura
3327 W. 7th Street
Fort Worth, TX 76107
Phone: (817) 332-4691
FAX: (817) 877-4205
Contact: Gordon Dee Smith, President
Services: U.S.-U.S.S.R. Museum exhibition exchange program.

Kennan Institute for Advanced Russian Studies
370 L'Enfant Promenade, SW
Suite 704
Washington, DC 20024-2518

Phone: (202) 287-3400
FAX: (202) 287-3772
Contact: Blair Ruble, Director

Lawyers Alliance for World Security (LAWS)
[formerly Lawyers Alliance for Nuclear Arms Control, Inc.]
1120 19th Street, NW
Suite 615
Washington, DC 20036
Phone: (202) 296-6054
FAX: (202) 296-6049
Contact: Elizabeth Lyman, Executive Director
Services: The Lawyers Alliance sponsors educational seminars, exchanges, and conferences for U.S. and Soviet legislators, lawyers, and law professors on current topics of legislative process and procedure, Soviet legal developments (including trade law), constitutional and international law, and arms control policy and law. It is a national, nonprofit membership organization.

Massachusetts Soviet Trade Council
31 Kidder Avenue
Sommerville, MA 02144
Phone: (617) 628-9297
Contact: Carol J. Madsen, Vice President - Marketing
Services: The MSTC is a trade association which promotes improvement in business conditions in the Soviet Union and increasing East/West trade. The Council has co-hosted two annual conferences

"Doing Business with the Soviet Union" and sponsors American Soviet Trade Breakfasts designed to educate business people and promote networking among those interested in doing business in the U.S.S.R. and Central Europe. Trade missions are planned. A data base is being developed. A newsletter and corporate and individual memberships are available.

Meridian House International
1630 Crescent Place, NW
Washington, DC 20009
Phone: (202) 667-6800
FAX: (202) 667-1475
Contact: Nancy Matthews, Director, Public Affairs
Services: The organization is dedicated to promoting intercultural exchange programs. Its programs include the Washington International Center, the National Council for International Visitors Information, and the Visitors Program Service.

National Foreign Trade Council
1625 K Street, NW
Washington DC 20006
Phone: (202) 887-0278
FAX: (202) 452-8160
Contact: Frank D. Kittredge, President
Services: The Council was founded in 1914 by a group of U.S. industrial companies engaged in international trade and investment. The Council's membership now consists of just under 500 U.S. manufacturing corporations, financial institutions, and other U.S. firms having substantial international operations or interests. The fundamental goal of the Council is to develop policies reflecting the interests and consensus of the Council members, expand exports, protect U.S. foreign investment, enhance the competitiveness and profitability of U.S. industry, and promote and maintain a fair and equitable international trading system.

National Impact
100 Maryland Avenue, NE
Suite 502
Washington, DC 20002
Phone: (202) 544-8636
Services: National Impact is a legislative information organization sponsored by national church groups.

National Council of World Affairs Organization
1619 Massachusetts Avenue, NW
Washington, DC 20036
Phone: (202) 663-5950

New England Soviet Trade Council
P.O. Box 60
Boston, MA 02130
Phone: (617) 524-5454
Contact: Gerald Wright, President
Services: The New England Soviet Trade Council (NESTC) is a business

education program of the Boston/Kiev Sister City Association, Inc. Its purpose is to promote understanding between government and business entities in the Soviet Union and the United States. The NESTC has sponsored four annual conferences on doing business in the Soviet Union and Eastern Europe.

Organization for American-Soviet Exchanges, DC (OASES-DC)
1430 K Street, NW, Suite 1200
Washington, DC 20005
Phone: (202) 393-0985
FAX: (202) 393-0989
Telex: 6503291788 MCI UW; 6976209 OASES UW
Contact: Rudy D'Alessandro, Executive Director
Services: OASES-DC is a nongovernmental, nonprofit U.S. organization which facilitates professional, educational, and cultural exchanges on a mutual basis between peoples of the United States and the Soviet Union. Its activities include conferences; organizing travel for Americans to the Soviet Union; hosting Soviet citizens in the United States; arranging bilateral exchanges between counterparts in the United States and Soviet Union; and interpreting and translating services. OASES operates primarily on a fee-for-services basis.

People to People
Citizen Ambassador Program
Dwight D. Eisenhower Building
Spokane, WA 99202
Phone: (509) 534-0430
FAX: (509) 534-5245
Telex: 326328
Contact: Mr. K. Raymond Schoedel, Executive Director
Services: The organization sponsors a variety of delegations to the Soviet Union, which can include trade delegations. Although the Citizen Ambassador Program is affiliated with People to People International, they are structurally different, with the former a for-profit firm and the latter a nonprofit organization.

Slepak Foundation
230 S. 15th Street
Suite 300
Philadelphia, PA 19102
Phone: (215) 545-1098
FAX: (215) 893-0462
Contact: Steven L. Carter
Services: The Foundation advocates the position that human rights should be a priority in any exchange between the U.S. and the Soviet Union. Specifically regarding U.S.-Soviet trade, the Foundation has developed the "Slepak Principles," seven principles that American companies are asked to adhere to when trading with the Soviet Union.

U.S.-Ukraine Trade and Economic Council
New York - Princeton Office
P.O. Box 20347, Columbus Circle Station
New York, NY 10023-9991 USA
Phone: (609) 259-2754
Telex: 173 206 EXEC
FAX: (609) 588-4643
Contact: Dr. George Loguseh, Chairman
Services: The Council, known as AMUTEC represents leading banks, enterprises, and government organizations in Ukraine, for trade and investment opportunities with US counterparts.

U.S.-U.S.S.R. Trade and Economic Council Inc.
in New York:
805 Third Avenue
New York, NY 10022
Phone: (212) 644-4550
FAX: (212) 752-0889
Telex: 425053 U.S.S.R. UI
in Moscow:
3 Shevchenko Embankment
Moscow 121248
Phone: 243-5470
FAX: 230-2467
Telex: 871-413212 ASREC SU
Contact: Bill Forrester, Director (NY); Vladislav L. Malkevich, U.S.S.R. Co-chairman
Services: The Council concerns itself with the dual responsibility of general market development and individual trade facilitation for members. Through a bi-national Board of Directors and membership, it works to develop and implement new business projects. It provides a range of services for members through its New York and Moscow offices.

World Trade Center Washington DC (WTCW)
1101 King Street
Suite 700
Alexandria, VA 22314
Phone: (703) 684-6630
FAX: (703) 684-2918
Telex: 5106004086 WTC WASH
Contact: Kathleen Durkin
Services: Members of WTCW have access to a computerized international buyer-seller information network, databases on trade and investment opportunities, office support services, an international trade library, consultant services, seminars and conferences, and reciprocal membership services at World Trade Centers globally, including WTC in Moscow.

SECTION 14

CONFERENCES, SEMINARS, & EXHIBITIONS

Conferences and seminars on U.S.-Soviet trade are an excellent way of gaining timely information and insights into the intricacies of doing business in the Soviet Union. They also offer opportunities for networking with specialists in the field.

Some seminars are general and cover a wide range of topics, such as The Florida Conference on Trade and Investment with the Soviet Union & Eastern Europe held in Tampa in October, 1990. Others focus on specific industries or issues.

Trade shows are held frequently in the Soviet Union and provide opportunities to learn about the Soviet market and customer environment, advertise your products and services, and meet with prospective buyers or partners. Trade exhibitions are sponsored by Soviet organizations, usually Expocenter, as well as by Western organizations.

This section includes a listing of organizations that routinely sponsor and/or organize seminars and exhibits. For this year's events, contact them directly.

AMERICAN TRADE EXHIBIT AND CONFERENCE ORGANIZERS

American Exhibition Services International, Inc.
801 Chase Ave., Unit 1
Elk Grove Village, IL 60007
Mailing Address
P.O. Box 66373
Chicago, IL 60666
Phone: (708) 593-2462

Argus Trading, Ltd
6110 Executive Blvd.
Suite 502
Rockville, MD 20852

Center for International Cooperation
2601 Elliott Avenue
Suite 5146
Seattle, Washington 98121
Phone: (206) 728-1546
FAX: (206) 728-1563
Contact: Norman Swanson, President
Description: Primary focus is to establish a network of international associations to promote international understanding and cooperation.

Construction, Marketing & Trading, Inc.
8150 Leesburg Pike
Suite 2100
Vienna, VA 22180

Design and Production, Inc.
7110 Rainwater Pl.
Lorton, VA 22079
Phone: (703) 550-8640

"Expocentr" USSR CCI
107113 Moscow
Sokolnichesky val, 1a
Telex: 411185 EXPO SU

Glahe International
1700 K St., NW
Washington, DC 20006-3624
Phone: (202) 659-4557
(202) 457-0776
Attn: Peter McKenna

Global Trading Associates, Inc.
1155 Connecticut Avenue, NW
Suite 500
Washington, DC 20036
Phone: (202) 467-8589
FAX: (202) 452-8654
Contact: William S. Loiry

Robert Schwartz & Associates
5402 S. Dorchester #2
Chicago, IL 60615
Phone: (312) 947-8179
FAX: (312) 643-0923

Scott European Corp.
58 E. State St.
Montpelier, VT 05602

CONFERENCE SPONSORS

American Center for International Leadership
522 Franklin Street
Columbus, Indiana 47201
Phone: (812) 376-3456
Contact: Donna Brown, Vice President for Programs

American Committee on U.S.-Soviet Relations
Trade Forums
109 Eleventh St, SE
Washington DC 20003
Phone: (202) 546-1700
Contact: Margaret Chapman, Forum Director

APCO Associates
Suite 1000
1155 21st St,, NW
Washington, DC 20036
Phone: (202) 778-1000
Contact: Bronwyn Hughs

ASET Consultants, Inc.
8350 Greensboro Dr.
Suite 805
McLean, VA 22102
Phone: (703) 790-1922
Contact: Randall Morgan

BLOC Magazine
350 Broadway, Suite 1205
New York, NY 10013
Phone: (212) 966-0655
Contact: Richard Fuchs

Brown University
Center for Policy development
Box 1948
Providence, RI 02912
Phone: (401) 863-3465
Contact: Alan Sherr

Center for the Study of Joint
Ventures
SUNY Plattsburg
Redcay Hall
Plattsburg, NY 12901
Phone: (518) 564-4190

Geonomics Institute
P.O. Box 682
Middlebury Vermont 05753-9952
Phone: (201) 388-9619

Global Trading Associates, Inc.
1155 Connecticut Ave., NW
Suite 500
Washington, DC 20036
Phone: (202) 467-8589
Contact: William S. Loiry

Harvard University
Russian Research Center
1737 Cambridge St.
Cambridge, MA 02138
Phone: (617) 495-4037
Contact: Marshall Goldman

Harvard Ukrainian Research Center
1583 Massachusetts Ave
Cambridge, MA 02138
Phone: (617) 495-4053

International Executive Reports
717 D St., NW Suite 300
Washington DC 20004-2807
Phone: (301) 983-3149
(202) 628-6618
Contact: Mary Saba

PlanEcon, Inc.
1111 14th St., NW
Suite 801
Washington, DC 20005-5603
Phone: (202) 898-0471

Price Waterhouse
Southwark Towers
32 London Bridge St.
London SE1 9SY
Phone: (1) 407-8989

University of Michigan
Center for Russian & East European
Studies
Lane Hall
Ann Arbor, MI 48109
Phone: (313) 764-0351

APPENDIX 1

SELECTED LIST OF REGISTERED U.S.-SOVIET JOINT VENTURES[1]

Alba Inc.
Joint Venture: Alba
Registration No.: 765
Date of Registration: August 4, 1989
U.S. Partner: Alba Inc.
U.S. Investment: 880,000 rubles
JV Activity: Consumer goods

Alex Import-Export
Joint Venture: Sovamtekstil'
Registration No.: 831
Date of Registration: August 17, 1989
U.S. Partner: Alex Import-Export
U.S. Investment: 600,000 rubles
JV Activity: Consumer goods

American Laboratories
Joint Venture: Mono-Al
Registration No.: 393
Date of Registration: April 20, 1989
Location: Ul. Moskovskaya, 326 Riga 226065 Latvian SSR
Phone: 26-88-11
Telex: 161149
Partners: Cooperative "Mono" (U.S.S.R., 40%), American Laboratories, Inc. (U.S. 60%)
U.S. Partner: American Laboratories
U.S. Investment: 1.28 million rubles
JV Activity: Condoms, syringes, baby care products

American General Resources
Joint Venture: Interscrap
Registration No.: 183
Date of Registration: December 28, 1988
Location: Four shipping and fisheries organizations (U.S.S.R. 51%), American General Resources (U.S. 49%)
U.S. Partner: American General Resources
U.S. Investment: 30,000 rubles
JV Activity: Ship scrapping and sales of scrap and used equipment

---

[1]Many of the addresses of the U.S. firms with registered joint ventures were provided by Alan Sherr of the Center for Policy Development, Brown University. The Center maintains a database of registered joint ventures in the Soviet Union.

Amex Import-Export
Joint Venture: Adan
Registration No.: 387
Date of Registration: April 17, 1989
Location: Sumgait, Azerbaizhan
Partners: "Avtozapchast" Factory and "Glans" Cooperative
(U.S.S.R. 40%), Amex Import-Export (U.S. 60%)
U.S. Partner: Amex Import-Export
1320 Dakar St.
Elizabeth, NJ 07201
Phone: (212) 964-7460
U.S. Investment: 2.1 million rubles
JV Activity: Consumer goods production, import-export operations

Amsovinvest
Joint Venture: Amsovinvest
Registration No.: 363
Date of Registration: March 31, 1989
Location: Moscow
Partners: Komosomol Central Committee and three others
(U.S.S.R., 75%), Amsovinvest (U.S., 25%)
U.S. Partner: Amsovinvest
U.S. Investment: 300,000 rubles
JV Activity: Electronic products manufacture

Ansat
Joint Venture: Literari Gazett International
Registration No.: 691
Date of Registration: July 5, 1989
U.S. Partner: Ansat

U.S. Investment: 430,000 rubles
JV Activity: Printing

APCO Associates
Joint Venture: MOST
Registration No.: 474
Date of Registration: May 24, 1989
Location: Ul. Pyatnitskaya 13/21 str 2, Moscow 103009
Partners: "Infeks" (U.S.S.R., 50%), APCO
(U.S., 50%)
U.S. Partner: APCO Associates
The Arnold Porter Consulting Group
1155 21st St., NW
Washington, DC 20036
Phone: (202) 778-1057
FAX: (202) 331-9832
U.S. Investment: Information, consulting, and intermediary services
JV Activity: 300,000 rubles

Aricard, Inc.
Joint Venture: Sinergiya-Internzinya
Registration No.: 878
Date of Registration: September 1, 1989
U.S. Partner: Aricard Inc.
JV Activity: Printing

Astra Consulting International
Joint Venture: Interdizain
Registration No.: 433
Date of registration: May 10, 1989
U.S. Partner: Astra Consulting

International
U.S. Investment: 60,000 rubles
JV Activity: Personal Computers

Atlantica, DG Electronic Contractor
Joint Venture: Tais Sport
Registration No.: 839
Date of Registration: August 22, 1989
U.S. Partner: Atlantica, DG Electronic Contractor
U.S. Investment: 20,000 rubles
JV Activity: Medical goods

Berusa
Registration No.: 411
Date of Registration: April 27, 1989
U.S. Partner: Berusa
2125 Center Ave., Suite 1034
Fort Lee, NJ 07024
U.S. Investment: 50,000 rubles
JV Activity: Personal computers

Berusa
Joint Venture: Interlink
Registration No.: 284
Date of Registration: March 2, 1989
Location: Shosse Entusiastov, 62 Moscow
Partners: "Lechenie i Konsultatsiya" Cooperative (U.S.S.R. 49%), Berusa (U.S. 49%)
U.S. Partner: Berusa
2125 Center Ave.
Suite 1034
Fort Lee, NJ 07024

U.S. Investment: 250,000 rubles
JV Activity: Medical diagnostics, production and sale of medical goods

Berusa
Joint Venture: Intersignal
Registration No.: 401
Date of Registration: April 21, 1989
Location: Shosse Narva, 28 Tallin
Partners: Association "Estagrostroy" (U.S.S.R., 52%), Berusa (U.S., 24%), Zig (West Berlin, 24%)
U.S. Partner: Berusa
2125 Center Ave., Suite 1034
Fort Lee, NJ 07024
U.S. Investment: 375,000 rubles
JV Activity: Chemicals, construction

Brownstone Production
Joint Venture: ASC
Registration No.: 287
Date of Registration: March 6, 1989
Location: Ul. Vasilyevskaya, 13 Moscow
Partners: Union of Cinematographers (U.S.S.R., 51%), Brownstone Productions (U.S., 49%)
U.S. Partner: Brownstone Productions
U.S. Investment: 25,000 rubles
JV Activity: Production and sale of movies, videos, animated films; production and marketing

Carlisle Syntec Systems
Registration No.: 509
Date of Registration: May 29, 1989
Location: Moscow
Partners: Production Organization "Soyuzpromstroykomplekt" (U.S.S.R., 51%), Carlisle Syntec Systems (U.S., 49%)
U.S. Partner: Carlisle Syntec Systems
P.O. Box 7000
Carlisle, PA 17013
Cincinnati, OH
U.S. Investment: 23.6 million rubles
JV Activity: Roofing and insulation materials

Classic Overseas Cyprus
Joint Venture: Esperanto
Registration No.: 621
Date of Registration: June 16, 1989
U.S. Partner: Classic Overseas Cyprus
U.S. Investment: 110,000 rubles
JV Activity: Consumer goods

Columbus
Joint Venture: Romos
Registration No.: 400
Date of Registration: April 21, 1989
Location: Staropanski Pereulok
Partners: U.S.S.R., 55%, UK (15%), FRG (15%), Columbus (U.S., 15%) *U.S. Partner:* Columbus
U.S. Investment: 370,000 rubles
JV Activity: Entertainment center

organization and operation

Combustion Engineering
Joint Venture: Tobolsk
Partners: Combustion Engineering Inc.,
U.S.; Neste OY, Finland
U.S. Partner: Combustion Engineering,(15%) 900 Long Ridge Rd.
Stamford, CT 06902
Phone: (203) 329-8771
U.S. Investment: $2,000,000,000
JV Activity: Production of polypropylene and butadiene-styrene elastomer

Combustion Engineering
Joint Venture: PRIS
Registration No.: 013
Date of Registration: November 26, 1987
Location: Moscow
Partners: Nyeftekhimavtomatika (U.S.S.R., 51%)
U.S. Partner: Combustion Engineering (U.S., 49%)
900 Long Ridge Rd.
Stamford, CT 06902
Phone: (203) 329-8771
U.S. Investment: 500 million rubles
JV Activity: Technology for oil refining and chemical processing

Considar Project Development
Registration No.: 423
Date of Registration: May 3, 1989
U.S. Partner: Considar Project Development

630 Third Ave.
New York, NY 10017
U.S. Investment: 3 million rubles
JV Activity: Waste oil recycling

Considar Project Engineering
Location: 1318 Beacon St.
Suite 7
Brookline, MA 02146
Joint Venture: Laiks
Registration No.: 065
Date of Registration: July 6, 1988
Partners: (617) 731-0200
Soviet Partners: Institute of
Electronics
and Computer Technology of the
Latvian Academy of Sciences,
Council of Ministers of the Latvian
SSR, (U.S.S.R., 75%); Considar
Project
Engineering (U.S., 25%)
Phone: (617) 439-5396
FAX: (617) 439-5396
U.S. Investment: 100,000 rubles

Cook Products International
Joint Venture: Stik
Registration No.: 626
Date of Registration: June 20, 1989
U.S. Partner: Cook Products
International
15 West Strong St., Suite 10A
Pensacola, FL 32501
U.S. Investment: 140,000 rubles
JV Activity: U.S. investment; toys,
trading

Crystalltec International, Inc.
Joint Venture: Intertest
Registration No.: 529

Date of Registration: June 1, 1989
Location: Tzvetnoi Blvd, 2
Moscow 103051
Partners: U.S.S.R., 50%;
Crystalltec (U.S., 50%)
U.S. Partner: Crystalltec
International, Inc.
13 Murray St.
New York, NY 10017
U.S. Investment: 50,000 rubles
JV Activity: Computer services

Dentsply International
Joint Venture: Stomadent
Registration No.: 793
Date of registration: August 9,
1989
U.S. Partner: Dentsply
International
570 W. College Ave.
York, PA 17405
U.S. Investment: 940,000 rubles
JV Activity: Dental fillings

Douglas Production International
Joint Venture: Start
Registration No.: 497
Date of Registration: May 29, 1989
Location: Ul. Druzhnikovskaya 15
Moscow 123376
Partners: Union of
Cinematographers and two others
(U.S.S.R., 60%), Douglas
Production International (U.S.,
40%)
U.S. Partner: Douglas Production
International
U.S. Investment: 40,000 rubles
JV Activity: Printing, publishing,
advertising

217

Dresser Industries
Joint Venture: Dresser Soviet Engineering
Registration No.: 147
Date of Registration: December 2, 1988
Location: 1 Ul. Lunacharskovo 7 Floor 6, Apt 16/17, Moscow
Partners: Scientific production association "Bolshevik: and Kazankompressormash, FTO "Soyuzkhimexport" (U.S.S.R., 60%), Dresser Industries (U.S., 40%)
U.S. Partner: Dresser Industries 1505 Elm St., Dallas TX 75221
Phone: (214) 740-6000; Moscow 203-0055
U.S. Investment: 150,000 rubles
JV Activity: Engineering

East-West Arts & Entertainment
Joint Venture: XXX-Arts
Registration No.: 478
Date of Registration: May 24, 1989
Location: Prospekt Rustaveli, 27 Tbilisi 380008
Partners: "Rustaveli" Association (U.S.S.R., 50%), East-West Arts & Entertainment Group (U.S., 50%)
U.S. Partner: East-West Arts & Entertainment
U.S. Investment: 30,000 rubles
JV Activity: Cinema, concerts, video products

Economic Development Partners Corporation
Registration No.: 627
Date of Registration: June 20, 1989

U.S. Partner: Economic Development Partners Corporation
U.S. Investment: 23.8 million rubles
JV Activity: Construction

Elan International
Joint Venture: Solavan Aroma
Registration No.: 037
Date of Registration: April 12, 1988
Location: Moscow
Partners: U.S.S.R. Research Institute for Sea Fisheries and Oceanography (U.S.S.R., 80%);
U.S. Partner: Elan International (U.S., 20%)
268 Doremus Ave.
Newark, NJ 07105
Phone: (201) 344-8014

Ergo Group
Joint Venture: Tbilisoft
Registration No.: 281
Date of Registration: March 1, 1989
Location: Ul. Lenina, 77, Tbilisi
Partners: Lenin Polytechnical Institute
(Georgian Republic, U.S.S.R., 75%), Ergo
Group (U.S., 25%)
U.S. Partner: Ergo Group
U.S. Investment: 20,000 rubles
JV Activity: Data processing, software development

Ernst & Young
Joint Venture: Vneshaudit
Location: Moscow

Partners: Vneshconsult
U.S. Partner: Ernst & Young
787 7th Ave.
New York, NY 10019
Phone: (212) 830-6000
JV Activity: Auditing and accounting work,
especially for other joint ventures in Moscow

Eugene Enterprises
Joint Venture: Rantarin
Registration No.: 301
Date of Registration: March 15, 1989
Location: Ul. Tashkentskaya, 22
Khabarovsk 680001
Partners: RFSFR State Agricultural Committee (U.S.S.R., 50%), Eugene Enterprises, Inc. (U.S., 50%)
U.S. Partner: Eugene Enterprises
U.S. Investment: 210,000 rubles
JV Activity: Reindeer horn processing and distribution
Farmingham, MA 01701
U.S. Investment: 180,000 rubles
Information, exhibition organization, consulting

FD Processing and Machinery
Joint Venture: Interpribor
Registration No.: 847
Date of Registration: August 24, 1989
U.S. Partner: FD Processing and Machinery
U.S. Investment: 20,000 rubles
JV Activity: Machine building

Forbes & Co.
Joint Venture: Forbesprogres
Registration No.: 873
Date of Registration: August 31, 1989
U.S. Partner: Forbes & Co.
Homers's Wharf
New Bedford, MA 02740
U.S. Investment: 550,000 rubles
JV Activity: Machine building

Foster Wheeler
Joint Venture: Hi-Tech
Registration No.: 179
Date of Registration: December 28, 1988
Partners: Grozny Petrochemical Scientific Production Association (U.S.S.R., 55%), Foster Wheeler (U.S., 45%)
U.S. Partner: Foster Wheeler
Perryville Corporate Park
Clinton, NJ 08809-4000
Phone: (201) 730-4000
U.S. Investment: 320,000 rubles
JV Activity: Engineering services for the petroleum industry

GJI, Inc.
Joint Venture: Sovamtest
Registration No.: 310
Date of Registration: March 17, 1989
Location: UL Tulinskaya, 27
Moscow
Partners: Central Council of Soviet Inventors Union (U.S.S.R., 51%), GJI (U.S. 49%)
U.S. Partner: GJI, Inc

U.S. Investment: 10,000 rubles
JV Activity: Non-invasive engineering diagnostics

Global Technology Group
Joint Venture: Kvorui
Registration No.: 415
Date of Registration: April 27, 1989
U.S. Partner: Global Technology Group
156 5th Ave.
Suite 1034
New York, NY 10010
Phone: (212) 741-5027
U.S. Investment: 3.35 million rubles
Activity: Personal computers

Global Technology Group
Joint Venture: Spindulis
Registration No.: 282
Date of Registration: March 1, 1989
Location: Kaunas
Partners: Lithuanian Publishing House "Pozhely" (U.S.S.R., 52%), Global Technology (U.S., 48%)
U.S. Partner: Global Technology Group
156 5th Ave. Suite 1034
New York, NY 10010
Phone: (212) 741-5027
U.S. Investment: 5.75 million rubles
JV Activity: Advertising, printing

Great Lakes Paper Company
Joint Venture: Intra-Union

Registration No.: 773
Date of Registration: August 4, 1989
U.S. Partner: Great Lakes Paper Company
308 W. Erie
Chicago, IL 60610
U.S. Investment: 1.26 million rubles
JV Activity: Building materials

Hemisphere Publishing
Joint Venture: Ekoenergetika
Registration No.: 659
Date of Registration: June 27, 1989
U.S. Partner: Hemisphere Publishing
79 Madison Ave.
New York, NY 10016-7892
U.S. Investment: 100,000 rubles

Hemisphere Publishing
Joint Venture: Tempo
Registration No.: 339
Date of Registration: March 27, 1989
Location: Ul. Petra Brovki, 15 Minsk 220728
Partners: Belorussian Academy of Sciences (U.S.S.R., 50%), Hemisphere Publishing (U.S., 50%)
U.S. Partner: Hemisphere Publishing
79 Madison Ave.
New York, NY 10016-7892
Phone: (212) 725-1999
U.S. Investment: $150,000
JV Activity: Scientific publishing

Honeywell Inc. and Honeywell of Austria
Joint Venture: STERH-Avtomatizatsiya
Registration No.: 046
Date of Registration: May 13, 1988
Location: Moscow, Tryokhprudny Per. 11/13, 3rd Floor
Partners: Orgminudobreniya Trust and Experimental Design Office Wineral
(U.S.S.R., 51%)
U.S. Partner: Honeywell Inc., and Honeywell of Austria (49%)
Paul Lomauro, Director, Moscow Office
Honeywell, Inc.
7900 Westpark Drive A521
McLean, VA 22102-4299
Phone: (612) 870-5200; Moscow: 299-6543
TELEX: 290651 HON SU
JV Activity: Production control systems, software development for efficiency improvement

Hudson Street International
Joint Venture: Mebinvest
Registration No.: 514
Date of Registration: May 30, 1989
Location: Ul. Tanevykh 7a Moscow
Partners: State Committee for Inventions and the Sintez Cooperative (U.S.S.R., 60%),
Hudson St. International (U.S., 40%)
U.S. Partner: 90 Hudson St., #7E New York, NY 10017
Phone: (212) 966-7540

FAX: (212) 966-5762
U.S. Investment: 40,000 rubles
JV Activity: Patents and licensing

IDG Communications
Joint Venture: Information Computer Enterprise
Registration No.: 492
Date of Registration: May 26, 1989
Location: Moscow 105826 E-37, Informelektro
Partners: Radio and Communications Publishing House (U.S.S.R., 51%), IDG Communications (U.S., 49%)

Interconcepts
Joint Venture: Intermedbio
Registration No.: 108
Date of Registration: October 10, 1988
Location: Ul. Konyukovskaya, 31 Moscow 123342
Partners: Leningrad Pharmaceutical Production association "Oktyabr" (U.S.S.R., 21%), "Universervis" cooperative (U.S.S.R., 30%), Interconcepts (U.S., 49%)
U.S. Partner: Interconcepts
10 E. 21st St.
New York, NY

International Joint Venture Consultants
Joint Venture: Ekopsi
Registration No.: 779
Date of Registration: August 4, 1989
U.S. Partner: International Joint

Venture Consultants
P.O. Box 1147
Plattsburg, PA 12901
U.S. Investment: 190,000 rubles
JV Activity: Intermediary services

ITI Trading International Inc.
Joint Venture: Khad-Don
Registration No.: 649
Date of Registration: June 23, 1989
U.S. Partner: ITI Trading International Inc.
575 Madison Ave., Suite 1006
New York, NY 10022
U.S. Investment: 4.93 million rubles
JV Activity: Consumer goods, tourism

King Furniture Manufacturing
Joint Venture: King-Paiufakturi Oktuabr'
Registration No.: 651
Date of Registration: June 23, 1989
U.S. Partner: King Furniture Manufacturing
U.S. Investment: 110,000 rubles
JV Activity: Consumer goods

Kofman Equities
Registration No.: 629
Date of Registration: June 20, 1989
U.S. Partner: Kofman Equities
U.S. Investment: 150,000 rubles
JV Activity: Consumer goods

Lotus Trading International
Joint Venture: Fleks International, Ltd.
Registration No.: 761
Date of Registration: August 2, 1989
U.S. Partner: Lotus Trading International
U.S. Investment: 100,000 rubles
JV Activity: Construction

Management Partnerships International, Inc.
Joint Venture: World Dialog
Registration No.: 021
Date of Registration: December 29, 1987
Location: Moscow
Partners: Manufacturing Association
(Kamaz, 32.6%), (IKI, 72%), (CEMI, 13%), (GDVIC, U.S.S.R. Economic Exhibition, 2.6%), (V/O Vneshtechnika, 9.8%)
U.S. Partner: Management Partnerships International, Inc. (U.S., 21.8%) CR&TG
440 South LaSalle St.
33rd Floor
Chicago, IL 60605
Phone: (312) 431-3000
FAX: (312) 431-3089
Pyotr Zrelov, General Director; Jack Byers, General Director
JV Activity: Production and marketing of software products utilizing Soviet computer science expertise.

Marine Resources
Joint Venture: Kamchatka Pacific Company
Registration No.: 335
Date of Registration: March 24, 1989
Location: Vladivostok
Partners: Ministry of the Fishing Industry and the Kolkhoz Union Fishing Association (U.S.S.R., 51%), Marine Resources (U.S., 49%)
U.S. Partner: Marine Resources
4215 21st Ave. West
Room 201
Seattle, WA 98199
Phone: (206) 285-6424
U.S. Investment: 80,000 rubles
JV Activity: Shipbuilding, aquaculture

Matrix Corp.
Joint Venture: Para-Graf
Registration No.: 677
Date of Registration: June 28, 1989
U.S. Partner: Matrix Corp.
U.S. Investment: 300,00 rubles
JV Activity: Personal computers

Metvac
Joint Venture: Intermet Engineering
Registration No.: 317
Date of Registration: March 21, 1989
Location: Leninskiy Prospekt, 4 Moscow
Partners: Moscow Institute of Steel and Alloys and the State Committee for Public Education (U.S.S.R., 50%), Metvac (U.S., 50%)
U.S. Partner: Metvac
U.S. Investment: 340,000 rubles
JV Activity: Metallurgy R&D, licensing

MG Import-Export International
Joint Venture: Soviet Brend
Registration No.: 892
Date of Registration: September 5, 1989
U.S. Partner: MG Import-Export International
U.S. Investment: 50,000 rubles
JV Activity: Intermediary services

Mobile Fidelity Sound
Joint Venture: Art and Electronics
Registration No.: 223
Date of Registration: January 24, 1989
Location: Moscow
Partners: Three Soviet organizations, 50%, Mobile Fidelity Sound Lab (U.S., 50%)
U.S. Partner: Mobile Fidelity Sound
U.S. Investment: 375,000 rubles
JV Activity: Concert promotion, organization

Neva Ltd.
Joint Venture: Bistro
Registration No.: 542
Date of Registration: June 2, 1989

Location: Leningrad
Partners: U.S.S.R., 60%, Neva Ltd.
(U.S., 40%)
U.S. Partner: Neva Ltd.
U.S. Investment: 20,000 rubles
JV Activity: Development and operation of fast food outlets, import-export of non-processed food.

Ogilvy and Mather
Joint Venture: Tisza
Registration No.: 203
Date of Registration: January 12, 1989
Location: Moscow
Partners: U.S.S.R., 65%, Ogilvy and Mather (U.S., 35%)
U.S. Partner: Olgilvy and Mather
309 W. 49th St.
New York, NY 10019
Phone: (212) 237-5813
FAX: (212) 237-5123
U.S. Investment: 150,000 rubles

Ollsten Trading
Joint Venture: PGD
Registration No.: 389
Date of Registration: April 19, 1989
Location: Ul. Amurskaya, 44
Moscow 107241
Partners: Cooperative "Russkaya pchela" (U.S.S.R., 50%), Ollsten Trading Company (U.S., 50%)
U.S. Partner: Ollsten Trading
Los Angeles, CA
U.S. Investment: 10,000 rubles
JV Activity: Software products

Olympian Embroidery
Joint Venture: Olimpiya AMROS
Registration No.: 760
Date of Registration: August 2, 1989
U.S. Partner: Olympian Emroidery
414 W. Pico Blvd.
Los Angeles, CA 90015
U.S. Investment: 250,000 rubles
JV Activity: Consumer goods

P. Citron Trading
Joint Venture: Suvenir Treiding
Registration No.: 709
Date of Registration: July 13, 1989
U.S. Partner: P. Citron Trading
U.S. Investment: 10,000 rubles
JV Activity: Consumer goods

Pen Enterprises
Joint Venture: Ideya
Registration No.: 788
Date of Registration: August 8, 1989
U.S. Partner: Pen Enterprises
U.S. Investment: 150,000 rubles
JV Activity: Personal computers

Perch Electronic
Joint Venture: ASTA
Registration No.: 508
Date of Registration: May 29, 1989
Location: Ul. Belomorskaya, 26
Moscow 125195
Partners: FTO "Vneshagropromexport" (U.S.S.R., 50%), Perch Electronics (U.S., 50%)

U.S. Partner: Perch Electronics
Far Rockaway, NY
U.S. Investment: 1.02 million
rubles
JV Activity: Consumer goods
production

Phargo Information Inc.
Joint Venture: Repko
Registration No.: 883
Date of Registration: September 1,
1989
U.S. Partner: Phargo Information
Inc.
369 Wayside Road
Portola Valley, CA 94028
U.S. Investment: 250,000 rubles
JV Activity: Printing, personal
computers

Phoenix Radiology
Joint Venture: COMED
Registration No.: 240
Date of Registration: February 7,
1989
Location: Ul. Timiryazevskaya 1
Moscow 125422
Partners: Scientific Production
Association "Ekran" (U.S.S.R.,
25%), All Union Research Institute
for Medical Instruments (U.S.S.R.,
25%), Phoenix Radiology (U.S.,
25%)
U.S. Partner: Phoenix Radiology
1100 Glendon, Suite 2045
Los Angeles, CA 90024
Phone: (213) 824-1124
FAX: (213) 824-0675
U.S. Investment: 100,000 rubles
JV Activity: Medical technology.

Polaroid Corporation
Joint Venture: Svetazor
Registration No.: 735
Date of Registration: July 28, 1989
U.S. Partner: Polaroid Corporation
International Business Development
Cambridge, MA 02139
Phone: (617) 577-2000
U.S. Investment: 900,000 rubles
JV Activity: Cameras

R&L International, CC Food Products
Joint Venture: Eri-si-vi Prodakts
International
Registration No.: 843
Date of Registration: August 23,
1989
U.S. Partner: R&L International,
CC Food Products
U.S. Investment: 100,000 rubles
JV Activity: Foodstuffs

Robert A. Weaver
Joint Venture: Inform-Pravo
Registration No.: 116
Date of Registration: November 1,
1988
Location: Ul. Druzhby, 10
Moscow
Partners: Union of Scientific and
Engineering Societies and the
Collegium of Moscow Lawyers
(U.S.S.R., 51%), Robert Weaver
(USA) et. al.
combined total 49%.
U.S. Partner: Robert A. Weaver
U.S. Investment: 20,000 rubles
JV Activity: Management consulting

Ruff Fur Dressing
Joint Venture: ATMPO
Registration No.: 456
Date of Registration: May 17, 1989
Location: Ul. Charigaron 10a
Dushanbe 734005 Tadzhikistan SSR
Partners: Dushambe Leather and
Shoe Factory (U.S.S.R., 50%), Ruff
Fur Dressing (U.S., 50%)
U.S. Partner: Ruff Fur Dressing
251 West 30th St.
New York, NY
U.S. Investment: 720,000
JV Activity: Fur processing,
clothing manufacturer

Sabey Corporation
Joint Venture: SiT
Registration No.: 698
Date of Registration: July 7, 1989
U.S. Partner: Sabey Corporation
U.S. Investment: 1.2 million rubles
JV Activity: Consumer goods,
printing

Sheldon Trading Company
Joint Venture: SAGOER
Registration No.: 538
Date of Registration: June 1, 1989
Location: Ul. Miaskovskogo, 20
Moscow 121019
Partners: "Foreign Gas"
Association (U.S.S.R., 50%),
Sheldon Trading (U.S., 50%)
U.S. Partner: Sheldon Trading
Company
Alamuchi, ND 07820
U.S. Investment: 10,000 rubles
JV Activity: Marketing services for
gas production, transport
processing, etc.

Sibir
Joint Venture: PSTI
Registration No.: 274
Date of Registration: February 27,
1989
Location: Ul. Pyatnitskaya, 45
Tashkent
Partners: The "Parus" Cooperative
(U.S.S.R., 51%), Sibir Inc. (U.S.,
49%)
U.S. Partner: Sibir
U.S. Investment: 50,000 rubles
JV Activity: Computer assembly,
software development

Slava International
Joint Venture: Sovet Broker
Registration No.: 632
Date of Registration: June 20,
1989
U.S. Partner: Slava International
510 L St., Suite 200
Anchorage, AK 99501
FAX: 30,000 rubles
JV Activity: Tourism

Space Commerce Corp.
Joint Venture: SKK
Registration No.: 675
Date of Registration: June 28,
1989
U.S. Partner: Space Commerce
Corp.
504 Pluto Dr.
Colorado Springs, CO 80906
U.S. Investment: 100,000 rubles
JV Activity: Scientific research,
design

Spec International
Joint Venture: Spekturi
Registration No.: 429
Date of Registration: May 5, 1989
U.S. Partner: Spec International
U.S. Investment: 125,000 rubles
JV Activity: Personal computers

Summit Ltd.
Joint Venture: Azsum
Registration No.: 531
Date of Registration: June 1, 1989
Location: Rostovskaya Oblast
Partners: Agroindustrial plant "Azov"
(U.S.S.R., 50%), Summit LTD (U.S., 50%)
U.S. Partner: Summit Ltd.
Omaha, NE
U.S. Investment: 125,000 rubles
JV Activity: Production and distribution of corn and soy

Thurston Sails
Joint Venture: Aquation
Registration No.: 315
Date of Registration: March 21, 1989
Location: Odessa
Partners: Cooperative "Aquamarine" (U.S.S.R., 51%), Thurston Sails (U.S., 49%)
U.S. Partner: Thurston Sails
U.S. Investment: 50,000 rubles
JV Activity: Sails for yachts

TIW Systems
Joint Venture: Inteks
Registration No.: 841

Date of Registration: August 22, 1989
U.S. Partner: TIW Systems
Parallel Graphics
Phone: 424 W. Grand
Ponca City, OK 74601
U.S. Investment: 50,000 rubles
JV Activity: Personal computers

Transatlantic Agency
Joint Venture: Hermitage
Registration No.: 313
Date of Registration: March 20, 1989
Location: Dvortsovskaya Nab.
Leningrad 191065
Partners: Hermitage Museum (U.S.S.R., 45%), Transatlantic Agency (U.S., 55%)
U.S. Partner: Transatlantic Agency
U.S. Investment: 520,000 rubles
JV Activity: Organization of art exhibits

Transcisco Industries
Joint Venture: Sovfinaitraks
Registration No.: 562
Date of Registration: June 5, 1989

Twain Trading Company
Joint Venture: IMC Corporation
Location: Moscow
Partners: Dedal Scientific-Technical Center
U.S. Partner: Twain Trading Company
2 West End Ave., Suite 4D
Brooklyn, NY 11235
Phone: (718) 236-8398,

(718) 891-3922
FAX: (718) 645-9596

Unicorn Investments International.,
Joint Venture: Sovaminko
Registration No.: 104
*Date of Registration: September
21, 1988*
Location: Moscow
Partners: Izdatelstvo "Mir",
Obedinenie
"Rekord", Kooperativ "Sintez",
(USSR, 51%)
U.S. Partner: Unicorn Investments
International, (USA, 49%)
16902 Bolsa Chica Rd. Suite 203
Huntington Beach, CA 92649
JV Activity: Mir Publishing House
(U.S.S.R., 21%), "Rekord"
Association
(U.S.S.R., 20%), "Sintez"
Cooperative
(U.S.S.R., 10%), Unicorn
Investment
(U.S., 49%)

USCO Investment
Joint Venture: Sovinterinvest
Registration No.: 172
Date of Registration: December
26, 1988
Partners: U.S.S.R., 87.7%, USCO
(U.S., 12.3%)
U.S. Partner: USCO
JV Activity: 500,000 rubles

User International
Joint Venture: Sovmestnii Put'
Registration No.: 546

Date of Registration: June 2, 1989
U.S. Partner: User International
U.S. Investment: 840,000 rubles
JV Activity: Computers

Winsome Food Technology
Joint Venture: Daguinaks
Registration No.: 483
Date of Registration: May 24, 1989
Location: Ul. Buynakskogo, 5
Makhachkala 367025
Partners: "Dagvino" Production
Organization (U.S.S.R., 75%),
Winsome Food Technology (U.S.,
25%)
U.S. Partner: Winsome Food
Technology
4340 150th Ave., NE
Redmond, WA 98052
U.S. Investment: 1.5 million rubles
JV Activity: Fruit juice production
and marketing

World Crafts Inc.
Registration No.: 820
Date of Registration: August 15,
1989
U.S. Partner: World Crafts Inc.
U.S. Investment: 15 million rubles
JV Activity: Building materials

World Ethnic Art Entertainment
Registration No.: 412
Date of Registration: April 27,
1989
U.S. Partner: World Ethnic Art
Entertainment
U.S. Investment: 170,000 rubles
JV Activity: Restaurants, trade

Worsham
Joint Venture: Perestroika
Registration No.: 056
Date of Registration: June 6, 1988
Location: Moscow
Partners: Main Administration for Construction of Engineering Buildings, Administration of High-Rise Buildings and Hotels, Main Administration for Urban Construction and Architecture and "Dialog" (U.S.S.R., 80%)
U.S. Partner: Worsham (U.S., 20%)
Chantilly Dr., Suite 200
Atlanta, GA 30324
Phone: (404) 634-1615
U.S. Investment: 7,500,000 rubles
JV Activity: Construction and renovation of buildings and office services

Young & Rubicam
Joint Venture: Young & Rubicam/Sovero
Registration No.: 455
Date of Registration: May 17, 1989
Location: 1404 Sovincentr
12 Krasnopresnenskaya Nab.
Moscow 123610
Partners: "Vneshtorgreklama" (U.S.S.R., 50%), Young and Rubicam (U.S., 50%)
U.S. Partner: Young & Rubicam
255 Madison Ave.
New York, NY 10017-6486
U.S. Investment: 370,000 rubles
Activity: Advertising

229

APPENDIX 2

SOVIET DECREES & RESOLUTIONS

Decree of January 13, 1987, No. 6362-XI, USSR Supreme Soviet, *On Questions Concerning the Establishment in the Territory of the USSR and Operation of Joint Ventures, International Amalgamations and Organizations with the Participation of Soviet and Foreign Organization, Firms and Management Bodies*

Decree of January 13, 1987, No. 49, USSR Council of Ministers, Decree of the USSR Council of Ministers On the Establishment in the Territory of the USSR and Operation of Joint Ventures with the Participation of Soviet Organizations and Firms from Capitalist and Developing Countries

Decree of December 2, 1988, No. 1405, USSR Council of Ministers, *On the Further Development of the Foreign Economic Activity of State, Cooperative and Other Public Enterprises, Association, and Organizations*

Decree of September 17, 1987, No. 1974, CPSU Central Committee and the USSR Council of Minsters, *On Additional Measures to Streamline Foreign Economic Activity in the New Conditions of Economic Management*

Instruction of November 24, 1987, No. 224, USSR Ministry of Finance, *On the Procedures for Registering Joint Ventures, International Amalgamations and Organizations Established in the Territory of the USSR with the Participation of Soviet and Foreign Organizations, Firms and Authorities*

Instruction of May 4, 1987, No. 124, USSR Ministry of Finance, *On Taxation of Joint Ventures*

Resolution of March 7, 1989, No. 203, USSR Council of Ministers, *On Measures of State Regulation of External Economic Activity*

The first six documents may be available from Baker & McKenzie in Washington. The final document may be available from APCO Associates in Washington.

231

U.S.-SOVIET TRADE YELLOW PAGES

Abakanovich, Svetlana M., Chairman of the Board, Prometey, 29, build 4, Checkhow str, 103006 Moscow. Phone 299-84-85

Accord Consulting Group, 444 Castro Street, Suite 400, Mountain View, CA 94041, Phone: (415) 940-1896, FAX: (415) 969-8660, Contact: Keith Rosten

Adams, Joyce B., P.O. Box 2893, New Britain, CT 06050, Phone: (203) 232-1248

AD-EX Translations, 525 Middlefield Road, Suite 250, Menlo Park, CA 94025, Phone: (415) 854-6732, FAX: (415) 325-8428, Telex: 171425

Aeroflot, 630 Fifth Ave., Suite 241, New York, NY 10111, Phone: (212) 397-1660 through - 1664, FAX: (212) 397-1667, Telex: (212) 495-0721

Aeroflot, 630 Fifth Ave, Suite 241, New York, NY, 10111, Phone: (212) 397-1660, (800) 535-9877, (800) 5-FLY-USSR, FAX: (212) 397-1660, Telex: (212) 459-0721

Agency for International Development (AID), Office of Business Relations, Department of State Building, 320 21st Street, NW, Washington, DC 20523-1414, Phone: (202) 647-1850; (703) 875-1551, FAX: (703) 875-1498, Contact: John Wilkinson, Director

Agropromservice, Per. Chernyshevskovo, 1, 103030 Moscow, Phone: 281-22-01, Telex: 411624

Akin, Gump, Strauss, Hauer & Feld, 1333 New Hampshire Avenue, NW, Suite 400, Washington, DC 20036, Phone: (202) 887-4000, FAX: (202) 887-4288, Contact: Daniel Spiegel

Alabama, 2015 2nd Avenue, N., Berry Building, 3rd Floor, Birmingham, Alabama 35203, Phone: (205) 264-1331

Alaska, U.S. & FCS, ITA, Anchorage DO, 222 N. 7th Avenue, Box 32, Anchorage, AK 99513-7591, Phone: (907) 271-5041, FAX: (907) 271-5173, Contact: Charles F. Becker, Director

Allied Travel, Inc., 11 E. 44th Street, New York, NY 10017, Phone: (212) 661-7200, (800) 843-2446, Telex: 236098

All World Travel, 131 State Street (India Street side), Boston, MA 02109, Phone: (617) 720-2000, (800) 343-2123, FAX: (617) 720-3909, Telex: 8100071150, Contact: Rita Cuker, President

American Association of Exporters and Importers (AAEI), 11 W. 42nd Street, New York, NY 10036, Phone: (212) 944-2230, FAX: (212) 382-2606, Contact: Eugene Milosh, President (formerly Vice-President of Operations, U.S.-U.S.S.R. Trade & Economic Council)

American Association of Exporters and Importers (AAEI), 11 West 42nd Street, New York, NY 10036, Phone: (212) 944-2230

American Bar Association, Soviet Lawyer Internship Program, 1800 M Street, NW, Washington, DC 20036, Phone: (202) 331-2280, FAX: (202) 331-2220, Contact: Steven G. Raikin, Esq., Program Director

American Center for International Leadership, 522 Franklin Street, Columbus, Indiana 47201, Phone: (812) 376-3456, Contact: Donna Brown, Vice President for Programs

American Center for International Leadership (ACIL), 401 East Pratt Street, Suite 2415, World Trade Center, Baltimore, MD 21202, Phone: (301) 539-2245, Contact: Donna Veatch, Vice President for Programs

American Committee on U.S.-Soviet Relations, 109 Eleventh Street, SE, Washington, DC 20003, Phone: (202) 546-1700, Contact: Margaret Chapman, Director U.S.-U.S.S.R. Trade Program

American Council of Learned Societies, 800 Third Avenue, New York, NY 10022, Phone: (212) 888-1759

American Embassy, Moscow, Mailing address: APO New York, NY, 09862-5438 Street address: Ul. Chaykovskogo, Moscow, Phone: 252-24-51 through 252-24-59; 230-20-01,

American Enterprise Institute for Public Policy Research, 1150 17th Street, NW, Washington, DC 20036, Phone: (202) 862-5800, FAX: (202) 862-7178, Contact: Paul Vizza

American Exhibition Services International, Inc., 801 Chase Ave., Unit 1, Elk Grove Village, IL 60007, Mailing Address, P.O. Box 66373, Chicago, IL 60666, Phone: (708) 593-2462

American Express Company, Sadovo-Kudrinskaya Ul. 21-A, Moscow, Phone: 254-43-05, Telex: 413075 AMEXM SU

American-Soviet Medical Market Journal, Sales Office, Suite 408, 374 Congress St., Boston, MA 02210, Phone: (617) 451-6633, FAX: (617) 451-6182, Contact: Richard P. Mills

American Trade Consortium, in New York: 375 Park Avenue, Suite 3200, New York, NY 10152, Phone: (212) 751-8066, Contact: Susan Bird, in Moscow: Sovincentr 1603A, Krasnopresnenskaya Nab. 12, Moscow, Phone: 253-94-96, 255-18-30, Contact: Rick Spooner

American Translators Association, 109 Croton Avenue, Ossining, NY 10562, Phone: (914) 941-1500

American-Ukrainian Trade Corporation, Inc., 2509 Rio DeJaneiro Avenue, Port Charlotte, FL 33983, Phone: (813) 627-5800, FAX: (813) 624-4023, Contact: Misha Nywelt

Amtorg Trading Company, in the U.S.: 1755 Broadway, New York, NY 10019, Phone: (212) 956-3010, FAX: (212) 856-2995, Telex: 422400, Contact: Yuri Mashkin, President, in Moscow: General Representative of Amtorg in the Soviet Union, Trubnikovskiy Pereulok, dom 19, 121069 Moscow, U.S.S.R., Phone: 202-57-49, FAX: 871-411-257

Amtrade Associates International, 420 Lexington Avenue, Suites 1624-27, New York, NY 10170, Phone: (212) 697-2467, FAX: (212) 599-0839, Telex: 6503764897, Contact: Stephen B. Van Campen, President

Anniversary Tours, 330 Seventh Avenue, Suite 700, New York, NY 10001, Phone: (212) 465-1200, (800) 366-1336, FAX: (212) 268-4855, Telex: 238608

APCO Associates, The Arnold and Porter Consulting Group, 1155 21st Street, NW, Suite 1000, Washington, DC 20036, Phone: (202) 778-1015, FAX: (202) 331-9832, Telex: 248303 ARPO UR, Contact: Randy Bregman, Director, Soviet and Eastern European Services

Aqua Air International, P.O. Box 164, Iselin, NJ 08830, Phone: (201) 283-2150, FAX: (201) 283-2171, Contact: J. Piazza

Aranda Corporation, 18 East Canal Avenue, Paoli, PA 19301, Phone: (215) 296-0111, FAX: (215) 640-0619, Contact: Michael S. Tomczyk, President

Ardis/Russian Literature, 2901 Heatherway, Ann Arbor, MI 48104, Phone: (313) 971-2367, Contact: Ellendea Proffer

Argus Trading Ltd., in the U.S.: 6110 Executive Boulevard, Suite 502, Rockville, MD 20852, Phone: (301) 984-4244, FAX: (301) 984-4247, Telex: 248209 ARGS UR, Contact: Michael Rae, President, in Moscow: Per. Sadovskikh 4, kv. 12, 103001 Moscow, Phone: 209-7071, 209-7843, FAX: 200-02-07, Telex: 413376 CIMOS SU, Contact: David Cant

Argus Trading, Ltd, 6110 Executive Blvd., Suite 502, Rockville, MD 20852

Arizona, Federal Building and U.S. Courthouse, 230 N. 1st Avenue, Room 3412, Phoenix, AZ 85025, Phone: (602) 254-3285

Arkansas, Savers Federal Building, Suite 635, 320 W. Capitol Avenue, Little Rock, AR 72201, Phone: (501) 378-5794

Armenian Chamber of Commerce, 24 Kutuzov Ul., 375033 Yerevan, Phone: (885) 27-73-90

Arnold & Porter, 1200 New Hampshire Avenue, NW, Washington, DC 20036, Phone: (202) 872-6929, FAX: (202) 331-9832, Telex: 89-2733, Contact: Jeffrey A. Burt

Arthur Anderson, in New York: 1345 Avenue of the Americas, New York, NY 10105, Phone: (212) 708-4125, FAX: (212) 708-3630, Contact: Paul W. Hoffman, in Moscow: Leninskaya Sloboda 26, 109068 Moscow, Phone: (095) 275-2126, FAX: (095) 275-2126, Contact: Hans Jochum Horn

ASET Consultants, Inc., American-Soviet Exchange and Trade, in Washington: 8350 Greensboro Drive, Suite 805, McLean, VA 22102, Phone: (703) 790-1922, FAX: (703) 883-1305, Telex: TWX 510-660-8023, Contact: Erika D. Nobel, President, in Moscow: Ul. Vernadskogo, 33/153, 117331 Moscow, Phone: 201-50-21, 138-05-04, FAX: 201-72-47, Telex: 412230 MPSM SU, Contact: Holly Smith, Director, Moscow Operations

Association of Joint Ventures, International Unions, and Organizations, 2-y Novopodmoskovnyy Per., 4, 125130 Moscow, Phone: 943-00-85, 159-01-47, Contact: Lev I. Weinberg, Chairman

Atmenintorg, 43, Ul. Chiraki, Yerevan 375086 U.S.S.R., Phone: 46-42-62, 46-41-64, 64-71-72, General Director: R. A. Sarkisyan

Auriema International Group, Inc., 747 Middleneck Rd., Great Neck, NY 11024, Phone: (516) 487-0700, FAX: (516) 487-0719, Telex: 62402 17505, Contact: Robert Auriema, President

Aviation Consulting Inc., 90 Moonachie Avenue, Teterboro, NJ 07608, Phone: (201)

288-1235, FAX: (201) 288-8400, Telex: 134408, Contact: John Dugan, Executive Vice President

Azerintorg, 4, Ul. Nekrasova, Baku 370004, Phone: 92-68-64, 92-29-40, Telex: 142127, General Director: A. M. Guseynov

Baholdin, Mark M., First Deputy General Director, Prometey, 29, build 4, Checkhow str, 103006 Moscow, Phone 299-84-85.

Baker & Botts, 555 13th Street, NW, Suite 500 East, Washington, DC 20004-1109, Phone: (202) 639-7700, FAX: (202) 639-7832, 639-7993, Telex: 6974881, 6502067689 BAKERBOTTS WAS, Contact: Paul Freedenberg

Baker & McKenzie, in Washington: 815 Connecticut Avenue, NW, Washington, DC 20006-4078, Phone: (202) 452-7012, FAX: (202) 452-7074, Telex: 89552, Contact: Eugene Theroux, in Chicago: One Prudential Plaza, 130 East Randolph Drive, Chicago, IL 60601, Phone: (312) 861-8179, FAX: (312) 861-2899, Telex: 25-4425, Contact: Preston M. Torbert, in Moscow: "Pushkin Plaza", Bolshoy Gnezdnykovskiy Pereulok, 7, 103009 Moscow, Phone: 200-61-67, 200-49-06, 200-61-86, FAX: 200-02-03, Telex: 413671 BAKER SU, Contact: Paul J. Melling, Arthur L. George, John P. Hewko

Baltic Shipping Company, U.S. Agent: Rice, Unruh, Reynolds Co., 232 S. Fourth Street, Philadelphia, PA 19106, Phone: (215) 629-1711, FAX: (215) 629-0242

Baltic Ventures, Inc., 1075 Washington Street, West Newton, MA 02165, Phone: (617) 527-2550, FAX: (617) 527-2823, Telex: 49605791

BALTIC, Contact: Paul D. Kalnins, President

Bank of America, 555 California Street, San Francisco, CA 94104, Phone: (415) 622-2073

Bank of New York, One Wall Street, New York, NY 10015, Phone: (212) 635-8130, Contact: Natasha Gurkinfel

Bank for Foreign Economic Affairs of the U.S.S.R., Vneshekonombank, 37 Plyuschikha Ul., 119121 Moscow, Phone: 256-67-80, 246-67-88, 246-67-98, 246-67-70, Telex: Telex 411174, Contact: Yuriy S. Moskovskiy, Chairman of the Board

Bankers Trust, 280 Park Avenue, New York, NY 10017, Phone: (212) 850-4882, Contact: Prudencio L. Vieira, Vice President, Barclays Bank PLC, 75 Wall Street, New York, NY 10265, Phone: (212) 412-3661, Contact: Gordon Hough

Barry Martin Travel, in New York: 19 West Street, Suite 3401, New York, NY 10004, Phone: (212) 422-0091, FAX: (212) 344-1997, Telex: 4952650, in Moscow: Hotel Mezhdunarodnaya 2 Kv. 940, Krasnopresnenskaya Nab., 12, Moscow, Phone: 253-29-40

Bashneftekhimexport, 14 Ul. Mira, 450064 Ufa, Cable: Bashneftekimzavody Ufa, Telex: 21429 Bonex SU, Phone: 43-25-14, General Director: L. G. Sushko

Batki, George, 208 Locksley Road, Syracuse, NY 13224, Phone: (315) 446-6451

BBDO Worldwide, in New York: 1285 Sixth Ave., New York, NY 10019, Phone: (212) 459-5000, FAX: (212) 459-6645, Contact: Sam

Johnson, in Moscow: c/o VTI Ad Center, 1, Ul. Fadeyeva, 125047 Moscow, Phone: 250-51-62, FAX: 253-97-94, Telex: 411-238 VTI SU, Contact: Bruce Macdonald

Bear, Stearns and Co., Inc., 245 Park Avenue, New York, NY 10167, Phone: (212) 272-3597, Contact: Brian Murray, Managing Director

Beerbaum, Mira S., 5881 Roblar Road, Petaluma, CA 94952, Phone: (707) 664-8535

Belarus, Inc., 7075 W. Parkland Ct., P.O. Box 23608, Milwaukee, WI 53223, Phone: (414) 355-2000, Telex: 177050 BELARUSNYK, Contact: Edward Ossinski, President

Belarus Machinery, Inc., 115 East 57th St., Suite 1450, New York, NY 10022, Phone: (212) 751-8550, FAX: (212) 371-4587, Telex: 177050 BELARUSNYK, and, Rt. 7 Box 7438R, Slidell, LA 70461, Phone: (504) 649-3000, Contact: Edward Ossinski, President

Belavtomaz, 3 Ul. Sotsialisticheskaya, 220831 Minsk, Cable: TF Belavtomaz Minsk, Telex: 252160 Maz, Phone: 46-96-08, General Director: A. N. Apukhtin

Belorusintorg, Dom Pravitelstva, Minsk 20010, Phone: 29-63-08, 29-63-09, 20-81-88, Telex: 252292, General Director: V. V. Andryushin

Belorussian Chamber of Commerce, 65 Ya. Kolasa, 220843 Minsk, Phone: (017) 66-04-60

Berlitz Translation Services, 6415 Independence Avenue, Woodland Hills, CA 91367, Phone: (818) 340-5147, FAX: (818) 340-5425, in Washington 1050 Connecticut Avenue, NW, Washington, DC 20036, Phone: (202) 331-1163, in New York: 257 Park Avenue, South,

New York, NY 10010, Phone: (212) 777-7878

BERUSA Corporation, in New York: 5411 Queens Boulevard, Woodside, NY 11377, Phone: (718) 779-0500, Contact: Tom Aman, in Milwaukee: 7075 W. Parklawn Ct., Box 23608, Milwaukee, WI 53223, Phone: (414) 355-2000

Bessmertnykh, Alexander, Soviet Ambassador to the United States, Embassy of the USSR, 1125 Sixteenth Street, NW, Washington, DC 20036. Phone (202) 628-7551

BET Trading Associates, in the U.S.: P.O. Box 771909, Houston, TX 77215-1909, Phone: (713) 266-5881, FAX: (713) 266-5985, Telex: 774697, in Moscow: Hotel National, Rm. 315, 103001 Moscow, Phone: 203-5303, 203-5335, Contact: Bobby E. Taylor, President

Bethesda Institute for Soviet Studies (BISS), 4400 East-West Hwy., Suite 806, Bethesda, MD 20814, Phone: (301) 652-2722, FAX: (301) 951-6435, Contact: Isaac Tarasulo

Beverly International Travel, Inc., 4630 Campus Drive, Suite 205, Newport Beach, CA 92660, Phone: (714) 474-7582, FAX: (714) 756-2169, Telex: 4996456

Biokard, 15/1 Tretya Cherepkovskaya Ul., 121552 Moscow, Cable: Biokard Moscow, Telex: 411355 EKE, Phone: 499-61-37, General Director: Yu. N. Chernikov

BLOC Magazine, 350 Broadway, Suite 1205, New York, NY 10013, Phone: (212) 966-0655, Contact: Richard Fuchs

Bloomstein, Elena, 7813 Pickard Avenue, NE, Albuquerque, NM 87110, Phone: (505) 291-

237

9812 (h); (505) 766-4700 (w)

Bobruiskshinaexport, Minskoye Shosse, 213824 Bobruisk, Mogilevskaya oblast, Cable: Bobruiskshinaexport Bobruisk Mogilevskoi, Telex: 252167 Wheel SU, Phone: 3-50-65, General Director: V. V. Alekseyev

Bojes & Bruchs, Financial Services, Ltd., 8000 Towers Crescent Drive, Suite 900, Vienna, VA 22812, Phone: (703) 506-3298, FAX: (703) 506-3291, Contact: Gary Bojes

British Airways, in Moscow: Hotel Mezhdunarodnaya II, Krasnopresnenskaya Nab. 12, Kv. 1905, Moscow, Phone: 253-27-01; (800) 247-9297 (U.S.), Telex: 413197

BRM International Division, U.S. Advertising, 2700 Rt. 22, Union NJ 07083, Contact: George Black

Brookings Institution, 1775 Massachusetts Avenue, NW, Washington, DC 20036, Phone: (202) 797-6000, FAX: (202) 797-6004, Contact: Ed Hewett, Senior Fellow

Brown University, Center for Policy development, Box 1948, Providence, RI 02912, Phone: (401) 863-3465, Contact: Alan Sherr

Bryan, Cave, McPheeters & McRoberts, 700 13th Street, NW, Washington, DC 20005-3960, Phone: (202) 508-6000, FAX: (202) 508-6200, Telex: 440321 BCMM UI, Contact: Peter D. Ehrenhaft, Anita C. Esslinger

Bureau of Export Administration (BXA), U.S. Department of Commerce, Washington, DC 20230, Phone: (202) 377-2000, Contact: Quincy M. Krosby

Burevestnik, 68 Malookhotinskiy Prosp., 195272 Leningrad, Cable: FTF Burevestnik Leningrad, Phone: 528-11-23, General Director: Ye. P. Sharanov

Business America, International Trade Administration, U.S. Department of Commerce, Room 3414, 14th and Constitution, NW, Washington, DC 20230, Phone: (202) 377-3251

Business Eastern Europe, Business International S.A., Schwarzenbergplatz 8/7, A-1030 Vienna, Austria, Phone: (0222) 72-41-61/65, Telex: 133 931

Business Service Desk, Mezhdunarodnaya Hotel I and II, Krasnopresnenskaya Nab. 12, Moscow, Phone: 253-32-82, Contact: The office provides telex, photocopying, secretarial, translation, and interpretation services.

California, Room 9200, 11000 Wilshire Boulevard, Los Angeles, CA 90024, Phone: (213) 575-7103, 116-A, W. 4th Street, Suite 1, Santa Ana, CA 92701, Phone: (714) 836-2461, P.O. Box 81404, San Diego, CA 91238, Phone: (619) 557-5395, Federal Building, Box 36013, 450 Golden Gate Avenue, San Francisco, CA 94102, Phone: (415) 556-5860

Cambridge East-West Consulting Group, Inc., University Place, 124 Mt. Auburn Street, Harvard Square, Cambridge, MA 02138, Phone: (617) 576-5724, FAX: (617) 547-1431, Contact: David J. Kramer

CAMCO Trading Co., in the U.S.: P.O. Box 14484, Houston, TX 77221, Phone: (713) 747-4000, FAX: (713) 747-6751, Contact: Roger Parrish, in Moscow: CAMCO, Hotel

Mezhdunarodnaya, Krasnopresnenskaya Nab., 12, Room 1340, 123610 Moscow, Phone: 253-15-75, FAX: 253-13-40, Telex: 413205 U.S. CO

Catskills Agency, Box 484, Rt. 28, Arkville, NY 12406, Phone: (914) 586-2900, (800) 537-7265, Contact: David Zeiset

Cauvin-Higgins, Catherine Marie, 6318 Rutgers, Houston, TX 77005, Phone: (713) 666-5944

CAWT, in San Francisco: 4 Embarcadero Center, Suite 2150, San Francisco, CA 94111, Phone: (415) 781-8520, FAX: (415) 781-0622, Telex: 330452, in New York: 245 Park Avenue, New York, NY 10167, Phone: (212) 856-1228, FAX: (212) 856-1694, Telex: 424700, Contact: Donald Asadorian, Manager

Center on East-West Trade, Investment and Communication, Duke University, 2114 Campus Drive, Durham, NC 27706, Phone: (919) 684-5551, Contact: Dr. Jerry Hough

Center for East-West Trade Policy, University of Georgia, 204 Baldwin Hall, Athens, GA 30602, Phone: (404) 542-2985, Contact: Dr. Gary Bertsch and Dr. Martin J. Hillenbrand

Center for Foreign Policy Development, Brown University, Box 1948, Providence, RI 02912, Phone: (401) 863-3465, FAX: (401) 274-8440, Telex: 3792135 CFPD, Contact: Dr. Alan Sherr, Associate Director

Center for International Business and Trade, Georgetown University, 1242 35th Street, Suite 501, Washington, DC 20057, Phone: (202) 687-6993, FAX: (202) 687-4031

Center for International Business and Travel, 2185 Wisconsin Avenue, NW, Washington, DC 20001, Phone: (202) 333-5550, (800) 424-2429, FAX: (202) 333-4753

Center for International Cooperation, 2601 Elliott Avenue, Suite 5146, Seattle, Washington 98121, Phone: (206) 728-1546, FAX: (206) 728-1563, Contact: Norman Swanson, President

Center for International Policy, Room 500, 1755 Massachusetts Avenue, NW, Washington, DC 20036, Phone: (202) 232-3317

Center for International Research, Bureau of the Census, Scuderi Bldg., Room 710, Washington DC 20233, Phone: (202) 763-4020, FAX: (301) 763-7610, Contact: Matthew Sagers, Branch Chief; Jeanine Braithwaite

Center for Russian and East European Studies, University of Michigan, Lane Hall, Ann Arbor, MI 48109, Phone: (313) 764-0351, Contact: Don K. Rowney

Center for the Study of Joint Ventures, SUNY Plattsburgh, Redcay Hall, Plattsburgh, NY 12901, Phone: (518) 564-4190, Contact: Dr. M. Zubaidur Rahman, Director

Centrally Planned Economics Branch, Economic Research Service, U.S. Department of Agriculture, 1301 New York Avenue, NW Washington, DC 20005-4788, Phone: (202) 786-1620, Contact: Ed Cook

Centre for Russian and East European Studies, University of Toronto, 100 St. George Street, Rm. 1022, Toronto, Ontario, Canada, M5S 1A1, Editors: Yuri Luryi and Peter Solomon

239

Chadbourne, Hedman & Raabe & Advocates CCCP, International Lawyers, 123610 Krasnopresnenskaya Nab. 12., Mezhdunarodnaya-2, Kv. 1421, Moscow, Phone: 253-14-21, FAX: 253-16-51, Contact: Robert E. Langer, Resident Attorney

Chadbourne & Parke, 30 Rockefeller Plaza, New York, NY 10112, Phone: (212) 408-5100, FAX: (212) 541-5406, Telex: 620520, Contact: William E. Holland and Eugene R. Sullivan, Jr.

Chamber of Commerce and Industry of the United States of America, U.S. Chamber of Commerce, 1615 H Street, NW, Washington DC 20062, Phone: (202) 463-5482

Chase Manhattan, One Chase Manhattan Plaza, 14th Floor, New York, NY 10081, Phone: (212) 552-4676, Contact: Gail Buyske, Vice President

Chemical Bank, 277 Park Avenue, New York, NY 10172, Phone: (212) 310-5370, Contact: Mauri Kutila, Vice President

Chestnoy, Vladimir Ivanovich, One Penn Plaza, Suite 100, New York, NY 10119, Phone: (201) 332-8783, or (212) 467-8669

Chilewich International Corp., in the U.S.: 12 Water Street, White Plains, NY 10601, Phone: (914) 997-2000, FAX: (914) 997-2122, Telex: 232088 CSC, Contact: Simon Chilewich, President, in Moscow: Kursovoy Pereulok #9, Phone: 119034 Moscow, 203-51-92, FAX: 200-12-15, Telex: 413211 CHILWSU

Chubb and Son, 15 Mountain View Road, Warren, NJ 07061-1615, Phone: (201) 580-2000, FAX: (201) 580-2003

Citibank, 399 Park Avenue, New York, NY 10172, Phone: (212) 559-8577, Telex: 235530, Contact: Miljenko Horvat

Citicorp's East-West Services, Vienna, Austria, Phone: 772-1450, Telex: 112105

Citizen Exchange Council, 12 W. 31st Street, New York, NY 10001-4415, Phone: (212) 643-1985, FAX: (212) 643-1996, Telex: 4900001648 CEC UI, Contact: Michael C. Brainerd, Ph.D., President

C & M International LTD, 1001 Pennsylvania Avenue, NW, Washington, DC 20004-2505, Phone: (202) 624-2895, FAX: (202) 628-5116, Contact: Doral S. Cooper

Cole Corette & Abrutyn, in the U.S.: 1110 Vermont Avenue, NW, Washington, DC 20005, Phone: (202) 872-1414, FAX: (202) 296-8238; (202) 872-1396, Telex: 64391, Contact: Edward H. Lieberman, in London: 21 Upper Broot Street, London W1Y 1PD, Phone: 44 71 491-3735, FAX: 408-0843, Telex: 264598, Contact: Robert Stan

Colorado, Room 119, U.S. Customhouse, 721 19th Street, Denver, CO 80202, Phone: (303) 844-3246

Columbia Shipping, Inc., 138-01 Springfield Boulevard, Jamaica, NY 11413, Phone: (718) 656-5900, FAX: (718) 712-3622, Telex: 645045, Contact: Loretta Block

COMECON, Trade and the West, Author: Wallace and Clarke, Publisher: St. Martin's Press Scholarly and Reference Division, New York, NY

Commercial Bank for Innovation, 5 Khashirskoye Shosse, Moscow, Phone: 393-73-64

Commercial Bank for Railway Transport, Moscow, Phone: 258-48-93

Commersant, in the U.S.: c/o Refco, Inc., 111 West Jackson Boulevard, Suite 1700, Chicago, IL 60604, Phone: (312) 930-6500, FAX: (312) 930-6534, Telex: 253322 REFCO CGO, In Moscow: Khoroshevskoye Shosse, 41, Moscow, 123308, FAX: 335-28-25, Telex: 411712 POSTF SU

Commodity Credit Corporation, Foreign Agricultural Service, U.S. Department of Agriculture, 14th & Independence Avenue, SW Room 4509, Washington, DC 20250, Phone: (202) 447-3224, FAX: (202) 447-2949, Contact: Richard Godsey

Communications House, Prospekt Kalinina 22, Moscow, Phone: 202-03-01

Connecticut, Federal Building, Room 610-B, 450 Main Street., Hartford, CT 06103, Phone: (203) 722-3530

Conner, R. Michael, 8008 Gault Street, Austin, TX 78758, Phone: (512) 467-8870

Construction, Marketing, & Trading, Inc., 8150 Leesburg Pike, Suite 1200, Vienna, VA 22180, Phone: (703) 761-3188, FAX: (703) 790-5933, Telex: 3792650 COMCORTY 1200, Contact: Eric Crabtree

Consulting Commodities Marketing International, Ltd., 1880 Commonwealth Avenue, Suite 6, Brighton, MA 02135, Phone: (617) 731-3433, FAX: (617) 731-3433, Telex:

940103 WU PUBTLX BSN, Contact: Amrit Russ

Contract Law in the U.S.S.R. and the United States, Author: Allan Farnsworth and Viktor P. Mozolin

Costello, Sally L., 6 Mill Lane, Rockport, MA 01966, Phone: (617) 546-7140

Coudert Brothers, in the U.S.: 200 Park Avenue, New York, NY 10166, Phone: (212) 880-4400, FAX: (212) 557-8137, 557-8136, Telex: 666764, Contact: Douglas R. Aden, in Moscow: Ulitsa Petrovka, 15, Second Floor, Phone: 230-2547, 928-7838, FAX: 200-1228, 200-0268, Telex: 413-310; 413-329, 413-267 IPATC-SU, Contact: Richard N. Dean

Council on International Educational Exchange (CIEE), 205 E. 42nd Street New York, NY 10017, Phone: (212) 661-1414, FAX: (212) 972-3231, Telex: 423227/6730395, Contact: Adele Donchenko, Chairperson

Covington & Burling, 1201 Pennsylvania Avenue, NW, Washington, DC 20044, Phone: (202) 662-5172, FAX: (202) 662-6288, Telex: 89593 COVLANG WSH, Contact: Russell H. Carpenter

Creskoff, Ellen Hood, 605 Westbury Apartments, 271 S. 15th Street, Philadelphia, PA 19102, Phone: (215) 545-1977

Daniels, Ernestine R., 610B Gadd Road, Hixson, TN 37343, Phone: (615) 870-1473

Daniels, Guy, 315 E. 86th Street, Apt. 11LE, New York, NY 10028, Phone: (212) 289-7207

Danzas Corp., 330 120th Avenue, NE, Bellevue, WA 98005, Phone: (206) 646-7171, FAX: (206) 646-7188

Dearner, Dolly A., 2405 NW 17th Street, Oklahoma City, OK 73107, Phone: (405) 528-5618

Debevoise & Plimpton, 875 Third Avenue, New York, NY 10022, Phone: (212) 909-6421, FAX: (212) 909-6836, Telex: (RCA) 234400 DEBS UR, Contact: Roswell Perkins, Jonathan H. Hines

Delaware, Serviced by Philadelphia office.

Delphi Travel Unlimited, in Washington: 1019 19th Street, NW, Suite 900, Washington, DC 20036, Phone: (202) 466-7951, (800) 826-0196, FAX: (202) 466-4113, Telex: 413931, in Moscow: Bolshaya Pereyaslavskaya 7-41, Moscow, Phone: 280-5441

Delphic Associates, Inc., 7700 Leesburg Pike, Suite 250, Falls Church, VA 22043, Phone: (703) 556-0278, FAX: (703) 556-0494, Contact: Gerold Guensberg, Director

Design and Production, Inc., 7110 Rainwater Pl., Lorton, VA 22079, Phone: (703) 550-8640

Design Dynamics, 5525 Twin Knolls Road, Suite 323, Columbia, MD 21045, Phone: (301) 995-3022, FAX: (301) 995-0805, Contact: Alex Koorbanoff

Dhalfelt International, in the U.S.: 120 Potter Road, Scarsdale, NY 10583, Phone: (914) 472-2084, Contact: Ulf Nofelt, President, in Moscow: ICA-Soviet-American Foundation, Moscow, 170778, B-87, Phone: 245-02-03, Contact: Alexander Churkin, Associate

DHL Worldwide Express, 333 Twin Dolphin Drive, Redwood City, CA 94065, Phone: (800) 225-5345

Diamant, Gabriel G., 6600 Boulevard East, W. New York, NJ 07093, Phone: (201) 861-2065

Dilson, Jesse, 201 E. 30th Street, New York, NY 10016, Phone: (212) 685-3121

Dilworth, Paxson, Kalish & Kauffman, 1001 Pennsylvania Avenue, NW, Suite 275 North, Washington, DC 20004, Phone: (202) 624-5900, FAX: (202) 624 -5904, Contact: Martin Mendelsohn

Diomedes, Inc., 3105 Washington Street, San Francisco, CA 94115, Phone: (415) 563-4731, FAX: (415) 931-0915, Telex: 4931349 ESAL UI, Contact: Jim Garrison, CEO

Diplomatic Language Services, Inc., 1111 N. 19th Street, Suite 525, Arlington, VA 22209, Phone: (703) 243-4855, FAX: (703) 358-9189

District of Columbia, Serviced by Baltimore office.

Dittrich, Terence W., President, Global Trading Associates, Inc., 1155 Connecticut Avenue, NW, Suite 500, Washington, DC 20036. Phone (202) 467-8589. FAX (202) 452-8654. Telex 4933729 WASH UI

Dr. Dvorkovitz & Associates, P.O. Box 1748, Ormond Beach, FL 32175-1748, Phone: (904) 677-7033, FAX: (904) 677-7113, Telex: 4940321, Contact: Anne Klenner

DRG International, Inc., in the U.S.: 1167 Route 22 East, P.O. Box 1178, Mountainside, NJ 07092, Phone: (201) 233-2075, FAX:

(201) 233-0758, Telex: 178110 DRG INTL, in Moscow: Inpred, Krasnopresnenskaya Nab., 12, 123610 Moscow, Telex: 411813 REPR SU, Contact: Cyril Geacintov, President

Duncan, Albert H., P.O. Box 669, Bodega Bay, CA 94923, Phone: (707) 875-3900

East European Markets, Financial Times Business Information, Tower House, Southampton Street, London WC2E 7MA, Phone: 071-240 9391, FAX: 071-240-7946, Telex: 296926

East-West Business Analyst, Debos Oxford Publications, Ltd., Kennett House, Suite 2, 108-110 London Road, Oxford OX3 9 AW, UK

East-West Concepts, Inc., 196 Tamarack Circle, Skillman, NJ 08558, Phone: (609) 924-6789, (800) 637-0201, FAX: (609) 466-0864, Telex: 408568 EWC/HVS, Contact: Janos Samu

East-West Development Corporation, Minsk, Belorussian SSR, Phone: 23-34-27, Contact: V. Semyonov, President

East-West Initiatives, Inc., 30 South 17th Street, Philadelphia, PA 19103, Phone: (215) 636-4961, FAX: (215) 636-4990, Contact: Julie Swift, President

East/West Technology Digest, Welt Publishing Company, 1413 K Street, NW, Suite 800, Washington, DC 20005, Phone: (202) 371-0555, Telex: 281 409, ISSN: 0145-1421

East-West Trade Development, Ltd., 2025 I Street, NW, Suite 606, Washington, DC 20006, Phone: (202) 296-3598, FAX: (202) 296-3599, Contact: William Barlow, President

Eastern Europe TIMES, 1401 Wilson Boulevard, 5th Floor, Arlington, VA 22209, Business Phone: (703) 527-0039, Business FAX: (703) 527-8679, Editorial Phone: (703) 527-1207, Editorial FAX: (703) 527-0321

Eastern European & Soviet Telecom Report (EESTR), 2940 28th Street, NW, Washington, DC 20008, Phone: (202) 234-2138, FAX: (202) 483-7922

Economic Newsletter, Russian Research Center, Harvard University, 1737 Cambridge Street, Cambridge, MA 02138, Phone: (617) 495-4037, FAX: (617) 495-8319, Telex: 4948261

Ecotass, Pergamon Press, Maxwell House, Fairview Park, Elsmford, NY 10523, Phone: (703) 487-4630

Ekonomika i zhizn, Bumazhniy proezd, 14, 101462, GSP-4, Moscow, Phone: 212-23-89, Telex: 112314 ROGOZA

Elektron, 68-A Komsomolskaya Ul., 244030 Sumy, Cable: Spektr Sumy,
Telex: 131473 KRON, Phone: 2-14-14, Director: V. N. Kaplichnyy

Elektronintorg, Ul. Usiyevicha 24/2, 125315 Moscow, Telex: 411362 EZP SU, Phone: 155-40-26, 155-40-38

Elektrosila, 139 Moskovskiy Prosp., 196105 Leningrad, Cable: TF Elektrosila Leningrad, Telex: 121588 Motor, Phone: 298-2075, Director: N. B. Filippov

Elmashintorg, 73 Petergofskoye Shosse, 198206 Leningrad, Cable: Elmashintorg Leningrad, Phone: 130-80-77, Director: O. E.

243

Rumyantsev

Embassy of the U.S.S.R., 1125 Sixteenth Street, NW Washington, DC 20036, Phone: (202) 628-7551, Contact: Alexander Kluyev

Emery Worldwide, (A Consolidated Freight Company), 3350 West Bay Shore Road, Palo Alto, CA 94303, Phone: (800) HI-EMERY (Service)

Energomashexport, 19 Prosp. Kalinina, 121019 Moscow, Telex: 411965, Phone: 203-15-71, General Director: V. I. Filimonov

Ernst & Young, in New York: East European Division, 787 7th Avenue, New York, NY 10019, Phone: (212) 830-6000, FAX: (212) 977-9358, Telex: 7607796, Contact: Stan Polovets, Manager, in Moscow: 119034 Moscow, Kursovoy Pereulok 9

Ernst & Young, East European Division, 787 7th Avenue, New York, NY 10019, Phone: (212) 830-6000, FAX: (212) 977-9359, 977-9159, Telex: 7607796, Contact: James E. Searing, National Director of International Business Services

Esalen Institute on Soviet-American Relations, 3105 Washington Street, San Francisco, CA 94115, Phone: (415) 563-4731, FAX: (415) 931-0915, Telex: 4931349 ESAL SU, Contact: Dulce Murphy, Director

Estimpex, Ul. Tolly 3, 200001 Tallinn, Phone: 60-14-62, Telex: 173288 ANTIK, General Director: O. M. Kaldre

Estonian Chamber of Commerce, 17 Toomkooli Ul., 200001 Tallinn, Phone: (014) 44-49-29

Expertech, in the U.S., c/o Wavetech International, 1600 Broadway, Suite 550, Denver, Colorado 80202, Phone: (303) 839-9488, FAX: (303) 839-9497, Contact: Edward Gendelman, in Moscow: Ul. Krasikogo, 32, 117418 Moscow, Phone: 095-129-16-33, FAX: 129-26-27, Contact: Dr. Igor N. Shokin, Director General

Expocenter, 1a Sokolnicheskiy Val, 107113 Moscow, Phone: 268-5874, Telex: 411185 EXPO SU

Expocourier, 1a Sokolnicheskiy val, Moscow 107113, Phone: 268-64-93, Telex: 411185 EXPO SU

Export-Import Bank of the United States, 811 Vermont Avenue, NW, Washington, DC 20571, Phone: (202) 566-8898

Export Network Inc., 7315 Wisconsin Avenue, Suite 300W, Bethesda, MD 20814, Phone: (301) 961-8770, FAX: (301) 961-8775, Contact: Linda Price

Exportkhleb, 32/34 Smolenskaya-Sennaya Pl., 121200 Moscow, Cable: Exportkhleb Moscow, Telex: 411145 E-KHLEB; 411146 E-KHLEB; 411147 E-KHLEB, General Director: O. A. Klimov

Exportles, 19 Trubnikovskiy Pereulok, 121803 GSP Moscow, Cable: Exportles Moscow G-69, Telex: 411229 Eles SU, Phone: 291-58-15; 291-61-16, General Director: Yu. V. Vardashkin

1st American Bank, 740 15th Street, NW, Washington, DC 20005, Phone: (202) 637-4670, FAX: (202) 637-7923, Telex: 197638 ISTAM UT, Contact: Marilyn Sohl Labriny

FAM Translations, 104 E. 40th Street, New York, NY 10016, Phone: (212) 986-5627, Contact: Sally Johns

FBIS (Foreign Broadcast Information Service): U.S.S.R. Serial Reports, U.S. Department of Commerce, NTIS 5285 Port Royal Road, Springfield, VA 22161, Phone: (703) 487-4630

Feofanov, Alexander N., Head of Customs Control Department, Prometey, 29, build 4, Checkhow str, 103006 Moscow. Phone 299-84-85

Feshbach, Murray, 232 Poulton Hall, Georgetown University, 37th & P Street, NW, Washington, DC 20057, Phone: (202) 687-6811, Contact: Murray Feshbach

Field, Mark G., Harvard Russian Research Center, Harvard University, 1737 Cambridge Street, Cambridge, MA 02138, Phone: (617) 495-1719, (617) 495-4037, (617) 862-8322, (603) 284-6437, FAX: (617) 495-8319, Telex: 4948261, Contact: Mark G. Field

Financial Times, FT Publications, 14 East 60th Street, New York, NY 10022, Phone: (212) 752-4500

Finnair, in New York: 10 East 40th Street, New York, NY 10016, Contact: Borje A. Sandberg, Phone: (212) 689-9300, (800) 950-5000, FAX: (212) 481-0569, in Moscow: Proyezd Khudozhestvennogo, Teatra 6, SU-103009 Moscow, Phone: 292-33-37, 292-87-88, FAX: 230-29-88

First National Bank of Chicago, One First National Plaza, Mail Suite 0040, Chicago, IL 60670, Phone: (312) 732-6796, Contact: Robert

L. Thomas, Assistant Vice President, International Structured Finance Group

Fiske, William K., 454 W. 44th Street, Apt. 4RW, New York, NY 10036, Phone: (212) 265-0210

Five Star Touring, 60 E. 42nd Street, Suite 612, New York, NY 10165, Phone: (212) 818-9140 (in NY); (800) 792-STAR (outside NY), Telex: 4972143

Fletcher, George R., c/o CompuLingua Translation, Services, 198 Broadway, Suite 1107, New York, NY 10038, Phone: (718) 788-7782, (212) 227-1994, FAX: (212) 693-1489

Flick, Cathy, 302 S.W. Fifth Street, Richmond, IN 47374, Phone: (317) 962-3427

Florida, 224 Federal Building, 51 SW 1st Avenue, Miami, FL 33130, Phone: (305) 536-5267, 128 N. Osceola Avenue, Clearwater, FL 33515, Phone: (813) 461-0011

FOLEY LARD MIL, Contact: John W. Brahm, in Washington: 1775 Pennsylvania Avenue, Washington, DC 20006-4680, Phone: (202) 862-5300, FAX: (202) 862-5339, Telex: 904136 (FOLEY LARD WASH), Contact: Peter C. Linzmeyer

Foley & Lardner, in Milwaukee: First Wisconsin Center, 777 East Wisconsin Avenue, Milwaukee, WI 53202-5367, Phone: (414) 289-3586, FAX: (414) 289-3791, Telex: 26819

Foreign Agricultural Service, U.S. Department of Agriculture, 14th & Independence Avenue, SW, Washington DC, 20250-1000, Phone: (202) 447-6219, FAX: (202) 382-6140,

Contact: Margie Bauer

Fox, Leonard, 278-A Meeting Street, Charleston, SC 29401, Phone: (803) 722-2531

Frank B. Hall & Co of California, Soviet and East European Risk Insurance Facility (SEERIF), One Market Plaza, Spear Street Tower, Suite 2100, San Francisco, CA 94105, Phone: (415) 543-9360, FAX: (415) 543-5628, Telex: 4937656, Contact: Price G. Lowenstein

Frentz, L. Brand, Rt. 2, Box 18A, Mankato, MN 56001, Phone: (507) 947-3268, (507) 345-4505

Fried, Frank, Harris, Shriver & Jacobson, 1001 Pennsylvania Avenue, Suite 800, Washington, DC 20036, Phone: (202) 639-7000, FAX: (202) 639-7003, 639-7004, 639-7008, Contact: David Birenbaum

FYI Information Resources, 735 8th Street, SE, Washington, DC 20003, Phone: (202) 544-2394, FAX: (202) 543-9385, Contact: Jonathan Halperin

Gallagher, Paul B., 2106 1/2 N. High Street #3, Columbus, OH 43201, Phone: (614) 294-3091

Gallagher, William B., M.D., 3891 N. Hillwood Cir., Tucson, AZ 85715, Phone: (602) 298-3489

Garrity, John K., 36 Linnaean Street, Suite 12A, Cambridge, MA 02138, Phone: (617) 868-2080, FAX: (617) 864-8002, Telex: 324168 OAKS CAMB, Contact: John K. Garrity

Gaston and Snow, 1511 K Street, NW, Suite 1200, Washington DC 20005, Phone: (202) 347-230, FAX: (202) 347-4819, Telex: 3725451 COMCOR WASH DC, Contact: James Gallatin

General Tours, 770 Broadway, New York, NY 10003, Phone: (212) 598-1800, (800) 221-2216, FAX: (212) 598-0117

Geonomics Institute, 14 Hillcrest Avenue, Middlebury, VT 05753, Phone: (802) 388-9619, FAX: (802) 388-9627, Contact: Michael P. Claudon, President

Georgia, Suite 504, 1365 Peachtree Street, NE, Atlanta, GA 30309, Phone: (404) 881-7000

Georgian-American Medical & Economic Development Corporation, 3419 Barger Drive, Falls Church, VA 22044, Phone: (703) 941-5264, FAX: (703) 658-2807, Contact: Alexander M. Van Doren-Shulkin

Georgian Chamber of Commerce, 1 I. Chavchavadze Prospect, 380079 Tbilisi, Phone: (883) 22-25-54

Geotech International, 714 S. Dearborn, Suite 3, Chicago, IL 60605, Phone: (312) 939-7162, FAX: (312) 427-4504, Telex: 271 001 GEOTECH UR, Contact: Dr. Marshall Silver, President

Gibson, Dunn and Crutcher, in the U.S.: 1050 Connecticut Avenue, NW, Washington, DC 20036, Phone: (202) 955-8500, FAX: (202) 467-0539, Telex: 197659 GIBTRASK WSH, Contact: Paul R. Harter, in London: 30/35 Pall Mall, London SW1Y 5LP, Phone: (071) 925-0440, FAX: (071) 925-2465, Telex: 27731 GIBTRK G

Gingold, Kurt (Dr.), 35 Windsor Ln., Cos Cob, CT 06807, Phone: (203) 869-2742

Glahe International, 1700 K St., NW, Washington, DC 20006-3624, Phone: (202) 659-4557, (202) 457-0776, Attn: Peter McKenna

Global Concepts, 2860 Walnut Hill Lane, Suite 104, Dallas, TX 75229, Phone: (214) 351-0001, (800) 322-4552, FAX: (214) 902-9020, Telex: 163410 PROBUS UT

Global Concepts, Inc., P.O. Box 540007, Dallas, TX 75354-0007, Phone: (214) 351-0001, FAX: (214) 902-9020, Telex: 163410 PROBUS UT, Contact: L. C. Smith

Global Trading Associates, Inc., in Washington: 1155 Connecticut Avenue, NW, Suite 500, Washington, DC 20036, Phone: (202) 467-8589, FAX: (202) 452-8654, Telex: 4933729 WASH UI, Contact: William S. Loiry, Chairman; Terence W. Dittrich, President, in Moscow: 29, Guild 4, Chekhow str., 103006 Moscow, Phone: 299-84-45, FAX: 200-22-12 (Attn: Anton E. Pronin), Telex: 411700 VAPRO 0310, Contact: Anton E. Pronin

Globus-Gateway/Cosmos, 150 South Los Robles, Suite 860, Pasadena, CA 91101, Phone: (818) 449-0919, (800) 556-5454, FAX: (818) 584-9857, Telex: 215292, in New York: 95-25 Queens Boulevard, Rego Park, NY 11374, Phone: (718) 268-1700, (800) 221-0090, FAX: (718) 520-1735, Telex: 170903

Goldenberg, Laura, Director of Marketing, Global Trading Associates, 1155 Connecticut Avenue, NW, Suite 500, Washington, DC 20036. Phone (202) 467-8589. FAX (202) 452-8654. Telex 4933729 WASH UI

Goodwin & Soble, 1300 19th Street, NW, Suite 350, Washington, DC 20036, Phone: (202) 223-8282, FAX: (202) 223-8560, Telex: 272691 GOSO UR, Contact: Steve Soble

Gorzkowska, Regina, 908 S. 47th Street, Philadelphia, PA 19143-3619, Phone: (215) 724-6477

Graf, Angelia, Department of Foreign Language, Virginia Polytechnic Institute, Blacksburg, VA 24061, Phone: (703) 961-5361

Grier, Ella Feodorovna, 450 Noble Boulevard, Carlisle, PA 17013, Phone: (717) 245-2804

Grimes & Leonard, P.O. Box 55, Hingham, MA 02043, Phone: (617) 749-0772, Contact: William J. Grimes or Isabel A. Leonard

Grimes, William J., P.O. Box 55, Hingham, MA 02043, Phone: (617) 749-1540, FAX: (617) 749-8738

Gruzimpex, Prospekt Rustaveli 8, Dom Pravitelstva, Tbilsi 380018, Phone: 93-71-69, General Director: D. A. Veruleishvili

Gwirtsman, Joseph J., 21 Hemlock Terrace, Springfield, NJ 07081, Phone: (201) 379-3947

Hall, Dickler, Lawler, Kent & Friedman, 460 Park Avenue, New York, NY 10022, Phone: (212) 838-4600, FAX: (212) 935-3121, Telex: 239857 GONY UR, Contact: Mark A. Meyer

Hall, Marie J., Box 1745, Route 1, Bar Harbor, ME 04609, Phone: (207) 288-3104, FAX: (207) 288-9336

Hanff, Konstanty Z., 3 E. 15th Street, New York, NY 10003, Phone: (212) 255-0754

Harper College, Algonquin and Roselle Rd., Palatine, IL 60067, Phone: (312) 397-3000

Harvard Ukrainian Research Center, 1583 Massachusetts Ave, Cambridge, MA 02138, Phone: (617) 495-4053

Harvard University, Russian Research Center, 1737 Cambridge St., Cambridge, MA 02138, Phone: (617) 495-4037, Contact: Marshall Goldman

Hawaii, 4106 Federal Building, P.O. Box 50026, 300 Ala Moana Boulevard, Honolulu, HI 96850, Phone: (808) 546-8694

Hazard, John, 435 W. 116th Street, New York, NY 10027, Phone: (212) 854-2646, FAX: (212) 854-7946, Contact: John Hazard

Henry A. Raab Consulting, 10 Shore Boulevard, Manhattan Beach, NY 11235-4056, Phone: (718) 648-7570, (212) 691-3666, FAX: (718) 934-8392, Telex: 423029 SHRAZ, Contact: Henry A. Raab, President

Henson & Efron, 1200 Title Insurance Bldg., Minneapolis, MN 55401, Phone: (612) 339-2500, FAX: (612) 339-6364, Contact: Robert Bayer

Hetzel, Eustace P., 7612 Cecelia Street, Downey, CA 90241, Phone: (213) 927-4585

Hogan & Hartson, 555 13th Street, NW, Washington, DC 20004, Phone: (202) 637-5964, FAX: (202) 637-5910, Telex: 248370 (RCA), Contact: Alex Frishberg

Hoover Institution on War, Revolution and Peace, Stanford University, Stanford, CA 94305-2323, Phone: (415) 723-2300, Institute for Sino-Soviet Studies, The George Washington University, 6th Floor, 2130 H Street, NW, Washington, DC 20052, Phone: (202) 994-6340, Contact: James R. Millar, Director, Joseph H. Lauder

Hudson Shipping Company, Inc., 17 Battery Place, Suite 1230, New York, NY 10004, Phone: (212) 487-2600

ICD, 641 Lexington Avenue, 11th Floor, New York, NY 10022, Phone: (212) 644-1509, Contact: Daniel Kazdan, Product Manager Eastern Europe

Idaho, Statehouse, Room 113, Boise, Idaho 83720, Phone: (208) 334-2470

IDB Communications Group, Inc., IDB Sales-New York, 260 Madison Avenue, New York, NY 10016, Phone: (212) 953-0070, FAX: (212) 986-0132, Telex: 213770, Contact: Dennis Mallon; in Moscow: CCS Satellite Co., Phone: 234-28-29, Telex: 411405, Contact: George Korolev

Ignatiev, Konstantin K., First Deputy Director General, Prometey, 29, build 4, Checkhow str, 103006 Moscow. Phone 299-84-85

Illinois, 1406 Mid Continental Plaza Bldg., 55 East Monroe Street, Chicago, IL 60603, Phone: (312) 353-4450

Impuls, 2 Pl. Pobedy, 349940 Severodonetsk, Voroshilovgradskaya oblast, Cable: FTF Impuls Severodonetsk, Phone: 4-13-23, Director: V. I. Smolin

248

Inaudit, Konushkovskaya 28, 123242 Moscow, Phone: 921-03-25 (Moscow), (212) 708-4803 (for information -- New York), Contact: J. Kenneth Hickman (in New York)

Indiana, 357 U.S. Courthouse & Federal Bldg., 46 E. Ohio Street, Indianapolis, IN 46204, Phone: (317) 269-6214

Inform-Pravo, Ul. Druzhby, 10/32, Phone: 117330 Moscow, 143-17-95, 143-67-70, 938-21-20, Telex: 411734 INF SU

Ingosstrakh, Insurance Company of the U.S.S.R., 12 Pyatnitskaya Ul., 113184 Moscow, Phone: 231-16-77, Telex: 411144, Contact: Mikhail Safranov

Institute of Management and International Studies, The Wharton School of the University of Pennsylvania, 102 Vance Hall, Philadelphia, PA 19104-6361, Phone: (215) 898-6182, Library of Congress, 10 1st Street, SE, Washington, DC 20540, Phone: (202) 287-5000, European Reading Room, Reading Room: Al Graham, Grant Harris

Institute for Security and Cooperation in Outer Space, 1336 A Corcoran Street, NW, Washington, DC 20009, Phone: (202) 462-8887, FAX: (202) 462-3576, Contact: Connie Van Pratt

Institute for Soviet-American Relations (ISAR), 1601 Connecticut Avenue, NW, Washington, DC 20009, Phone: (202) 387-3034, Contact: Eliza Klose

Interconcepts, 10 E. 21st Street, New York, NY, Phone: (212) 254-8271

InterCultura, 3327 W. 7th Street, Fort Worth, TX 76107, Phone: (817) 332-4691, FAX: (817) 877-4205, Contact: Gordon Dee Smith, President

Interflo, P.O. Box 42, Maplewood, NJ 07040, Phone: (201) 763-9493, ISSN 0748-4631

Inter-Lavia, Ul. Lenina 85, Riga 2260001, Phone: 27-16-62, 33-28-46, General Director: M. A. Lotagr

Inter-Tours Corp., 5458 Wilshire Boulevard, Los Angeles, CA 90036, Phone: (213) 933-7153, (800) 366-5458, FAX: (213) 933-8317, Telex: 691370, Contact: Helen Stein

International Executive Reports, 717 D St., NW Suite 300, Washington DC 20004-2807, Phone: (301) 983-3149, (202) 628-6618, Contact: Mary Saba

International Leadership, American Center for International Leadership, 522 Franklin St, Columbus, IN 47201, Phone: (812) 376-3456

International Trade Administration (ITA), U.S. Department of Commerce, Room 1015 Washington, DC 20230, Phone: (202) 377-0550, Contact: J. Michael Farren, Under Secretary for International Trade

International Trade and Communications, Inc. (ITC), 1608 Walnut Street, Philadelphia, PA 19103, Phone: (215) 732-2844, FAX: (215) 790-0158, Telex: 4948598, Contact: Richard B. Price, President

International Trade Controls, U.S. Department of State, Room 3529, 2201 C Street, NW Washington DC, 20520, Phone: (202) 647-

1625, Contact: Mike Zacharia, Deputy Assistant Secretary

International Post Office, Komsomolskaya Pl., 1A, or, Varshavskoye Shosse, 37A, Moscow, Phone: 111-05-13

Internauchpribor, 26 Prospekt Ogorodnikova, 198103 Leningrad, Telex: 121549 NTO AN, Phone: 251-88-89; 135-50-38, Director: Yu. A. Konopaltsev

Intertorg, Inc., in the U.S.: 940 Sagamore Way, Sacramento, CA 95822, Phone: (916) 443-2981, FAX: (914) 443-2991, Telex: 176834, in Moscow: Gruzinskiy Pereulok 3, kv. 63, 123056 Moscow, Phone: 253-97-71, 254-31-62

Intertrans Corporation, 113 Executive Drive, Suite 101, Sterling, VA 22170, Phone: (703) 834-3116, FAX: (703) 834-5786, Contact: Dale Goodson

Intourist, 630 Fifth Ave., Suite 868, New York, NY 10111, Phone: (212) 757-3884, Contact: Yuri Bagrov, General Manager

Intracom, Inc., 6 New England Executive Park, Burlington, MA 01803, Phone: (617) 229-1685, FAX: (617) 229-1687

INTRAVCO Travel Centers, Inc., 211 East 43rd Street, New York, NY 10017, Phone: (212) 972-1155, (800) ITC-TRVL, FAX: (212) 983-2590, Telex: 201831 ITCNY UR, Contact: Clark Malcom

Iowa, 817 Federal Bldg., 210 Walnut Street, Des Moines, IA 50309, Phone: (515) 284-4222

ISPO, 1 Ul. Stankostroiteley, 153009 Ivanovo, Cable: Granit Ivanovo, Telex: 412687, Phone: 3-37-24, Director: A. V. Mayerov

ITS Tours & Travel, 1055 Texas Avenue, Suite 104, College Station, TX 77840, Phone: (409) 764-9400, (800) 533-8688, FAX: (409) 693-9673, Telex: 293148

Jacobson, Helen Saltz, 55 Thompson Hay Path, Setauket, NY 11733, Phone: (516) 751-0371

Jacolev, Leon, 30 The Fairway, Upper Montclair, NJ 07043, Phone: (201) 748-5673

Jarrett International, Inc., P.O. Box 132, Weston, MA 02193, Phone: (617) 893-5406, FAX: (617) 891-9316, Contact: Derek Jarrett

Johanson, Astrid, c/o Bell Laboratories, 600 Mountain Avenue, Murray Hill, NJ 07974, Phone: (201) 792-5826, (201) 582-6066

Johnson and Higgins, 125 Broad Street, New York, NY 10004-2400, Phone: (212) 574-7745, FAX: (212) 574-8993, Telex: 420027, Contact: Ken Horne, Vice President, Political Risk Unit

Jones, Day, Reavis, & Pogue, Metropolitan Square, 1450 G Street, NW, Washington, DC 20005-2088, Phone: (202) 879-3939, FAX: (202) 737-2832, Telex: 892410 - Domestic, 64363 - International, Contact: Michael R. Silverman or Charles Mathias, Jr.

Journal of Commerce, 110 Wall Street, New York, NY 10005, Phone: (212) 425-1616

Journal of the U.S.-U.S.S.R. Trade and Economic Council, U.S.-U.S.S.R. Trade and

Economic Council, Inc., 805 Third Avenue, New York, NY 10022, Phone: (212) 644-4550

JPRS (Joint Publication Research Service): U.S.S.R. Serial Reports, U.S. Department of Commerce, NTIS 5285 Port Royal Road, Springfield, VA 22161, Phone: (703) 487-4630.

Jurjans, Peteris, 38021 Euclid Avenue, Cleveland, OH 44094, Phone: (216) 951-6665, FAX: (216) 951-4797, Telex: 7101109209, Contact: Peteris Jurjans [Yuryans]

Kansas, 727 N. River Park Pl., Suite 565, Waco, KS 67203, Phone: (316) 259-6160

Karl, Ann Marie, 2880 N. Meridian Rd., Tallahassee, FL 32312, Phone: (904) 385-9747

Kawecki, Alicja T., 4AD Foxwood Drive, Morris Plains, NJ 07950, Phone: (201) 582-3817

Kazakhintorg, Ul. Gogol 111, 480003 Alma-Ata, General Director: S. Zh. Abishev

Keasbey, William P., 5031 Alta Vista Road, Bethesda, MD 20814, Phone: (301) 530-5031

Keesan, Cynthia, 504 Hiscock #1, Ann Arbor, MI 48103, Phone: (313) 995-9463

Kelly International, 120-65 168th Street, Jamaica, NY 11434, Phone: (718) 528-0540, (718) 656-5926, FAX: (718) 528-0510, Telex: 427889, Contact: Martin J. Kelly, President

Kennan Institute for Advanced Russian Studies, 370 L'Enfant Promenade, SW, Suite 704, Washington, DC 20024-2518, Phone: (202) 287-3400, FAX: (202) 287-3772, Contact: Blair Ruble, Director

Kent Group International, 131 State Street, Boston, MA 02109, Phone: (617) 232-8008, FAX: (617) 730-6485, Telex: 8100071150, Contact: George Cuker, President

Kentucky, Rm 636B, U.S. Post Office and Courthouse Bldg., Louisville, KY 40202, Phone: (502) 582-5066

Kertesz, Francois, 112 Wendover Cir., Oak Ridge, TN 37830-8246, Phone: (615) 483-6225

KFC Corporation, 1441 Gardiner Lane, Louisville, KY 40213, Phone: (502) 454-2169, FAX: (502) 456-8323, Contact: R. Scott Toop

Kirghizvneshtorg, Ul. Kirova 205, Frunze 72000, Phone: 26-63-66, General Director: E. A. Mochayev

Kirgiz Chamber of Commerce, 435 Frunze Ul., 720345 Frunze, Phone: (331) 26-49-42

Kirishinefteorgsintez, 187110 Kirishi, Leningradskoy oblasti, Cable: Kirishinedteorgsintez Kirishi Leningradskaya FTF, Phone: 2-11-90; 9-12-30, Director: A. P. Smirnov

Kiser Research, Inc., 1233 20th Street, NW, Suite 505, Washington, DC 20036, Phone: (202) 223-5806, FAX: (202) 452-9571, Telex: 4991601 ITT, Contact: John Kiser

Klineburger Worldwide Travel, 3627 1st Avenue South, Seattle, WA 98134, Phone:

251

(206) 343-9699, FAX: (206) 682-8868, Telex: 185283

KLM Royal Dutch Airlines, Hotel Mezhdunarodnaya II, Krasnopresnenskaya Nab. 12, Kv. 1307 Moscow, Phone: 253-21-50-51, 230-23-04; (800) 777-5553 (U.S.), Lufthansa, in New York: 750 Lexington Avenue, New York, NY 10022-1208, Phone: (212) 745-0701, (800) 645-3880, FAX: (212) 745-0899, in Moscow: Kuznetskiy Most, 3, Moscow, Phone: 923-04-88

Kniga Printshop, 50 Gorky Street, Moscow 125047, Phone: 251-1215, FAX: 230-2207

KOMPASS Intercontinental Publishing, Inc., in Boston: 418 Commonwealth Ave. Boston, MA 02215, Phone: (617) 266-1214, FAX: (617) 247-3008, in Moscow: Sovietskaya Hotel, Leningradskiy Prospekt 32, Moscow

Koorbanoff, Alex, 5525 Twin Knolls Road, Suite 323, Columbia, MD 21045, Phone: (301) 995-3022, FAX: (301) 995-0805

Krasitel, 2 Prospekt Khimikov, 349870 Rubezhnoye Voroshilovgradskoy oblasti, Cable: Rubezhnoye 70 Voroshilovgradskoy Rubin, Director: S. P. Pushkin

Krayan, 2 Ul. Yanvarskogo Vosstaniya, 270017 Odessa, Cable: Podem Odessa, Telex: 232714 Kran, Phone: 66-01-03, Director: V. V. Larionov

KRI, Kiser Research, Inc., 1233 20th Street, NW, Suite 505, Washington, DC 20036, Phone: (202) 223-5806, FAX: (202) 452-9571, Telex: 499160 (ITT), Contact: John W. Kiser

Kutak, Rock & Campbell, The Omaha Building, 1650 Farnam Street, Omaha, NE 68102, Phone: (402) 346-6000, FAX: (402) 346-1148, Telex: 484 415 Kuroc, Contact: William E. Holland

Latvian Chamber of Commerce, 21 Ul. Lenina, 226189 Riga, Phone: (013) 33-22-05

Laurel Industries, in the U.S., 280 Laurel Avenue, Highland Park, IL 60035, Phone: (708) 432-8204, FAX: (708) 432-8243, Telex: 720457 CRL INC HLPK, Contact: Catherine Lambrecht, in Moscow: Hotel Mezhdunarodnaya 2, Krasnopresnenskaya Nab., 12, 123610 Moscow, Phone: 437-54-64, FAX: 437-54-64

Lawyers Alliance for World Security (LAWS), [formerly Lawyers Alliance for Nuclear Arms Control, Inc.], 1120 19th Street, NW, Suite 615, Washington, DC 20036, Phone: (202) 296-6054, FAX: (202) 296-6049, Contact: Elizabeth Lyman, Executive Director

LeBoeuf, Lamb, Leiby & MacRae, 520 Madison Avenue, New York, NY 10022, Phone: (212) 715-8000, FAX: (212) 371-4840, Telex: 423416, Contact: John I. Huhs

Lenfintorg, 98 Moskovskiy Prosp., 196084 Leningrad, Cable: Lefintorg Leningrad M-84, Telex: 122724 Lenfin, Phone: 292-56-33; 296-1165, General Director: V. N. Gladkov

Leningrad Chamber of Commerce, 10 Krasnyy Flot Embankment, 190000 Leningrad, Phone: (812) 314-99-53

Licata, Arthur F., P.C., 20 Custom House Street, Suite 1010, Boston, MA 02110, Phone:

(617) 345-9588, (800) 777-0899, FAX: (617) 345-9787, Contact: Arthur F. Licata

LIC-CON Technologies, Inc., 655 3rd Avenue, Suite 1620, New York, NY 10017, Phone: (212) 818-9010, FAX: (212) 818-0463, Telex: CMC 66403 UW, Contact: Peter Walsh

Licensintorg, 11 Minskaya Ul., Moscow 121108, Cable: Licensintorg Moscow, Telex: 145-27-00; 145-29-00, General Director: V. V. Ignatov

Linguitronics, P.O. Box 9504, Arlington, VA 22209, Phone: (703) 920-7098, FAX: (703) 979-0467, Contact: Tamara Sherman

Linzmeyer, Peter C., Foley & Lardner, 1775 Pennsylvania Avenue, NW, Washington, DC 20006. Phone (202) 862-5300. FAX (202) 862-5399.

Lithuanian Chamber of Commerce, 31 Algirdo St., 232600 Vilnius, Phone: (012) 66-15-50

Litimpex, Prospekt Lenian 37, Vilnius 232600, Phone: 62-09-96; 62-14-53, Telex: 278128, 261148, General Director: A. A. Smagin

LMZ, 18 Sverdlovskaya Naberezhnaya, 195108 Leningrad, Cable: Leningrad 108 Turbina, Phone: 248-70-19, Director: A. I. Burgazliyev

Loiry, William S., President, Global Trade Books, 1155 Connecticut Avenue, NW, Suite 500, Washington, DC 20036, Phone (202) 467-8553. FAX (202) 452-8654. Telex 4933729 WASH UI

Loiry, William S., Chairman & CEO, Global Trading Associates, Inc., 1155 Connecticut Avenue, NW, Suite 500, Washington, DC

20036. Phone (202) 467-8589, FAX: (202) 452-8654. Telex 4933729 WASH UI

Loiry, William S., President, The Foundation for Citizen Diplomacy, 1155 Connecticut Avenue, NW, Suite 500, Washington, DC 20036. Phone (202) 467-8587. FAX (202) 452-8654. Telex 4933729 WASH UI

Lord Day & Lord, Barrett Smith, 1675 Broadway, New York, NY 10019-5874, Phone: (212) 969-6000, FAX: (212) 969-6100, Telex: 62589, Contact: Peter Pettibone, Polina Smith, Jonathan Pavluk

Lotyczewski, Agnieszka T., 11 Terrace Street, Norwich, NY 13815, Phone: (607) 334-9070

Louis & Johnson, Chartered, 7611 Lexington Avenue, Laurel, MD 02707, Phone: (301) 498-9404, FAX: (301) 604-7348, Telex: 6504339454, Contact: Zakhar Matlin

Louisiana, 432 International Trade Mart, No. 2 Canal Street, New Orleans, LA 70130, Phone: (504) 589-6546

LTZ, 2 Krasnogvardeyskaya Ul., Lipetsk, Cable: Lipetsk 30 Proton, Phone: 23-74-64, Director: V. V. Antonov

Madsen Marketing Strategies, 31 Kidder Avenue, Somerville, MA 02144, Phone: (617) 628-9297, Contact: Carol J. Madsen, Principal

Main Customs Administration, 9 Komsomolskaya Ploshchad 1a, 107140 Moscow, Phone: Protocol 208-24-41; Information 208-44-62

Maine, Memorial Circle, Casco Bank Bldg., Augusta, ME 04330, Phone: (207) 622-8249

253

Malmgren Group, 2001 L Street, NW, Suite 1040, Washington, DC 20036, Phone: (202) 466-8740, FAX: (202) 872-1529, Telex: 440555, Contact: Harald B. Malmgren

Manufacturer's Hanover, 270 Park Avenue, New York, NY 10022, Phone: (212) 286-3314, Contact: Roger Codat, Vice President

Marcinik, Roger, P.O. Box 060411, Palm Bay, FL 32906, Phone: (305) 725-1610

Margo's International Travel Service, 1812 Irving Street, San Francisco, CA 94122, Phone: (415) 665-4330; (800) 33 MARGO, FAX: (415) 665-4942, Telex: 340649

Marsh and McLennan Worldwide, 1221 Avenue of the Americas, New York, NY 10020-1011, Phone: (212) 345-4000, FAX: (212) 345-4054, Contact: Frank Gunderson, Managing Director

Martin, Joan M., 922 Shirley Manor Road, Reisterstown, MD 21136, Phone: (301) 833-3248

Maryland, 415 U.S. Custom House, Gay & Lombard Streets, Baltimore, MD 21202, Phone: (301) 962-3560

Mashpriborintorg, 32/34 Smolenskaya-Sennaya Pl., 121200 Moscow, Cable: Mashpribor Moscow, Telex: 411235; 411236, Phone: 244-27-75, General Director: V. F. Klimov

Massachusetts, 10th Fl., 441 Stuart Street, Boston, MA 02116, Phone: (617) 223-2312

Massachusetts Port Authority, Trade Development Unit, World Trade Center, Suite 321, Boston, MA 02210, Phone: (617) 439-5560

Massachusetts Soviet Trade Council, 31 Kidder Avenue, Sommerville, MA 02144, Phone: (617) 628-9297, Contact: Carol J. Madsen, Vice President - Marketing

Matekon, M.E. Sharpe, Inc., 80 Business Park Drive, Armonk, NY 10504, Phone: (800) 541-6563 or (914) 273-1800

Mayer, Brown & Platt, 787 7th Avenue, New York, NY 10019, Phone: (212) 554-3000, FAX: (212) 262-1910, Telex: 701842, Contact: Michael G. Capatides

Mayer, Claudius Francis, 5513 39th Street, NW, Washington, DC 20015, Phone: (202) 966-3723

MB International, 9704 Burke View Avenue, Burke, VA 22015, Phone: (703) 425-0024, FAX: (703) 425-0025

McAulay Fisher Nissen & Goldberg, 261 Madison Avenue, New York, NY 10016, Phone: (212) 986-4090, FAX: (212) 818-9479, Telex: 427294, Contact: J. Harold Nissen, international patent and trademark attorney

McGlothlin, William C., 717A Old County Road, Belmont, CA 94002, Phone: (415) 591-2875

Medical Consortium, 1055 Washington Boulevard, Stamford, CT 06901, Phone: (203) 327-0900, FAX: (203) 325-3127, Contact: Dennis A. Sokol, President

Meridian House International, 1630 Crescent Place, NW, Washington, DC 20009, Phone:

(202) 667-6800, FAX: (202) 667-1475, Contact: Nancy Matthews, Director, Public Affairs

Meta-Filtr, 77 Ul. Frunze, 600016 Frunze, Cable: Poisk SU, Telex: 218291 Poisk SU, Phone: 1-56-74, Director: V. B. Kryukovskiy

Mezhdunarodnaya kniga, 39 Ul. Dmitrova, 113095 Moscow, Cable: Mezhkniga Moscow, Telex: 411160, Phone: 238-46-00, General Director: S. V. Ostapishin

MG Trade Finance Corporation, 520 Madison Avenue, New York, NY 10016, Phone: (212) 826-5506, Contact: Huang Hung, Vice President

Michigan, 445 Federal Bldg., 231 W. Lafayette, Detroit, MI 48226, Phone: (313) 226-3650

Midwest Enterprises, Inc., 8493 16th Road, Almond, WI 54909, Phone: (715) 366-8800, FAX: (715) 366-4400, Contact: Mark Dzulynsky, President

Milbank, Tweed, Hadley & McCloy, International Square Building, 1825 Eye Street, NW, Suite 900, Washington DC 20006, Phone: (202) 835-7500, FAX: (202) 835-7586, Telex: 440887, Contact: Stanley J. Marcus/Fred W. Reinke

Miller & Chevalier, 655 15th Street, NW, Washington DC 20005, Phone: (202) 626-5800, FAX: (202) 628-0859, Telex: 440250, Contact: Homer E. Moyer, Jr.

Ministry of Automotive and Agricultural Machine Building (Minavtoselkhozmash) Kuznetskiy Most, 21-5, 100031 Moscow

Ministry of Aviation (Minaviaprom), 16 Ulanskiy Per., 101849 Moscow, Phone: Foreign Relations Department 207-02-73

Ministry of Communications (Minsvyaz), 7 Ul. Gorkogo, 103375 Moscow, Phone: Foreign Relations Department 295-51-08;, Protocol Section 229-98-78, 292-25-58

Ministry of Civil Aviation (MGA), 37 Leningradskiy Prosp., 125167 Moscow, Phone: Foreign Relations Department 155-57-28; Protocol Section 155-54-94

Ministry of Culture (Minkultury), 35 Ul. Arbat, 121835 Moscow, Phone: Foreign Relations Department 248-12-80;, Protocol Section 248-10-26, 248-10-14, FAX: 411290 MUZA SU

Ministry of Defense (Minoborony), 37 Ul. Kirova, 103160 Moscow, Phone: 223-61-08, Telex: The Ministry is concerned with the defense of the Soviet Union.

Ministry of Energy and Electrification (Minelektrotekhprom), 19 Prospekt Kalinina, 121908 Moscow G-19, Phone: Foreign Relations Department 291-50-48;, Protocol Section 291-50-45, Telex: 411390 METR SU

Ministry of Finance (Minfin), 9 Ul. Kuybysheva, 103097 Moscow, Phone: Foreign Relations Division 298-51-88;, Protocol Section 298-51-45, Telex: 411144 INGS SU

Ministry of Foreign Affairs (MID), 32/34 Smolenskaya-Sennaya Ploshchad, 121200 Moscow, Phone: Information Department 244-41-19; Protocol Department 244-43-03, Telex: 411458 OPMID S

Ministry of Foreign Economic Relations (MVES), 32/34 Smolenskaya-Sennaya Ploshchad, 121200 Moscow, Phone: Protocol Section 244-34-83, 244-34-80, Telex: 411931 TIOJP SU

Ministry of General Machine Building (Minobshchemash), 3 Miusskaya Pl., 125833 Moscow, Phone: Foreign Relations Department 251-68-50

Ministry of Geology (Mingeo), 4/6 Bolshaya Gruzinskaya Ul., 123242 Moscow, Phone: Foreign Relations Department 254-11-33

Ministry of Health (Minzdrav), Rakhmanovskyy Per., 3, 101431 Moscow, Phone: Protocol Section 921-46-72; Information 228-44-78, Telex: 411355

Ministry of Heavy, Power and Transport Machine Building (Mintyazhmash), 5 Nizhne-Kislovskiy Per., 103906 Moscow, Phone: Foreign Economic Relations Administration 291-09-70;, Protocol Section 291-27-52, Telex: 411337

Ministry of Installation and Special Construction (Minmotazhspetsstroi), B. Sadovaya 8, 103379 Moscow, Phone: 209-10-09

Ministry of Internal Affairs (MVD), 6 Ul. Ogareva, 103009 Moscow, Phone: Foreign Relations Division 222-68-2

Ministry of Justice, 4 Ul. Obukhova, 129028 Moscow

Ministry of Land Reclamation and Water Conservation (Minvodkhoz), 10 Novobasmannaya Ul., 107803 Moscow, Phone:

Foreign Relations Department 267-34-71;, Protocol Section 265-91-87, Telex: 411857 WODA SU

Ministry of Local Industries, Uzbek S.S.R., Department of International Economic Relations, 5 Alleya Paradov, 700017 Tashkent, Phone: (371) 33-62-44, Contact: U. K. Ismailov

Ministry of Metallurgy (Minmet), 27 Prosp. Kalinina, 121911 Moscow

Ministry of Trade (Mintorg), 14 Ul. Razina, 103688 Moscow-Centre, Phone: Foreign Relations Department 298-39-34;, Protocol Section 298-47-76, Telex: 411424 BAM SU

Ministry of Transport Construction (Mintransstroy), 21 Sadovaya-Spasskaya Ul., 107217 Moscow

Ministry of the Chemical and Petroleum Machine Building (Minkhimmash), 25 Bezbozhnyy Per., 129833 Moscow, Phone: Foreign Relations Department 288-64-33; Protocol 288-40-10

Ministry of the Coal Industry (Minugleprom), 23 Kalinina Prosp., 121910 Moscow, Phone: Foreign Relations Department 202-87-67, 202-87-58; Protocol Section 202-26-94

Ministry of the Defense Industry (Minoboronprom), 35 Ul. Gorkogo, Moscow, Phone: 209-85-87

Ministry of the Electronics Industry (Minelektronprom), 7 Kitayskiy Proyezd, 103074 Moscow, Phone: Foreign Relations Department and Protocol Section 155-40-35, Telex: 411390 METP SU

256

Ministry of the Fishing Industry (Minrybkhoz), 12 Rozhdestvenskiy Bulvar, 103031 Moscow, Phone: Foreign Relations Department 228-28-73, 228-12-96, Telex: 411208, 411210 SRF SU

Ministry of the Forestry Industry (Minlesbumprom), 1 Telegraphnyy Per., 101934 Moscow-Centre, Phone: Foreign Relations Department and Protocol Section 207-96-43, 208-02-57

Ministry of the Machine Tool and Instrument Building Industry (Minstankoprom), 20 Ul. Gorkogo, 103789 Moscow GSP-3, Phone: Foreign Relations Department 209-79-65;, Protocol Section 209-55-17, 209-23-86, Telex: 411053 MINST SU

Ministry of the Maritime Fleet (Minmorflot), Ul. Zhdanova, 1/4, 103759 Moscow GSP, Phone: 226-10-00

Ministry of the Medical Industry (Minmedprom), Prospekt Khudozhestvennogo Teatra, 2, 103823 Moscow GSP

Ministry of the Oil and Gas Construction Industry (Minneftegazstroy)

Ministry of the Radio Industry (Minradioprom), 7 Kitaysky Proyezd, 103074 Moscow, Phone: Main Administration for Economic, Scientific, and Technical, Cooperation with Foreign Countries 925-24-21; Protocol Section 207-96-27, Services: Minradioprom is involved in research and production of television sets, radios, tape recorders, computers, radio instruments, and other electronic gear.

Ministry of the Railways (MPS), 2 Novobasmannaya Ul., 107174 Moscow, Phone:

Foreign Relations Department 262-16-28, Telex: 411 832 CIMPS

Ministry of the Shipbuilding Industry (Minsudprom), 11 Sadovo-Kudrinskaya Ul., 123231 Moscow, Phone: Foreign Relations Department 252-07-40, V/O Sudozagranpostavka 254-98-29, Telex: 411116 KURS SU

Minnesota, 108 Federal Bldg., 110 S. 4th Street, Minneapolis, MN 55401, Phone: (612) 349-3338

Mir Corporation, 3603 S. Hanford, Seattle, WA 98144, Phone: (206) 722-1633, FAX: (206) 624-7360

Missouri, 120 S. Central Avenue, Street Louis, MO 63105, Phone: (314) 425-3302

MK Technology Deltac, 1920 N Street, NW, Suite 600, Washington, DC 20036, Phone: (202) 463-1250, FAX: (202) 429-9812, Telex: 6503140383

MK Technology Deltac, 1920 N Street, NW, Suite 650, Washington, DC 20036, Phone: (202) 463 0904, FAX: (202) 429-9812, Contact: Mitchell Eisen

Moldex, Ul. Botanicheskaya 15, 277018 Kishinyev, Telex: 163125 KODRU SU, Phone: 55-70-36, General Director: V. D. Volodin

Montana, Phone: Serviced by Denver, CO office.

Morgan Grenfell & Co. Limited, USSR Team, Banking Division, 23 Great Winchester Street, London EC2P 2AX, UK, Phone: 588-4545, FAX: 1-826-7130, Telex: 896106 MG BFI G,

257

Contact: Olimpia Cuomo, in Moscow: USSR Representative Office, Morgan Grenfell & Co. Limited, Pokrovsky, Bulvar 4/17, kv. 34, Phone: 230-23-86; 207-59-98, FAX: 230-23-86, Telex: 413121 MINBRO SU, Contact: Neil Jenkins

Morrison & Foerster, 1290 Avenue of the Americas, New York, NY 10104, Phone: (212) 468-8057, FAX: (212) 468-7900, Contact: James R. Silkenat

Morrow, Theodore E., 1663 Woodford Way, Blue Bell, PA 19422, Phone: (215) 277-0672

Mortekhinformreklama, Ul. Rozhdestvenka 1/4, 103759 Moscow, Telex: 411197 MMF SU, Phone: 158-2553

Moscow Boston International, Ltd., P.O. Box 1327, Cambridge, MA 02238 U.S.A., Phone: (617) 868-2080, FAX: (617) 864-8002, Contact: John K. Garrity, Chairman of the Board; Yuri A. Brazhenko, President

Moscow Central Post Office, Ul. Kirova, 26A 101000 Moscow, Phone: 228-63-11, 924-02-50, 924-95-29

Moscow Central Telephone and Telegraph, Ul. Gorkogo, 7, Moscow, Phone: 924-05-20, 924-90-40,

Moscow Chamber of Commerce, 13-17 Ul. Chekova, 103050 Moscow, Phone: 299-76-12

Moscow City Council (Mossoviet), 13 Ul. Gorkogo, 103789 Moscow, Phone: 229-79-51, Contact: S. I. Dolgoshljbov, Director of Foreign Relations Department

Moscow International Business Network, 119 Peterborough Street, #4, Boston, MA 02215,

Phone: (617) 262-4010, Contact: George Laughead

Moscow Narodnyy Bank, Pokrovskyy Bulvar 4/17 Suite 34, Moscow, Phone: 230-2386, Telex: 413121 MNBRO SU

Moscow Narodnyy Bank Press Bulletin, Economics Department, Moscow Narodnyy Bank, 32 King William Street, London EC4P JS, England

Moscow News, 16/2 Ul. Gorkogo, Moscow 103829, Phone: 229-90-00 (information) and 209-12-49 (letters)

Moscow Project Management, 131 State Street, Boston, MA 02109, Phone: (617) 720-2000, FAX: (617) 720-3909, Telex: 8100071150, Contact: Rita Cuker

Moskvitch, 46-A Volgogradskiy Prosp., 109316 Moscow, Cable: FTF Moskvitch Moscow, Phone: 276-87-32, Director: V. K. Fedulov

MPO Elektrozavod, 21 Ul. Elektrozavodskaya, 105023 Moscow, Telex: 411589 Mez SU, Phone: 369-30-78, Director: S. L. Ponamaryov

MSPO, 16 Oktyabraskaya Ul., 220801 Minsk, Cable: Minsk Koltso, Phone: 22-00-32

National Council for Soviet and East European Research, 1755 Massachusetts Ave., Suite 304, Washington, DC 20036, Phone: (202) 387-0168, Contact: Robert H. Randolph

National Council of World Affairs Organization, 1619 Massachusetts Avenue, NW, Washington, DC 20036, Phone: (202) 663-5950

National Foreign Trade Council, 1625 K Street, NW, Washington DC 20006, Phone: (202) 887-0278, FAX: (202) 452-8160, Contact: Frank D. Kittredge, President

National Impact, 100 Maryland Avenue, NE, Suite 502, Washington, DC 20002, Phone: (202) 544-8636

National Institute of Standards and Technologies, 108 Bureau Drive, Gaithersburg, MD 20899, Phone: (301) 975-2000, FAX: (301) 975-2128

National Westminster, 175 Water Street, 28th Floor, New York, NY 10038, Phone: (212) 602-2120, Contact: Donna Gravier, Assistant Treasurer

Nebraska, 1st Fl., 300 S. 19th Street, Omaha, NE 68102, Phone: (402) 221-3664

Neftekhimbank, (Commercial Bank for the Petroleum and Chemical Production Sector), Ul. Gilyarskogo 31, 129832 Moscow, Phone: 284-81-22

Nelles, Peter, Nelles Translations, 18 S. Michigan Avenue, Suite 1000, Chicago, IL 60603, Phone: (312) 236-2788, FAX: (312) 236-0717

Nevmashexport, 52 Prosp. Obukhovskoy Oborony, 193029 Leningrad, Cable: Kit Leningrad 29, Telex: 121574, Phone: 221-04-85; 567-69-42, Director: V. I. Savoshchev

New England Soviet Trade Council, P.O. Box 60, Boston, MA 02130, Phone: (617) 524-5454, Contact: Gerald Wright, President

New Hampshire, Serviced by Boston office.

New Jersey, 3131 Princeton Pike, 4-D Suite 211, New Jersey, Trenton 08648, Phone: (609) 989-2100

New Mexico, 517 Gold SW, Suite 4303, Albuquerque, NM 87102, Phone: (505) 766-2386

New Outlook, American Committee on U.S.-Soviet Relations, 109 Eleventh Street, SE, Washington, DC 20003, Phone: (202) 546-1700

New Times, Pushkin Square, Moscow 103782, Phone: 229-88-72, 209-07-67, FAX: 200-41-92, 200-10-38, Telex: 411164a NEWT SU, Editor-In-Chief: Vitaliy Ignatenko, Editor of English Edition: N. Agaltsev

New York, 1312 Federal Bldg., 111 W. Huron Street, Buffalo, NY 14202, Phone: (716) 846-4191

New York/New Jersey Port Authority, 1 World Trade Center, Room 63 East, New York, NY 10048, Phone: (212) 466-8499

New York State Bar Association, Committee on Soviet and Eastern European Law, c/o Brian G. Hart, Simpson, Thacher & Bartlett, 425 Lexington Avenue, New York, NY 10017, Phone: (212) 455-2000, FAX: (212) 455-2502, Telex: 4552500, Contact: Brian G. Hart

NEXUS, Publisher: NEXUS Corp., 7700 Leesburg Pike, Falls Church, VA 22043, Phone: (703) 847-6644

North Carolina, 203 Federal Bldg., 324 W. Market Street, P.O. Box 1950, Greensboro, NC 27402, Phone: (919) 378-5354

North Dakota, Serviced by Omaha, NB office.

Nuclear Regulatory Commission, Public Document Room, Washington, DC 20555, Phone: (202) 634-3273

OASES-DC, 1430 K Street, NW, Suite 1200, Washington, DC 20005, Phone: (202) 393-0985, FAX: (202) 393-0989, Contact: Rudy Delassandro

O'Brien, Maureen, 1380 N.E. Miami Gardens Drive, Suite 220, North Miami Beach, FL 33179, Phone: (305) 949-0093, FAX: (305) 949-9325

Obshchemashexport, Ul. Krasnoproletarskaya, 9, 101444 Moscow, Telex: 411836, Phone: 258-19-70, 258-66-56

Office for Europe, Office of International Health, Parklawn Bldg. Rm 18-75, 5600 Fishers Lane, Rockville, MD 20857, Phone: (301) 443-4010

Office of East-West Economic Policy, U.S. Department of Transportation, 1550 Pennsylvania Ave, NW, Room 444, Washington DC 20220, Phone: (202) 556-5637

Office of East-West Trade, U.S. Department of State, Bureau of Economic Affairs, Room 3529 2201 C Street, NW, Washington DC, 20520, Phone: (202) 647-2875, Contact: Patrick Nichols, Director of East-West Trade

Office of Eastern Europe and Soviet Affairs, U.S. Department of Commerce, Room 3413,

Main Commerce Bldg., Washington, DC 20230, Phone: (202) 377-1104, 377-4655, FAX: (202) 377-2155, Telex: 892536, Contact: Jack Brougher, Leslie Brown, Susan Lewenz

Office of European Affairs, Soviet Desk, U.S. Information Agency, 301 4th Street SW, Washington DC 20547, Phone: (202) 485-8857

Office of Foreign Agricultural Affairs, U.S. Department of Agriculture, 14th Street & Independence Avenue, SW, Washington, DC 20250, Phone: (202) 447-6138, Contact: Wayne Sharp

Office of Import Investigations, U.S. Department of Commerce, Room 3047, Washington DC 20230, Phone: (202) 377-5497

Office of International Activities, Environmental Protection Agency, 401 M Street, SW, Mail Code A106, Washington, DC 20460, Phone: (202) 475-8597, FAX: (202) 382-4470, Contact: Gary Waxmonsky

Office of International Activities, U.S. Department of Housing and Urban Development 451 7th Street, SW, Room 7114 Washington, DC 20410, Phone: (202) 755-6422

Office of International Trade Policy, U.S. Department of Agriculture, Foreign Agricultural Service, Washington, DC 20250-1000, Phone: (202) 382-1289, Contact: Scott Bleggi

Office of International Transportation and Trade, U.S. Department of Transportation, 400 7th Street, SW, Room 10300, Washington DC 20590, Phone: (202) 366-4368, FAX: (202)

366-7483, Contact: Arnold Levine

Office of Joint Ventures, U.S. Department of Commerce, Room 4060, Main Commerce Bldg., 14th Street and Constitution Ave, NW Washington DC 20230, Phone: (202) 377-5695, FAX: (202) 377-0937, Contact: Surendra K. Dhir

Office of Soviet Union Affairs, Economic Section, U.S. Department of State, EUR/SOV Room 4229, 2201 C Street, NW, Washington DC, 20520, Phone: (202) 647-8920, Contact: Edward J. Salazar

Office of Technology and Policy Analysis, U.S. Department of Commerce, Rm 4061, 14th Street and Constitution Ave, NW, Washington DC 20230, Phone: (202) 377-4516

Office of the United States Trade Representative, East-West and Non-Market Economies Division, Winder Bldg., 600 17th Street, NW, Washington, DC 20506, Phone: (202) 395-3074; (202) 395-3211, Contact: Gordana Earp, Michael Brownrigg

Ohio, 9504 Federal Bldg., 550 Main Street, Cincinnati, OH 45202, Phone: (513) 684-2944

Oklahoma, 6601 Broadway Ext., Suite 200, Oklahoma City, OK 73116, Phone: (405) 231-5302

Olaechea, Marilyn, 6140 Dayton Road, Springfield, OH 45502, Phone: H: (513) 864-5709, O: (513) 257-2891

Olkhovsky, Yuri, 12409 Braxfield Court, #4, Rockville, MD 20852, Phone: H: (301) 881-5326, W: (202) 994-6336, Contact: Yuri Olkhovsky

Oregon, Room 618, 1220 SW, 3rd Avenue, Portland, OR 97204, Phone: (503) 221-3001

Organization for American-Soviet Exchanges, DC (OASES-DC), 1430 K Street, NW, Suite 1200, Washington, DC 20005, Phone: (202) 393-0985, FAX: (202) 393-0989, Telex: 6503291788 MCI UW; 6976209 OASES UW, Contact: Rudy D'Alessandro, Executive Director

Osorio, Pedro, 133 66th Street, W. New York, NJ 07093, Phone: (201) 868-4984

Osporad, 6 Ul. Lomonosova, 302018 Oryel, Cable: Rele Oryol, Telex: 412505 Prima, Phone: 22-13-54; 22-10-86, Director: K. M. Manenkov

Outlook, 1782 Wyrinck Avenue, San Jose, CA 95124, Phone: (408) 723-5135, FAX: (408) 371-4474

Overseas Private Investment Corporation (OPIC), 1615 M Street, Washington, DC 20527, Phone: (202) 457-7093

P.D.I.-Barcon Inc., 25 W. 43rd Street, New York, NY 10036, Phone: (212) 764-8800, FAX: (212) 764-8850, Telex: 6790550, Contact: Joseph H. Filner, CEO; Jacob Pollock, Chairman, in Ohio: 3200 W. Market Street, Akron, OH 44313, Phone: (216) 869-8734, FAX: (216) 869-8726, Telex: 205938 BARMET

Pan American Airways, Mezhdunarodnaya/Sovincenter, Krasnopresnenskaya 12, Kv. 1102A, Moscow, Phone: 253-26-58, 253-26-59, in New York: (800) 221-1111, Percival Tours, Hurst Bldg.,

Suite 1025, 5 Third Street, San Francisco, CA 94103, Phone: (415) 442-1815, (800) 537-8600 (CA); (800) 451-0800 (outside CA), FAX: (415) 442-1824, Telex: 3717748

Panalpina, Inc, Harborside Financial Center, 34 Exchange Place-Plaza II, Jersey, NY 07201, Phone: (201) 451-4000, Telex: 22-2874 PANNY UR, Cable: PANALPINA

Papinako, Ilya, 14100 W. 94th Terrace, Lenexa, KS 66215, Phone: (913) 492-6076

Parsons Friedmann Stephan & Rose, 418 Commonwealth Ave., Boston, MA 02215, Contact: John M. Rose, Jr., President

Paul, Hastings, Janofsky & Walker, 1050 Connecticut Avenue, NW, Twelfth Floor, Washington, DC 20036, Phone: (202) 223-9000, FAX: (202) 452-8149, Telex: 710-822-9062, Contact: G. Hamilton Loeb

PC World USSR, International Marketing Services, IDG Communications, Inc., 5 Speen St., Framingham, MA 01701-9192, Phone: (508) 879-0700, Contact: Frank Cutitta, Managing Director

Peat Marwick, 559 52nd Street, New York, NY 10055, Phone: (212) 909-5596, FAX: (212) 751-1760, Contact: Aidan Walsh

Pennsylvania, 9448 Federal Bldg., 600 Arch Street, Philadelphia, PA 19106, Phone: (215) 597-2866

People to People, Citizen Ambassador Program, Dwight D. Eisenhower Building, Spokane, WA 99202, Phone: (509) 534-0430, FAX: (509) 534-5245, Telex: 326328,

Contact: Mr. K. Raymond Schoedel, Executive Director

Pepper, Hamilton & Scheetz, 1300 19th Street, NW, Suite 700, Washington, DC 20036, Phone: (202) 828-1200, FAX: (202) 828-1665, Telex: 1240653 ITT, Contact: Stephen B. Ives, Jr.

Perspectives on U.S.-Soviet Joint Ventures, Author: Erika D. Nobel and H. Randall Morgan

Phargo Information, Inc., 369 Wayside Rd., Portola Valley, CA 94028, Phone: (415) 851-2102, FAX: (415) 851-2353, Contact: Donna Carano, Project Director

Philadelphia National Bank, Offshore Banking Division/Trade Finance and Advisory, P.O. Box 7618, Philadelphia, PA, Phone: (215) 973-7336, Contact: Gerald F. Rama

Philipp Brothers, Inc., 1221 Avenue of the Americas, New York, NY 10020, Phone: (212) 790-5127, 575-5900, FAX: (212) 790-6810, Telex: 233031, 420808, Contact: Gary Marcus, Managing Director

Pioneer Travel, 203 Allston Street, Cambridge, MA 02139, Contact: Frank "Paco" Norall

PlanEcon, Inc., 1111 14th Street, NW, Suite 801, Washington, DC 20005-5603, Phone: (202) 898-0471, FAX: (202) 898-0445, Contact: Dr. Jan Vanous

PlanEcon Report, PlanEcon, Inc., 1111 4th Street, NW, Suite 801, Washington, DC 20005-5603, Phone: (202) 898-0471, FAX: (202) 898-0445

262

Polimir, Vitebskoy oblasti, 211440 Novopolotsk, Phone: 5-73-38; 5-11-05, Director: N. N. Markovich

Poljot, 34 Ul. Marksistkaya, 109147 Moscow, Cable: FTF Polyot Moscow 147, Telex: 411989 Polex, Phone: 272-01-08, Director: Yu. N. Nikitin

Polmark, Inc., 150 West 56th Street, Suite 4101, New York, NY 10019, Phone: (212) 262-1212, FAX: (212) 956-5022, Telex: 650 379 6500 MCI UW, Contact: George M. J. Meller, President

PO MTZ V.I. Lenin, 61 Ul. Dolgobrodskaya, 220668 Minsk-GSP, Cable: Nord Minsk, Phone: 44-12-64, Director: P. Ya. Lyubchevskiy

Ponomarev, Valeriy, Trade Representation of the USSR in the USA, 2001 Connecticut Avenue, NW, Washington, DC 20008. Phone (202) 232-5988

Potomac Group International, Ltd., P.O. Box 18226, Washington, DC 20036, Phone: (703) 538-4553, FAX: (703) 538-6007, Telex: 510 601 7467, Contact: Scott M. Blacklin

Potyomkina, Anna, 50 The Lynnway, Apt. 826, Lynn, MA 01902, Phone: (617) 581-3011

Predicasts Funk and Scott Index Europe Annual, Author: Predicasts, Inc.

Premier Global Group, Ltd., The Toomey Building, 47 South Hamilton Street, Poughkeepsie, NY 12601, Phone: (914) 454-4111, FAX: (914) 473-0305, Contact: Lev Fedyniak, President

President's U.S.-Soviet Exchange Initiative, United States Information Agency, Office of the Coordinator, Room 751, 301 4th Street SW, Washington DC 20547, Phone: (202) 619-4548, FAX: (202) 619-5958, Contact: Gregory Guroff, Coordinator

Price Waterhouse, in London: Southwark Towers, 32 London Bridge Street, London SE1 9SY, United Kingdom, Phone: (1) 407-8989, FAX: (1) 378-0647, Telex: 884657/8, Contact: Bruce Edwards; in Moscow: Kursovoy Pereulok, Office 4, 119034 Moscow, Phone: 202-17-17, FAX: 200-12-34, Telex: 413526 SUL SU, Contact: Susan Shale

Price Waterhouse, in Moscow: Kursovoy Pereulok 9, Office 4, 119304 Moscow, Phone: 202-17-17, 202-17-29, FAX: 200-12-34, Telex: 413526 SULSU, Contact: Susan Shale

Priest, Peter F. H., P.O. Box 3180, Terre Haute, IN 47083

Prodintorg, 32/34 Smolenskaya-Sennaya Pl., 121200 Moscow, Cable: Prodintorg Moscow, Telex: 411206, Phone: 244-26-29, General Director: A. K. Krivenko

Project Development International, Inc., 25 W. 43rd Street, New York, NY 10036, Phone: (212) 764-8800, FAX: (212) 764-8850, Telex: 6790550, Contact: Joseph H. Filner, CEO

Prometey, 29, build 4, Checkhow str., 103006 Moscow, Phone: 299-84-45, FAX: 200-22-12 (Attn: Anton E. Pronin), Telex: 411700 VAPRO 0310, Contact: Anton E. Pronin

Pronin, Anton, Prometey, 29, build 4, Checkhow str, 103006 Moscow. Phone 299-84-85

Puerto Rico, Rm. 659 Federal Bldg., (Hato Rey) San Jan, PR 00918, Phone: (809) 753-4555

Radix Group International, Inc., 301 East Grand Avenue, South San Francisco, CA 94080, Phone: (415) 742-8231, FAX: (415) 875-3794, Telex: 210620, Contact: Val Anderson

Raduga, 106 Ul. B. Khmelnitskogo, 290024 Lvov, Cable: Stroimaterialintorg Moscow, Telex: 411887; 411889, Phone: 269-05-54; 269-05-55, Director: A. I. Burgazliyev

Radzai, Ronald B., 6304 Monadnock Way, Oakland, CA 94605, Phone: (415) 562-3882, FAX: (415) 562-1187

Rahim Tours, Inc., 12 South Dixie Highway, Lake Worth, FL 33460, Phone: (407) 585-5305, (800) 556-5305, FAX: (407) 582-1353

Rausch, Ted L. Co., P.O. Box 77147, San Francisco, CA 94107, Phone: (415) 348-5923

Raznoexport, 15 Verkhnaya Krasnoselskaya Ul., 107896 Moscow, Cable: Raznoexport Moscow, Telex: 411408, Phone: 264-56-56; 264-01-83; 264-04-83, General Director: Yu. Kostrov

Raznoimport, 32/34 Smolenskaya-Sennaya Pl., SU-121200 Moscow, Phone: 220-18-49, Director: Vyacheslav N. Semin

Red Excavator, 83/2 Prosp. Pobedy, 252062 Kiev, Cable: Krex Kiev, Phone: 433-69-18

Renfield, Richard L., 2200 Leeland Drive, Falls Church, VA 22043, Phone: (703) 532-5271

Reuters Information Services, Publisher: Reuters Europe, 85 Fleet Street, London, England, FAX: (1) 353-9909, Contact: Gregory Kats

RHA Group, 2182 Dupont Drive, Suite 23, Irvine, CA 92715, Phone: (714) 851-0623, FAX: (714) 851-0623 (auto FAX)

Rhode Island, 7 Jackson Walkway, Providence, RI 02903, Phone: (401) 528-5104

Riga-American, Ltd., in the U.S.: 1201 West Main Street, Waterbury, CT 06708, Phone: (203) 757-5052, FAX: (203) 596-8073, Telex: 62806768, Contact: Baxter K. Walsh, in Riga: Latvian Orthopaedic Institute, Duntes Ul. 12/22, 226005 Riga, Latvian S.S.R., Phone: 39-26-23, 39-30-00, FAX: 39-26-23, Contact: Maris O. Toms

Rigaselmash, 23-A Daugavrivas, 226007 Riga, Cable: Riga TF Rigaselmash, Phone: 246-55-51, Director: S. S. Yatsenko

Riggs National Bank of Washington, DC, International Division, 1913 Massachusetts Avenue, NW, Washington, DC 20036, Phone: (202) 835-5391, Telex: 897455, 197660, Contact: Paul Cushman, III, Vice President

Robert Schwartz & Associates, 5402 S. Dorchester #2, Chicago, IL 60615, Phone: (312) 947-8179, FAX: (312) 643-0923

Robert T. Creutz & Co., P.O. Box 490, S. Weymouth, MA 02190, Phone: (617) 331-8421, FAX: (617) 331-8421, E-mail: MCI mail: CREUTZ; Compuserve: 70611,3147

Roder, Antonio, 3875 Magnolia Drive, Palo Alto, CA 94306, Phone: (415) 493-5168

ROI Research & Analysis, Inc., 39C1 Roswell Road, Suite 133, Marietta, GA 30062, Phone: (404) 578-0474, FAX: (404) 578-0527, Contact: Alan Urech

Rosmedintorg, Ul. 25 let Oktyabrya 19, Moscow, Phone: 924-49-29, Director: V. E. Schkapkin

Rossa, Reklamo-Kommercheskoye Agentstvo, Dmitrovskiy Proezd 4, Moscow, Phone: 216-34-18

Rothschild Travel Consultants, 900 West End Avenue, Suite 1B, New York, NY 10025, Contact: Kathy Rothschild

RSEEA: Newsletter for Research on Soviet and East European Agriculture, Center for Business and Economic Research, School of Business, Economics, and Management, University of Southern Maine, 96 Falmouth Street, Portland, ME 04103, Phone: (207) 780-4411, ISSN 8756-8942

Russart Travel Service, 291 Geary Street, Suite 511, San Francisco, CA 94102, Phone: (415) 781-6655, (800) 232-RUSS (CA); (800) 338-RUSS (outside CA), FAX: (415) 781-6134, Telex: 255718

Russian and East European Center, University of Illinois at Champaign-Urbana, 1208 West California Avenue, Urbana, IL 61801, Phone: (217) 333-1244

Russian and East European Studies Program, University of Washington/Seattle, DR-05, Seattle, WA 98195, Phone: (206) 436-0250

Russian Language Services, Inc., 423 Feather Rock Drive, Rockville, MD 20850, Phone: (301) 424-0158, FAX: (301) 738-9411, Contact: Mark Berkovich

Russian Travel Bureau, Inc., 225 E. 44th Street, New York, NY 10017, Phone: (212) 986-1500, (800) 847-1800, FAX: (212) 490-1650

Russian Research Center (RRC), Harvard University, 1737 Cambridge Street, Cambridge, MA 02138, Phone: (617) 495-4037, Contact: Marshall Goldman, Associate Director

Ruzanov, Robert, Trade Representative of the USSR in the USA, 2001 Connecticut Avenue, NW, Washington, DC 20008. Phone (202) 232-5988

Saatchi & Saatchi, 375 Hudson St. New York, NY 10014-3620, Phone: (212) 463-2000

Safonov, Dr. Sidonie H., 1643 Krameria Street, Denver, CO 80220, Phone: (303) 394-4360 (Home); (303) 236-6956 (Office)

Salans, Hertzfeld & Heilbronn, in the U.S.: 1270 Avenue of the Americas, New York, NY 10020, Phone: (212) 974-8400, FAX: (212) 974-8318, Telex: RCA 839554, in Paris: 9 rue Boissy d'Anglas, Paris 75008, Phone: (1) 42-68-48-00, Telex: 280 990 Parilex, Contact: Jim Hogan or Jeff Hertzfeld

Samu, Janos, 46 Shaftsbury Avenue, Hopewell, NJ 08525, Phone: (609) 466-9105, (609) 924-6789, FAX: (609) 466-0864

San Francisco/Moscow Teleport, in San Francisco: 3278 Sacramento Street, San Francisco, CA 94115, Phone: (415) 931-8500, FAX: (415) 931-2885, Telex: 9103804097

TELEPORT, in Moscow: Ul. Nezhdanovoy, 2a, Moscow 103009, Phone: 229-96-63, FAX: 229-41-21, Contact: Deborah L. Miller, Data Communications Manager, SFMT

Sargent, Peter, Rt. 1 Box 447, Hamilton, VA 22068, Phone: (703) 338-4875

SAS Scandinavian Airlines System, in Moscow: Kuznetskiy Most, 3, Moscow, Phone: 925-47-47; (202) 833-3131 (Washington), Telex: 413077 MOWSK SU

Satra Corp., in the U.S.: 645 Madison Avenue, New York, NY 10022, Phone: (212) 355-3030, FAX: (212) 758-6366, Telex: 225747, Contact: Ara Oztemal, President, in Moscow: 11/13 Tryekhprudnyy Per., 103001 Moscow, Phone: 299-9164, Telex: 413129 SATRA SU

Schenkers International Forwarder, 147-29 182nd Street, Jamaica, NY 11413, Phone: Ocean (212) 432-3031, Air (718) 632-7300, FAX: Ocean (718) 432-3092, Air (718) 632-1929

School of Advanced International Studies, The Johns Hopkins University, 1740 Massachusetts Ave., NW, Washington, DC 20036, Phone: (202) 663-5700

Schuldt, M. Lesley, 4645 NW Kahneeta Drive, Portland, OR 97229, Phone: (503) 645-3615

Schultz, Arlo A., 16450 NE 18th Street, Bellevue, WA 98008, Phone: (206) 747-1325, FAX: (206) 641-0408

Schwartz, Marian B., 1207 Bickler Road, Austin, TX 78704, Phone: (512) 442-5100

Science in the USSR, Omni Magazine, 1965 Broadway, New York, NY 10133-0116, Phone: (212) 496-6100

Scott European Corp., in the U.S.: 58 E. State Street, Montpelier, VT 05602, Phone: (802) 223-0262, FAX: (802) 223-0265, Telex: 5101011983, Contact: Robert L. Krattli, in Moscow: Inpred, Krasnopresnenskaya Nab., 12/501, 123610 Moscow, Phone: 253-10-94, FAX: 253-93-82, Telex: 411813 REPR SU, Contact: Andrei Zelenov

Scott European Corp., 58 E. State St., Montpelier, VT 05602

Security Pacific Trade Finance, 595 Madison Avenue, 12th Floor, New York, NY 10022, Phone: (212) 644-0020, Contact: Jeffrey Malakoff, Sr., Vice President

Selkhozpromsexport, 32/34 Smolenskaya-Sennaya Pl., SU-121200 Moscow

Shaw, Pittman, Potts & Trowbridge, 2300 N Street, NW, Washington DC 20037, Phone: (202) 663-8136, FAX: (202) 663-8007, Telex: 892693 SHAWLAW WSH, Contact: Robert B. Robbins

Sherr, Alan B., 39 Blaney Street, Swampscott, MA 01907, Phone: (617) 581-7651, (401) 863-3465, FAX: (617) 581-7651, (401) 274-8440, Contact: Alan B. Sherr

Shillinglaw, Thomas, Division Counsel, Corning Inc., Corning, NY 14830, Phone: (607) 974-8164, FAX: (607) 974-6135, Telex: 192809010, Contact: Thomas Shillinglaw

Shkolnik, Alexander, 962 S. El Camino Real #202, San Mateo, CA 94402, Phone: (415) 343-3805, FAX: (415) 342-8723

Sidley & Austin, 1722 I Street, NW, Washington, DC 20006, Phone: (202) 429-4101, FAX: (202) 429-6144, Telex: 8-9463 (SIDLEY AUS WSH), Contact: Robert B. Shanks

Simpson, Thacher & Bartlett, 425 Lexington Ave, New York, NY 10017, Phone: (212) 455-2000, FAX: (212) 455-2502, Telex: 4552500, Contact: Brian G. Hart

Silliman, Emily, 2434 Rock Street, #1, Mountain View, CA 94043, Phone: (415) 968-9099, FAX: (415) 968-7423, Contact: Emily Silliman

Skotoimport, 6 Ul. Makarenko, 103062 Moscow, Cable: Skotoimport Moscow, Phone: 221-64-79, General Director: B. F. Chutchev

Slepak Foundation, 230 S. 15th Street, Suite 300, Philadelphia, PA 19102, Phone: (215) 545-1098, FAX: (215) 893-0462, Contact: Steven L. Carter

Small Business Administration (SBA), Office of International Trade, 1441 L Street, NW, Washington, DC 20416, Phone: (202) 653-7794

Smikun, Emanuel, 805 Ditmas Avenue, Brooklyn, NY 11218, Phone: (718) 941-5703, FAX: (718) 941-5703

Smith & Williams, P.A., 712 South Oregon Avenue, Tampa, Florida 33606, Phone: (813) 253-5400, FAX: (813) 254-3459, Contact: Sam Mandelbaum

South Carolina, Federal Bldg. Suite 172, 1835 Assembly Street, Columbia, SC 29201, Phone: (803) 765-5345

South Dakota, Serviced by Omaha

Sovfracht (U.S.A), Inc., 477 Madison Avenue, New York, NY 10022, Phone: (212) 355-6280, Contact: S. Karachkov, President, in Moscow: 1/4 Rozhdestvenka Ul., 103759 Moscow, Phone: 926-11-18, Telex: 411168, Cable: SOVFRACHT MOSCOW, Contact: V. L. Schutov, President

Soviet-American Trade, P.O. Box 18394, Washington, DC 20036, Phone: (301) 907-8125

Soviet Business and Trade With News From Eastern Europe, Welt Publishing Company, 1413 K Street, NW, Suite 800, Washington, DC 20005, Phone: (202) 371-0555, Telex: 281 409 TAOA UR, ISSN 0731-7727

Soviet Business Center, Yaroslavskaya Ulitsa, 13, Moscow 129366, Phone: 282-42-07, FAX: 200-22-16, 200-22-17, Telex: (095) 2889587 ECHO, Contact: Dr. Vladimir S. Shustikov, President; Yuri V. Korkin, Vice President

Soviet Business Connections, P.O. Box 925, Oneonta, NY 13820, Phone: (607) 433-2654, FAX: (607) 433-2654, Contact: Tom Scholet, President

Soviet Business Law Report, 1350 Connecticut Avenue, NW, Suite 1000, Washington, DC 20036, Phone: (202) 862-0990, FAX: (202) 862-0999

Soviet Consular Office, 1852 Phelps Place, NW Washington, DC 20009, Phone: (202) 939-

267

8916, FAX: (202) 483-7579

Soviet Consulate, 1825 Phelps Place, NW, Washington, DC 20036, Phone: (202) 939-8916, FAX: (202) 483-7579, in San Francisco: 2790 Green Street, San Francisco, CA, Phone: (415) 922-6642

Soviet Information Department, 1706 18th St., NW, Washington, DC 20009, Phone: (202) 328-3234, Contact: Oleg Benyukh, Head

Soviet Life, 1706 18th Street, NW, Washington DC 20009, Phone: (202) 328-3237

Soviet Mission to the UN, 136 E. 67th St., New York, NY 10021, Phone: (212) 861-4900

Sovincentr, 12 Krasnopresnenskaya Nab., 123610 Moscow, Telex: 411486 SOVIN SU, Phone: 256-63-03, 255-64-01

Sovintersport, 5 Bolshoy Rzhevskiy Per., 121069 Moscow, Cable: 114108 SPIDV, Telex: 411578 PIK SU, Phone: 291-91-49; 291-98-37, Acting General Director: V. N. Zhukov

Sovkabel, 5 Shosse Entuziastov, 111112 Moscow, Cable: Sovkabel Moscow, Phone: 361-61-82, Director: A. D. Orlov

Sovkomflot, 1/4 Ul. Zhdanova, 103759 Moscow, Cable: Sovkomflot Moscow, Telex: 411168, Phone: 926-13-01, Director: I. S. Osminin

Sovryblot, 9 Rozhdestvenskiy Bulvar, 103045 Moscow, Telex: 411206, Phone: 208-40-57, General Director: G. V. Zhigalov

SOVSET' Computer Network, Publisher: Center for Strategic and International Studies-Soviet Studies, Washington, DC, Phone: (202)

775-3257, Contact: Dawn Mann

SOVUS, 40 West 67 Street, Suite 7C, New York, NY 10023, Phone: (212) 580-4973, FAX: (212) 580-4990, Contact: Grace Kennan Warnecke, President

Soyuzgazexport, 20 Leninskiy Prosp., 117071 Moscow, Cable: Sovgaz Moscow, Telex: 411987 Sgaz SU, Phone: 230-24-10; 230-24-40, General Director: V. N. Mikhaylov

Soyuzkarta, 45 Volgogradskiy Prosp., 109125 Moscow, Cable: Soyuzkarta Moscow, Telex: 411222 REN, Phone: 177-40-50, General Director: V. A. Piskulin

Soyuzpushnina, 1-y Krasnogvardeisky Per., 12, 103012 Moscow, Cable: Soyuzpushnina Moscow, Telex: 411150, Phone: 259-99-79; 259-99-85, General Director: Yu. M. Mashkin

Soyuzvneshstroyimport, 32/34 Smolenskaya-Sennaya Pl., SU-121200 Moscow, Phone: 290-00-98, Director: Grant G. Grigoryan

Soyuzvneshtrans, 17 Gogolevskiy Bulvar, 121019 Moscow, Cable: Vneshtrans Moscow, Telex: 411441, Phone: 203-11-79, General Director: V. I. Aliseichik

Soyuzzagranpribor, 5 Ul. Ogareva, K-9 Moscow 103918, Telex: 411437, Phone: 229-61-10, General Director: Yu. A. Agapov

Specan International, Inc., P.O. Box 652, Princeton, NJ 08542-0652, Phone: (609) 683-4900

Spiegler, Paul A., 7 Sierra Vista Lane, Valley Cottage, NY 10989, Phone: (914) 358-9443

Spindler, James W., 66 Weston Road, Lincoln, MA 01773, Phone: (617) 275-1269, FAX: (508) 658-2492

Squire, Sanders & Dempsey, 1201 Pennsylvania Avenue, NW, Washington, DC 20004, Phone: (202) 626-6600, FAX: (202) 626-6780, Contact: Charles A. Vanik, Stephen Bell

Stackhouse, Kathy, 300 S. Lang Avenue, Pittsburgh, PA 15206, Phone: (412) 391-0378

Stacy, Charles M., 2006 Reagan Boulevard, Carrollton, TX 75006, Phone: (214) 416-8039, (214) 418-3571, FAX: (214) 418-3833

Stafford Holding Company, P.O. Box 175, Colfax, NC 27235, Phone: (919) 996-4087, FAX: (919) 996-3225, Telex: 62034336, Contact: Suzanne Beane Stafford

Stanimpex, 2 Ul. B. Khmelnitskogo, 342042 Ulyanovsk, Cable: Granit Ulyanovsk, Telex: 214117, Phone: 6-15-87, Director: O. Ye. Benkovskiy

Stankiyev, 67 Prosp. Pobedy, 252062 Kiev, Cable: Patron Kiev, Telex: 131462, Phone: 442-83-24; 442-83-98, Director: S. A. Vdovichenko

Stankoimport, 34/63 Ul. Obrucheva, 117839 Moscow, Cable: Stankoimport Moscow, Telex: 411991; 411992; 411993, Phone: 333-51-01; 334-83-04, General Director: V. I. Marinin

State Bank of the USSR (GOSBANK), Ul. 12, Neglinnaya, Moscow, Phone: 923-20-38, 925-29-19

State Committee for Cinematography (Goskino), 7 Malyy Gnezdikovskiy Per., 103877 Moscow, Phone: Foreign Relations Department 229-13-30;, Protocol Section 229-04-74, Telex: 411417 KINO SU

State Committee for Computer Technology and Information Science (GKVTI)

State Committee for Construction (Goskomstroy), 26 Pushkinskaya Ul., 103828 Moscow, Phone: Foreign Relations Department 292-75-87;, Protocol Section 292-69-74

State Committee for Environmental Protection (Goskompriroda), Ulitsa Nezhdanovoy, 11, Moscow

State Committee for Hydrometerology (Goskomhydromet), 12 Per. Pavlika Morozova, 123376 Moscow, Phone: Foreign Relations Department 252-08-08;, Protocol Section 255-52-26

State Committee for Labor and Social Affairs (Goskomtrud), 1 Ul. Kuybysheva, 103706 Moscow K-12, Phone: Foreign Relations Department and Protocol Section 298-39-24

State Committee for Material and Technical Supply (Gossnab), 5 Orlikov Per., 107801 Moscow, Phone: Foreign Relations Department 208-33-18, 208-02-17

State Committee for Physical Culture and Sports (Goskomsport), 8 Luzhnetskaya Nab., 119270 Moscow, Phone: Protocol Section 201-14-10, 201-06-01, Telex: 411287

State Committee for Planning (Gosplan), 12 Prosp. Marksa, 103009 Moscow

State Committee for Prices (Goskomtsen), 20 Bersenevskaya Nab., 109072 Moscow ZH-72, Phone: Inquiries 231-02-45

State Committee for Production Quality and Standards (Gosstandart), 9 Leninskiy Prosp., 117049 Moscow G-49, Phone: Foreign Relations Department 236-40-44, 236-71-03

State Committee for Publications (Goskomizdat), 5 Strastnoi Bulv., 101409 Moscow K-6, Phone: Foreign Relations Department 295-58-42, Telex: 113428 CHTENIE

State Committee for Public Education, 51 Ul. Lyusinovskaya, Moscow, Phone: 237-77-95

State Committee for Science and Technology (GKNT), 11 Ul. Gorkogo, 103095 Moscow, Phone: Protocol Section 229-20-00, 229-20-39, 229-22-36, FAX: 229-47-30, Telex: 411241 GKNT SU, 411 354 DMNTS SU

State Committee for Statistics (Goskomstat), 39 Ul. Kirova, 103450 Moscow, Phone: Foreign Relations Division 207-49-17, (new office at Izmaylovskoye Shosse, Moscow)

State Committee for Supervision of Safety in Industry and Atomic Energy (Gospromatomnadzor), Taganskaya Ul., 34, 109147 Moscow

State Committee for Television and Radio Broadcasting (Gosteleradio), 25 Pyatnitskaya Ul., Moscow, Phone: Main Administration for External Relations 217-78-48, 217-70-09, 233-60-60, Telex: 411130 RADIO SU

State Committee for the Forestry (Goskomles), 18 Ul. Lesteva, 113808 Moscow GSP-230,

Phone: Foreign Relations Department 236-83-03

State Committee for the Utilization of Atomic Energy (GKAE), Staromonetnyy Per., 26, 109180 Moscow

State Register of Participants in the Foreign Economic Relations of the Soviet Union, Publisher: Mezhdunarodnaya Kniga, Ul. Dimitrova, Moscow 113095, FAX: 230-21-17

State Security Committee (KGB), 2 Ul. Dzerzhinskogo, 101000 Moscow

Steptoe & Johnson, in Washington: 1330 Connecticut Avenue, NW, Washington, DC 20036, Phone: (202) 429-3000, FAX: (202) 429-3000, Telex: 98-2503, Contact: Sarah Carey; in Moscow: 26 Rublevskoye Shosse, Moscow, U.S.S.R., Phone: 415-42-49, FAX: 415-29-20, Contact: Alexander Papachristou

Stone, Lydia Razran, Ph.D., 1111 Westmoreland Road, Alexandria, VA 22308, Phone: (703) 768-5441, (202) 488-5854, 863-6269

Stonehill, Paul, 5700 Etiwanda, Tarzana, CA 91356, Phone: (818) 344-7442, (213) 627-6171

Stromavtoliniya, 77 Ul. Pervomayskaya, 212648 Mogilev, Cable: Press Mogilev 212648, U.S.S.R., Telex: 252161 Liniya, Phone: 3-44-17, Director: A. A. Usenya

Stroock & Stroock & Lavan, 1150 Seventeenth Street, NW, Washington, DC 20036, Phone: (202) 452-9250, FAX: (202) 293-2293, Telex: 84238 STROOCK DC; 89401 STROOCK DC, Contact: George G. Lorinczi or, Michael H. Mobbs

Sudoexport, Ul. Chaykovskovgo 1, 123231 Moscow, Telex: 411116, Phone: 255-18-13, 255-48-04

Sudoimport, 10 Uspenskiy Per., 103006 Moscow, Telex: 411387 Sudo SU; 411443 Sudo SU, Phone: 299-68-49; 299-02-14; 299-58-77; Acting General Director: B. A. Yakimov

Summit Limited, The Omaha Building, 1650 Farnam Street, Omaha, NE 68102, Phone: (402) 346-5151, FAX: (402) 346-1148, Telex: 484415, Contact: Wallace Johnson, President

Superintendent of Documents, U.S. Government Printing Office, Washington, DC 20402

Surviving Together: A Journal on Soviet-American Relations, ISAR (Institute for Soviet-American Relations), 1601 Connecticut Avenue, NW, Washington, DC 20009, Phone: (202) 387-3034

Svetotechnika, 5 Shosse Svetotechnikov, 430023 Saransk, Cable: FTF Svetotechnikov Saransk, Telex: 412512 Svet, Phone: 4-89-68; 2-22-16, Director: D. S. Sozin

Swacker & Associates, P.C., 15950 Bay Vista Drive, Suite 240, Clearwater, FL 34620, Phone: (813) 530-0800, FAX: (813) 538-2080, Contact: Drucilla E. Bell

Swissair, in Moscow: Sovincenter, Krasnopresnenskaya Nab. 12, Room 2005, Moscow 123100, Phone: 253-89-88, 253-18-59; (800) 221-4750 (U.S.), FAX: 253-18-52, Telex: 413417

Tadjikvneshtorg, Pr. Lenina 42, Dushanbe 734051, Telex: 116119 SAWDO, Phone: 23-29-03, General Director: Yu. G. Gaytsgori

Tadzhik Chamber of Commerce, 31 Sh. Rustaveli Ul., 734025 Dushanbe, Phone: (377) 22-69-68

Tallex, 12 Ul. Mustomayae, 200105 Tallinn, Cable: FTF TALLEX Tallinn, Phone: 49-82-20, Director: E. A. Mark

Tapp, Linda, 1861 Mintwood Place, NW, Washington, DC 20009, Phone: (202) 328-3280

TASS News Agency, 50 Rockefeller Plaza, New York, NY 10020, Phone: (212) 245-4250, Contact: I. Makhurin, Editor

Tax Planning International Review, BNA International, Inc., 17 Dartmouth Street, London SW1H 9BL, Phone: International toll-free service 800 number 44-(1)997-4909

Teague, Ben, P.O. Box 129, Athens, GA 30603, Phone: (404) 543-0860, FAX: (404) 546-6539

Technoexport, 32/34 Smolenskaya-Sennaya, Su-121200 Moscow, Phone: 233-59-87 Director: Yuri V. Chugunov

Technointorg, 64 Pyatnitskaya Ul., M-95 113836 Moscow, Telex: 411200, Phone: 231-26-22, General Director: A. A. Vasilyev

Technology Contact International, 758 Lowell Street, Peabody, MA 01960, Phone: (617) 598-1753, Contact: Vladimir L. Tsivkin, President

Techsnabexport, 32/34 Smolenskaya-Sennaya Pl., 121200 Moscow, Cable: Techsnabexport Moscow, Telex: 411328 TSE SU, Phone: 244-32-85, General Director: V.I. Zharikov

Telex Service Center, Intourist Hotel, 3-5 Ul. Gorkogo, Moscow, Phone: 925-92-681, 925-15-88 (Inquiries), 924-47-50 (Telegraph)

Tennessee, 1114 Parkway Towers, 404 Jas. Roberston Pkwy., Nashville, TN 37219-1505, Phone: (615) 736-5161

Texas, Room 7A5, 1100 Commerce Street, Dallas, TX 75242, Phone: (214) 767-0542

Textilmash, 1 Proyezd Mashinostroiteley, 428022 Cheboksary, Cable: FTF Tekstilmash, Telex: 512502, Phone: 23-36-37, Director: Yu A. Cherkasov

The American Export Marketer, Welt Publishing Company, 1413 K Street, NW, Suite 800, Washington, DC 20005, Phone: (202) 371-0555

The American-Soviet Medical Market Journal, 374 Congress Street, Suite 408, Boston, MA 02210, Phone: (617) 451-6633, FAX: (617) 451-6182, Associate Publisher: Richard P. Mills

The Belorussian Railroad Experiment, Staff Paper 48, Author: Center for International Research (CIR)

The Byelorussian Republican Bank, 10 Ul. Zaslavskaya, 220035 Minsk., Cable address: Vneshbank Minsk

The Corporate Word, Inc., 18 South, Gateway Center 3, Pittsburgh, PA 15222, Phone: (412) 391-0378, FAX: (412) 391-3935

The Current Digest of the Soviet Press, 3857 North High Street, Columbus, OH 43214, Phone: (614) 292-4234

The Delphi International Group, 1019 19th Street, NW, Suite 900, Washington, DC 20036, Phone: (202) 466-7951, FAX: (202) 466-4113, Telex: 989989, Contact: Sam A. Mariam, Project Specialist

The Estonian Republican Bank, 7 Narvskoye Schosse, 200001 Tallinn., Cable address: Vneshbank Tallinn 911

The Florida Bar, Soviet and Eastern European Law Committee, c/o Maureen O'Brien, 1380 N.E. Miami Gardens Drive, Suite 200, North Miami Beach, FL 33179, Phone: (305) 949-0093, FAX: (305) 949-9325

The Foundation for Citizen Diplomacy, Inc., 1155 Connecticut Avenue, NW, Suite 500, Washington DC 20036, Phone: (202) 467-8587, FAX: (202) 452-8654, Telex: 4933729 WASH UI, Contact: William S. Loiry, President

The Harriman Institute Forum, The W. Averell Harriman Institute for Advanced Study of the Soviet Union, Columbia University, 420 West 118 Street, 12th floor, New York, NY 10027, ISSN: 0896-114X

The International Connection, P.O. Box 52332, Atlanta, GA 30344, Phone: (404) 233-8329, FAX: (404) 239-9102

The International Information Report, Washington Researchers Publishing, Ltd., 2612 P Street, NW, Washington DC 20007, Phone: (202) 333-3533

Thelen, Marrin, Johnson, & Bridges, One Kaiser Plaza, Suite 1950, Oakland, CA 94612, Phone: (415) 893-5195, FAX: (415) 891-9086, Contact: Richard N. Gary

The Lithuanian Republican Bank, 10/1 Gediminas Prospekt, 232629 Vilnius, Cable address: Vneshbank Vilnius

The Phargo Group, 33 Young Street, Suite 1150, Toronto, Ontario, M5E 1G4 CANADA, Phone: (416) 360-6003, FAX: (416) 360-7942, Contact: VP, Business Development

The Russian Business Center, P.O. Box 2332, Cambridge, MA 02238, Phone: (617) 492-1558, FAX: (617) 577-1209, Telex: 324168 OAKS CAMB, Contact: John Garrity

The Soviet Business Review, Dhalfelt International, 120 Potter Road, Scarsdale, NY 10583, Phone: (914) 472-2084

The Soviet Travel Newsletter, International Intertrade Index, Box 636 Federal Square, Newark, NJ 07101

The Stern Group, Inc., 1133 Connecticut Avenue, NW, Suite 1000 Washington, DC 20036, Phone: (202) 775-2379, FAX: (202) 833-8491, Contact: Paula Stern

The Ukrainian Republic Bank, 8 Ul. Kreshchatnik, 252001 Kiev, Cable address: Vneshbank Kiev

Thomas Butler Associates, 5A Ellsworth Drive, Cambridge, MA 02139

Tisza, Ogilvy & Mather, 309 West 49th St., New York, NY 10019, Phone: (212) 237-5813, FAX: (212) 237-5123, Contact: Deroy

Murdock, in Moscow: Ul. Vernadskogo 33, Moscow, Phone: 131-5743, FAX: 237-5123, Telex: 414511

TNT SKYPACK, 990 Stewart Avenue, Garden City, NY 11530, Phone: (800) 558-5555

Tornquist, David A., 2 Wilbur Avenue, Newport, RI 02840, Phone: (401) 846-9013, FAX: (401) 847-2970

Tour Designs, 510 H Street, SW, Washington, DC 20024, Contact: Dan Hays

Townsend, Sylvia Linner, 30 Ardmore Road, Kensington, CA 94707, Phone: (415) 524-5097

Trade Representative of the U.S.S.R. in the U.S.A., 2001 Connecticut Avenue, NW Washington, DC 20008, Phone: (202) 232-5988, Contact: Valeriy Ponomarev, Senior Economist

Traktoroexport, 43 Ul. Lesnaya, 103055 Moscow, Telex: 411273A TPEX SU; 111456/2 PAXO, Phone: 258-59-34; 258-18-74, General Director: D. N. Monayenkov

Transemantics, Inc., Van Ness Center #147, 4301 Connecticut Avenue, NW, Washington, DC 20008, Phone: (202) 686-5600, FAX: (202) 686-5603, Contact: M-L. Wax, Director

Travcoa, P.O. Box 2630, Newport Beach, CA 92658, Phone: (714) 476-2800, (800) 992-2004 (CA); (800) 992-2003 (outside CA), FAX: (714) 476-2538, Telex: 692483

Travel Advisers of America, 1413 K Street, NW, Suite 800, Washington, DC 20005, Phone: (202) 371-1440, FAX: (202) 682-5833

Travelling Shoes, P.O. Box 4410, Laguna Beach, CA 92652, Phone: (714) 752-9036, FAX: (714) 752-7105

Trenan, Simmons, Kemker, Scharf, Barkin, Frye & O'Neill, 2700 Barnett Plaza, Tampa, FL 33602, Phone: (813) 223-7474, FAX: (813) 229-6553, Telex: 6502251910   MCI UW, Contact: Richard A. Jacobson

Troika, Inc., 192 Nickerson Street, Suite 312, Seattle, WA 98109, Phone: (206) 281-9289, (800) 367-9928, FAX: (206) 281-9040, Telex: 256663 TRTR UR

Tschen, Jung, P.O. Box 753, Cary, NC 27512-0753, Phone: (919) 467-8346

Twain Trading Company, 2 W. End Avenue, Suite 4D, Brooklyn, NY 11235, Phone: (718) 236-8308, (718) 891-3922, FAX: (718) 645-9596, Telex: 178-384 or 289-793, Contact: Edward Dubrovsky, President, in Moscow: 8/4 Ulitsa Svoboda, Moscow 123362, Phone: 491-06-77

Ukrainian Business Outlook, Outlook International Inc., 213 Valley Street, Suite 254, South Orange, NJ 07079, Phone: (201) 672-6105, FAX: (201) 672-6105

Ukrainian Chamber of Commerce, 33 Zhitomirskaya Ul., 252625 Kiev, Phone: (044) 22-29-11

Ukrainian Research Institute, Harvard University, 1583 Massachusetts Ave., Cambridge, MA 02138, Phone: (617) 495-4053, FAX: (617) 495-8097

Ukrimpex, 22 Ul. Vorovskogo, 252054 Kiev, Cable: Ukrimpex Kiev, Telex: 216-21-74; 216-

25-13, General Director: S. T. Sokolenko

Ukrimpex, Ul. Vorovskogo 22, 242054 Kiev, Phone: 216-21-74, 131384, General Director: V. A. Vernigoroz

Union of the World Advisory Companies, 50 Milk Street, Boston, MA 02109, Phone: (617) 426-7671, FAX: (617) 451-2589, Telex: 951-131 HQ-BSN, Contact: J. Michael Any, President

Union Tours, Inc., 79 Madison Avenue, Suite 1104, New York, NY 10016, Phone: (212) 683-9500, (800) 451-9511, FAX: (212) 683-9511

United Parcel Service (UPS), Contact your local UPS office, Phone: (800) 595-9090

Universal Travel & Tours, Inc., 3495 Thomasville Road, Tallahassee, FL 32308, Contact: Lani Rodgers, Phone: (904) 222-7171, (800) 524-1524 (in Fla.), (800) 433-1333 (outside Fla.)

University of Michigan, Center for Russian & East European Studies, Lane Hall, Ann Arbor, MI 48109, Phone: (313) 764-0351Air-Sea Forwarders, Inc., P.O. Box 90637, Los Angeles, CA 90009, Phone: (213) 776-1611, FAX: (213) 216-2625

University Travel Services, Inc., 4534 11th Avenue, Seattle, WA 98105, Phone: (206) 296-3080, (800) 426-1419, FAX: (206) 296-3047

USA Today International, Phone: (212) 715-2051, Contact: Barbara Krasne

U.S. Commercial Office (USCO), Ulitsa

Chaikovskogo 15, Moscow, Phone: 255-4848, 255-4660, or 252-2451, x. 276, 277, 278, Telex: 413205 USCO SU, FAX: 230-2101, Contact: Maria Aronson

U.S. Consulate General, Ul. Pyetra-Lavrova, 15, Leningrad, Phone: 292-45-48, Telex: 64121527 AMCONSUL

U.S. Postal Express Service, Contact your local post office

U.S. International Trade Commission, 500 E Street, SW, Room 602, Washington DC 20436, Phone: (202) 252-1263, FAX: (202) 252-1789, Contact: Constance Hamilton, Chief, East-West Branch

U.S.-Soviet Trade Alert, Global Trading Associates, Inc., 1155 Connecticut Avenue, NW, Suite 500, Washington, DC 20036, Phone: (202) 467-8589, FAX: (202) 452-8654, Telex: 4933729 WASH UI, Contact: William S. Loiry, Chairman & CEO

U.S. Trade and Development Program, Room 309 SA-16, Washington, DC 20523-1602, Phone: (703) 875-4357, FAX: (703) 875-4009, Contact: Barbara Bradford, private sector, Fred Eberhard, public sector

U.S.-Ukraine Trade and Economic Council, P.O. Box 20347, Columbus Circle Station, New York, NY 10023-9991, Contact: Dr. George Loguseh, Chairman

U.S.S.R. Agriculture and Trade Report, To order call: (800) 999-6779

U.S.S.R. Chamber of Commerce and Industry, Ul. Kuybysheva, 6, 101000 Moscow, Phone:

298-3231, 223-4323, Telex: 411126 TPP SU, Contact: Victor Mishchenko

U.S.S.R. Currents, P.O. Box 65861, Washington, DC 20035-5861, Editor: Steven Stomski

U.S.S.R. Technology Update, 7700 Leesburg Pike, Suite 250, Falls Church, VA 22043, Phone: (703) 556-0278, FAX: (703) 556-0494, ISSN: 0892-497X

U.S.S.R.-U.S. Fisheries Claims Board, 1609 Decatur Street, NW, Washington, DC, Phone: (202) 726-3838, Contact: Gennady Chursin, Attache

U.S.-U.S.S.R. Marine Resources Company, in the U.S.: 192 Nickerson, Suite 307, Seattle, WA 98109, Phone: (206) 285-6424, FAX: (206) 282-9414, Telex: 277115MCR UR, Contact: James Talbot, President, in Moscow: SOVAM, National Hotel, kv. 450, Moscow, Phone: 230-2214, Telex: 413052 SOVAM, Contact: Paul Iremonger

U.S.-U.S.S.R. Trade and Economic Council Inc., in New York: 805 Third Avenue, New York, NY 10022, Phone: (212) 644-4550, FAX: (212) 752-0889, Telex: 425053 U.S.S.R. UI, in Moscow: 3 Shevchenko Embankment, Moscow 121248, Phone: 243-5470, FAX: 230-2467, Telex: 871-413212 ASREC SU, Contact: Bill Forrester, Director (NY); Vladislav L. Malkevich, U.S.S.R. Co-chairman

Utah, Room 340 U.S. Courthouse, 350 S. Main Street, Salt Lake City, UT 84101, Phone: (801) 524-5116

Uzbek Chamber of Commerce, 16 Leninskiy Prospekt, 700017 Tashkent, Phone: (371) 33-62-82

Uzbekintorg, Pr. Uzebkistani 18, 700115 Tashkent, Phone: 45-73-13; 45-78-42, Telex: 457313, General Director: A. I. Ikramov

V/O Atomenergoexport, 32/34 Smolenskaya-Sennaya Pl., 121200 Moscow, Phone: 220-14-36, Director: Vladimir D. Gulko

V/O Almazyuvelirexport, 25/1 Zubovskiy Bulvar, 119021 Moscow, Cable: Almazyuvelirexport Moscow, Telex: 411115, Phone: 245-02-59; 245-34-10; 245-34-20, General Director: I. S. Alekseev

V/O Aviaexport, 19 Trubnikovskiy Per., 121817 Moscow, Cable: Aviaexport Moscow, Telex: 411257, Phone: 290-01-71, General Director: V. S. Studenikin

V/O Avtoexport, 8 Ul. Marksa-Engelsa, 119902 Moscow, Cable: Avtoexport Moscow, Telex: 411135; 411253, Phone: 202-83-37; 202-85-35, General Director: E. N. Lyubinskiy

V/O Avtopromimport, 50/2 Ul. Pyatnitskaya, 109017 Moscow, Cable: Avtopromimport Moscow, Telex: 411961A API; 411961B API; 411961C API; 411961D API, Phone: 231-81-26, General Director: Yu. V. Kalashnikov

V/O Chimmashexport, 35 Mosfilmovskaya Ul., 114330 Moscow, Telex: 411068 Tehex SU; 411228 Tehex SU, Phone: 143-86-63; 288-36-90, General Director: A. I. Burgazliyev

V/O Elektronorgtechnika, 32/34 Smolenskaya-Sennaya Pl., 121200 Moscow, Telex: 411385;

411386, Phone: 205-00-33, General Director: V. F. Beresnev

V/O Expocentr, Sokolnicheskiy Val, 1a, 107113 Moscow, Telex: 411185 EXPO SU, Phone: 268-70-83, 268-63-52

V/O Exportljon, 33 Ul. Arkhitektora Vlasova, 117393 Moscow, Cable: Exportljon Moscow, Telex: 411204, Phone: 128-07-86; 128-18-24, General Director: I. N. Gorokhov

V/O Intourservice, 16 Prosp. Marksa, Moscow, Telex: 411211 INTOU SU, FAX: 200-12-43, Phone: 203-31-91, General Director: I. A. Feodorov

V/O Legpromexport, Prosp. Kalinina 29, Kor. 4, 121905 Moscow, Telex: 411859 NORD SU, Phone: 291-94-96, 259-99-79

V/O Mebelintorg, 35 Bolshaya Filyovskaya Ul., 121433 Moscow, Cable: Mebelintorg Moscow, Telex: 411282, Phone: 146-36-72, General Director: A. P. Grachev

V/O Promexport, Ul. Gorkogo, 37a, 125047 Moscow, Telex: 411045, Phone: 282-20-45

V/O Sovbunker, 10/12 Kaloshin Per., 121002 Moscow, Cable: Sovbunker Moscow, Telex: 411170, Phone: 248-23-40; 248-23-60, General Director: Yu. P. Drobinin

V/O Sovelectro, 1/4 Deguninskaya Ul., 127486 Moscow, Telex: 410003, Phone: 487-31-82, General Director: V. B. Ulyanov

V/O Sovexportkniga, Ul. Gorkogo 50, 125047 Moscow, Telex: 411069 SUPER SU, Phone: 251-72-76, 251-63-03

V/O Sovinteravtoservice Insititutsky, Per. 2/1, Moscow, Telex: 411008, Phone: 299-77-73, 299-59-00; Protocol Department: 971-03-37; Moscow-Helsinki Two-Way Courier Service: 299-77-73, 299-59-00, Fax: 230-24-50

V/O Soyuzagrokhimexport, Ul. Gritsevetskaya 2/16, 119900 Moscow, Telex: 411297 KHIM SU

V/O Soyuzkhimexport, Smolenskaya-Sennaya Pl., 32/34, 121200 Moscow, Telex: 411297 KHIM SU, Phone: 244-22-84, 224-41-83

V/O Soyuzkinoservice, Skatertnyy Per., 20, 121069 Moscow, Telex: 411114 INFLM SU, Fax: 200-12-86

V/O Soyuzkoopvneshtorg, 15 Bolshoy Cherkasskiy Per., 103626 Moscow, Cable: Soyuzkoopvneshtorg

V/O Soyuztorgoborudovaniye, Ul. Pushkinskaya 9, kor. 8, Telex: 471209, Phone: 229-34-48 Moscow, Telex: 411127, Phone: 924-81-71; 924-75-37, General Director: A. N. Starykh

V/O Soyuznefteexport, 32/34 Smolenskaya-Sennaya Pl., 121200 Moscow, Cable: Nafta Moscow, Telex: 411148, A, B, C, D, E, Phone: 244-40-48; 244-40-49, General Director: V. A. Arutyunyan

V/O Soyuzpatent, Ul. Kuybysheva, 5/2, 103684 Moscow, Telex: 411431 ATPP SU, Phone: 925-16-61, 925-68-00

V/O Soyuzplodoimport, 32/34 Smolenskaya-Sennaya Pl., 121200 Moscow, Cable: Plodoimport Moscow, Telex: 411262; 411329,

Phone: 244-22-58, General Director: L. P. Batov

V/O Soyuzregion, Ul. Kuybysheva, 6, 103864 Moscow, Phone: 525-48-73

V/O Soyuzzdravexport, 32/34 Smolenskaya-Sennaya, 121200 Moscow, Director: V. Zharikov

V/O Vneshekonomservice, 12, 1-ST Krasnogvardejskc Proezd, 123100 Moscow, Phone: 259-37-53, FAX: 921-53-97, Telex: 412138 VES SU, Contact: Valeriy Glazunov

V/O Vneshekonomservice, Ul. Kuybysheva, 6, 6103684 Moscow, Phone: 925-35-29, Telex: 411431 A, 411431 B TPP SU

V/O Vostokintorg, 32/34 Smilenskaya-Sennaya Pl., SU-121200 Moscow, Phone: 205-60-70, Director: Vladimir I. Brazhnikov

V/O Tyazhpromexport, 32/34 Smolenskaya-Sennaya Pl., SU-121200 Moscow, Phone: 220-16-10, Director: Valeri A. Yegorov

V/O Techmashimport, 19 Trubnikovskiy Per., 121819 Moscow, Cable: Techmashimport Moscow, Telex: 411194; 411195; 411306, Phone: 202-48-00; 248-83-00, General Director: V. I. Grib

V/O Vneshtorgreklama, Ul. Kakhovka 31, Kor. 2, 113461 Moscow, Telex: 411265 VTR SU, Phone: 331-83-11

V/O Vneshtorgizdat, 1 Ul. Fadeyeva, 125047 Moscow, Cable: Vneshtorgizdat Moscow, Telex: 411238 VTI, Phone: 250-51-62, Genral Director: Vladimir I. Prokopov

277

V/O Technopromexport, 32/34 Smolenskaya-Sennaya Pl., SU-121200 Moscow, Phone: 220-15-23, Director: Alexander S. Postovalov

V/O Technopromimport, 35 Mosfilmovskaya Ul., 117330 Moscow, Cable: Technopromimport Moscow, Telex: 411233, Phone: 147-22-85; 147-22-77; 143-87-85, General Director: V. I. Boiko

V/O Soyuzpromexport, 32/34 Smolenskaya-Sennaya Pl., 121200 Moscow, Cable: Promexport Moscow, Telex: 411268, Phone: 244-19-79; 244-47-68, General Director: Ye. F. Manakhov

V/O Promsyrioimport, 13 Ul. Chaykovskogo, 121834 Moscow, Cable: PSIM Moscow, Telex: 111824, Phone: 203-05-77; 203-05-95; 203-06-46, General Director: G. S Afanasyev

V/O Novoexport, 32/34 Smolenskaya-Sennaya Pl., SU-121200 Moscow, Phone: 128-68-59, Telex: 411204 NOVEX SU, Director: Igor N. Gorokhov

V/O Mashinoexport, 32/34 Smolenskaya-Sennaya Pl., 121200 Moscow, Phone: 147-15-42, Director: Vladimir V. Zasedatelev

V/O Mashinoimport, 32/34 Smolenskaya-Sennaya Pl., 121200 Moscow, Cable: Mashinoimport Moscow, Telex: 411231, Phone: 244-33-09, General Director: A. G. Yushkin

V/O Vneshtorgreklama, 31, Ul. Kakhovka, 113461 Moscow, Phone: 331-8311, 331-8801, FAX: 310-7005, Telex: 411625 VTR SU

V/O Stroidormashexport, Suvorovskiy Bulvar 7, Moscow, Telex: 411063 BREIM SU, Phone: 291-49-31

V/O Sovincentr, 12 Krasnopresnenskaya Nab., 123610 Moscow, Phone: 256-63-03, 255-64-01, Telex: 411486 SOVIN SU

V/O Metallurgimport, 33, Ul. Arkhitektora Vlassova, 117393 Moscow, Cable: Metallurgimport Moscow, Telex: 411388, Phone: 128-09-32, Acting General Director: A. V. Tverdokhlebov

V/O Medexport, Ul. Kakhovka 31, Kor. 2, 113461 Moscow, Telex: 411247 MEDEX SU, Phone: 331-82-00, 321-85-22

V/O Mosinter, Ul. Gorkogo 13, 103032 Moscow, Phone: 229-58-27

V/O Neftekhimexport, Ul. Gilyarovskogo 31, 129832 Moscow, Telex: 411615 NEXT, Phone: 284-8768, 284-8855

V/O Morsvyazsputnik, Ul. Rozhdestvenka 1/4, 103759 Moscow, Telex: 411197 MMF SU, Phone: 258-70-45

V/O Sovfracht, 1/4 Ul. Zhdanova, 103759 Moscow, Cable: Sovfracht Moscow, Telex: 41168, Phone: 926-11-18, General Director: V. L. Shutov

V/O Rosvneshtorg, 8/5 Ul. Barrikadnaya, 123242 Moscow, Cable: Rosvneshtorg Moscow, Telex: 411060 ROSST SU, Phone: 254-80-50, Chairman: I. V. Belotserkovskiy

V/O Stroimaterialintorg, 2 Sokolnicheskiy Val,

korpus 50, 107113 Moscow, Cable: Stroimaterialintorg Moscow, Telex: 411887; 411889, Phone: 269-05-54; 269-05-55, General Director: V. V. Devyatov

V/O UNEX, Ul. Kosygina 15, 117946 Moscow, Telex: 411049 UNEX SU, Phone: 939-88-67

V/O Vneshekonomservice, Ul. Kuybysheva 6, 103684 Moscow, Telex: 411126 TPP, Phone: 259-37-53

V/O Vneshtechnika, 6 Starokonyushennyy Pereulok, 119034 Moscow, Cable: Vneshtechnika Moscow, Telex: 411418 MLT, Phone: 201-72-60, General Director: V. I. Rybak

V/O Vnesheconomservice, 12, 1-ST Krasnogvardejskc Proezd, 123100 Moscow, Phone: 259-37-53, FAX: 921-53-97, Telex: 412138 VES SU

Valliere, Robert J., 10 Radcliff Road, Beverly, MA 01915, Phone: (617) 927-7784

Vencor, 1001 3rd Avenue, West, Suite 350, Bradenton, FL 22505, Phone: (813) 747-5700, FAX: (813) 748-1049, Contact: Michael T. Ligett

Vermont, Serviced by the Boston office

Victor Kamkin Bookstore, Inc., Boiling Brook Parkway, Rockville, MD 20852, Phone: (301) 881-5973

Vienna Agency of American International Underwriters: European American Underwriters, Bartensteingasse 2, Vienna, Austria 1010, Phone: 222-402-35560, FAX:

222-402-5160, Telex: 132303, Contact: Gerard Jansen, General Manager; Mujib Khan, Underwriting Manager; I. Polleheimer, Administrative Manager

Virden, Emerson H., Jr., 1541 Clearview Avenue, Blue Bell, PA 19422, Phone: (215) 272-0571

Virginia, 8010 Federal Bldg., 400 N. 8th Street, Richmond, VA 23240, Phone: (804) 771-2246

Vneshaudit, Vneshaudit can be contacted through Ernst and Young's New York office, Phone: (212) 830-6000

Vneshekonombank, Ul. Pushkinskaya 4/2, 103810 Moscos, Phone: Main Office 246-67-80, Moscow World Trade Center address: Krasnopresnenskaya Nab. 12, Moscow, Phone: 246-67-88, World Trade Center, 253-17-90; 253-81-82, Telex: 411174 (cable address: Vneshbank Moscow), 253-23-49

Vneshposyltorg, 32/34 Smolenskays-Sennaya Pl., SU-121200 Moscow, Phone: 271-05-05, Director: Vilik V. Khshtoyan

Vneshpromtechobmen, 9 Per Vasnetsova, 129090 Moscow, Cable: Vneshpromtechobmen Moscow, Telex: 411181, Phone: 284-72-41, General Director: Yu. I. Cherepanov

Vorys, Sater, Seymour and Pease, Suite 1111, 1828 L Street, NW, Washington, DC 20036-5104, Phone: (202) 822-8200, FAX: (202) 835-0699, Telex: 440693, Contact: Randal C. Teague

279

VPO Zarubezhstroi, Ul. Petrovka 14, 103031 Moscow, Telex: 411191, Phone: 200-45-25, 200-45-66

Vum E/I Elektronmash, 4 Bolshaya Okruzhnaya Ul., 252180 Kiev, Cable: Elektronmash Kiev, Phone: 487-06-28, Director: V. G. Sirota

W. Averell Harriman Institute for Advanced Study of the Soviet Union, Columbia University, 420 W. 118th Street, 12th Floor, IAB, New York, NY 10027, Phone: (212) 854-4623, Contact: Douglas A. Evans, Program Coordinator

Walsh, P. Hartley, 533 2nd Street, SE, Washington, DC 20003, Phone: (202) 707-7630

Walter, Conston, Alexander & Green, P.C., 90 Park Avenue, New York, NY 10018-1387, Phone: (212) 210-9400, FAX: (212) 210-9444, Telex: INTL 234435 RCA, DOM/INTL 125410 WU, Contact: Henry S. Conston

Washington, Rm 706, Lake Union Bldg., 1700 West Lake Avenue, N., Seattle, WA 98109, Phone: (206) 442-5616

Washington Resources International, 2101 Wilson Boulevard, Suite 900, Arlington, VA 22202, Phone: (703) 522-6900, Telex: 4933729 WASH UI, Contact: William Chastka, President

Washington Researchers, Ltd., 2612 P Street, NW, Washington, DC 20007, Phone: (202) 333-3533, Contact: Leila Kight, President

Weadon, Rehm, Thomsen, Scott, 1301 Pennsylvania Avenue, Suite 500, Washington, DC 20004, Phone: (202) 783-9200, FAX: (202) 783-9071, Telex: 6971742 WRTS UW, Contact: George Rehm

Weil, Gotshal & Manges, in Washington: 1615 L Street, NW, Suite 700, Washington, DC 20036, Phone: (202) 682-7000, FAX: (202) 857-0167, (202) 857-0930, (202)857-0940, Telex: ITT 440045, Contact: M. Jean Anderson; in New York: 767 Fifth Avenue, New York, NY 10153, Phone: (212) 310-8000, FAX: (212) 310-8007, Telex: ITT 424281, Contact: Robert Todd Lang, in London: 50 Stratton Street, London W1X 5FL, Phone: 1-493-9933, FAX: 1-629-7900, Contact: Peter D. Standish

Welt International, Inc., 1413 K Street, NW, Suite 800, Washington, DC 20005, Phone: (202) 371-0555, FAX: (202) 862-5833, Telex: 248599, Contact: Leo Welt, President

Weppner, Eileen, 1491 High Street, Boulder, CO 80302, Phone: (303) 494-8325

West Virginia, 3402 Federal Building, 500 Quarrier Street, Charleston, WV 25301, Phone: (304) 347-5123, Contact: James Pittard, Trade Specialist

White & Case, 1155 Avenue of the Americas, New York, NY 10036, Phone: (212) 819-8200, FAX: (212) 354-8113, Telex: 126201, Contact: Daniel J. Arbess

Williams, Kastner & Gibbs, Two Union Square 601 Union Street, Suite 4100, Seattle, WA 98111-0040, Phone: (206) 628-6600, FAX:

280

(206) 628-6611, Telex: 6286611, Contact: Michael Jay Brown

Willis, John M., 177 Doorack Lane, Kirkwood, MO 63122, Phone: (314) 822-4471

Wisconsin, Federal Bldg., U.S. Courthouse, 517 E. Wisc. Avenue, Milwaukee, WI 53202, Phone: (414) 291-3473

Womble, Carlyle, Sandridge & Rice, Charlotte Office, 3300 One First Union Center, 301 South College Street, Charlotte, NC 28202, Phone: (704) 331-4900, FAX: (704) 331-4955, Telex: 853609, Contact: Larry B. Coffey

World Patents Index Database, Publisher: Derwent Incorporated, McLean, VA, Phone: (703) 790-0400, FAX: (703) 790-1426

World Trade, 4940 Campus Drive, Newport Beach, CA 92660, Phone: (714) 641-1404, FAX: (714) 957-0922

World Trade Center Washington DC (WTCW), 1101 King Street, Suite 700, Alexandria, VA 22314, Phone: (703) 684-6630, FAX: (703) 684-2918, Telex: 5106004086 WTC WASH, Contact: Kathleen Durkin

Wyoming, Serviced by Denver

Young and Rubicam/Sovero, in Chicago: C/O Burson Marsteller, 1 East Wacker Dr., Chicago, IL 60601-1854, Phone: (312) 329-9292, FAX: (312) 329-7583, Telex: 6871 401, In Moscow: 1404 Sovincentr, 12 Krasnopolskaya Nab., 123610 Moscow, Phone: 253-1347, FAX: 253-1348, Telex: 412199 ADPR, Contact: Michael Adams, Chief

Executive Officer; Vladimir Vlasov, General Manager

Zane, Michael S., 3 Deer Run, Watchung, NJ 07060, Phone: (201) 754-6048

Zarubezhgeologiya, 10 Kaholshin Pereulok, 121002 Moscow, Telex: 411829 OZGEO, Phone: 241-15-15, General Director: M. I. Nikulshin

Zotov-Kondratov, Eduard S., President, Prometey, 29, building 4, Checkhow str, 103006 Moscow. Phone 299-84-85

ABOUT THE EDITOR

William S. Loiry is Chairman and CEO of Global Trading Associates, Inc., a Washington-based firm specializing in trade negotiations between U.S. companies and their Soviet and East European counterparts.

Global Trading's business facilitation services include the operation of Western-style business centers throughout the Soviet Union and the representation of U.S. companies seeking Soviet partners. The firm's information services include the sponsorship of conferences on Soviet trade and the publication of the *U.S.-Soviet Trade Alert*, the industry's main fax newsletter. Global is also involved in a variety of trading deals, ranging from high-tech products to natural resources.

Loiry sits on the boards of directors of four Soviet business centers and leads frequent business delegations throughout the Soviet Union.

During the late 1980s, Loiry served as President of one of the original U.S.-Soviet sister city programs, the Tallahassee-Krasnodar Sister City Program. During his leadership tenure, the document making the program official was signed, the first Soviet delegation visited Tallahassee, and a multi-part exchange program, including trade, was begun between the two cities. For his efforts, Loiry was presented with a Soviet peace medal from the Mayor of Krasnodar and an Award of Appreciation from the Mayor of Tallahassee. In 1989, Loiry launched The Foundation For Citizen Diplomacy, a Washington-based nonprofit organization which supports the U.S.-Soviet sister city movement.

The founding editor of a metropolitan business magazine, Loiry is the author of three other books, *The 1991 U.S.-East European Trade Directory,* for businesses entering the East European trade market, *Winning With Science*, an annual guide for high school students on science research and programs, and *The Impact Of Youth* (1984), a history of children and youth with recommendations for the future.